BEYOND TH

The Nicky English Story

With Vincent Hogan

Published by MedMedia Ltd.

Published in 1996 by
MedMedia Ltd.
99 Upper George's Street,
Dun Laoghaire,
Co Dublin.
Tel: 01-280 3967 Fax: 01-280 7076
e-mail: medmedia@indigo.ie

Design: Fiona Donohoe/MedMedia

Photographs courtesy of Ray McManus, David Maher and Brendan Moran, Sportsfile and John Kelly, Clonmel.

ISBN: 0-9523039-1-4

INTRODUCTION

FOR fifteen years, Nicky English has proudly worn the blue and gold of his native Tipperary. He has, almost certainly, been one of the greatest hurlers of his generation and, will no doubt, be an inspiration for generations to come.

AIB has a long tradition of GAA sponsorship with much of our support currently channelled towards the hugely successful AIB Hurling and Football Club Championships. Supporting the games at club level will, we believe, assist in ensuring the continuous strength and success of Gaelic games and indeed, encourage more young people to participate and aspire towards the greatness and achievements of the likes of Nicky English.

We are proud to be associated with this publication and congratulate the author on his foresight and honest interpretation of Nicky's career in hurling.

Hugh Cawley,
General Manager,
AIB Bank

ACKNOWLEDGEMENTS

ABOVE all else, I wanted to write an honest book. So much of my life has been given to hurling, I felt it would be a kind of betrayal to just churn out a glib, care-free chronicle of my years in the game.

I'm happy that the efforts of the last twelve months are reflected between these covers now. For that, I'd like to thank Vincent Hogan for teasing the memories from their cobwebs and putting structure on my reminiscence.

I'd like to thank my father, Donie, and my mother, Maura, for encouraging me so much when I was a fledgling hurler in the yard at home and my sisters, Eilish and Fionnuala, for filling in occasionally as markers.

I'd like to thank Hugh Cawley and Allied Irish Banks for their enthusiastic support of this book.

Anyone who looks through it will vouch immediately for the high standard of photography on display. For this, I thank Ray McManus and his team at Sportsfile as well as my good friend, John Kelly, from Clonmel.

And, finally, I'd like to thank Anne for always being there.

Nicky English

October 1996

HELPING this book come to fruition was a largely painless exercise for me. As a Tipperary man and a friend of Nicky's, stitching his thoughts together could never be categorised as any kind of chore.

Still, there were many hours of taped conversation that needed to be transcribed and, for this, I am indebted to Maura Quill.

I would like to thank Anne and Nicky for their hospitality and patience while we teased out the more distant memories.

I would also like to thank Maura English for supplying some of the photographs Nicky might have preferred not to have seen again.

I would like to thank MedMedia for a superbly professional effort in publishing the book.

And finally, I would like to thank my wife, Geraldine, and our two children, Nicholas and Laura, for their encouragement and support.

Vincent Hogan

October 1996

CONTENTS

PROLOGUE

WOKE up this morning sharing a room again with Pat Fox. Just like it used to be when we were kings of the castle.

But time has dragged us from our pedestals.

Pat was worrying about simply making the six substitutes, me about holding my own out on the field. Old codgers fighting back the demons.

Then I got physically ill before the game for the first time in maybe five years. A sign, I suspect, that I knew this would be my last shot.

Can't say the 70 minutes flew. Once Limerick got away from us, time seemed to drag by for a small eternity. Tipperary had plenty of the ball, but we couldn't seem to use it. 'Running to stand still' as the song goes.

When it ended, the Limerick people came spilling in from every corner. Stephen McDonagh and I embraced and he asked me to swap jersies. I declined.

'Probably my last one,' I told him. 'I'd like to keep it.'

As the field filled up, I couldn't find a way out. So I started wandering about, almost as if in a daze. Looking into the stand, thinking about how that was the place for me now.

And I met this little kid from Limerick, still wearing the green and white number nine jersey I had given him in the Gaelic Grounds seven days earlier. Sean O'Neill's jersey.

The kid had broken his arm in a hurling match during the week and, now, it was in a sling. He sounded proud.

Most of the lads were showered and changed by the time I got into the dressing-room. The floor was wet, the air sticky. Michael Cleary was sitting with his head down. Johnny Leahy too.

A few people chatted but their voices were no more than whispers. Tears were not far away from most eyes.

So I got into the shower and let the hot water splash down over me, washing away the grime of battle, trying to ease away the pain of defeat.

For the last time.

Nicky English

July 14, 1996

For Anne

I

COULD HAVE BEEN A HERO...

TALK is cheap.

I knew that's what the lads were thinking as I gave my little sermon. Early December in Dundrum House and the beer had begun to loosen inhibitions. It was the day of our annual golf challenge against Cork but a few hurling sores were now being dredged up and dissected.

Johnny Leahy and Declan Ryan sat listening to me, their agitation visible.

'Look lads, ye didn't do what ye should have done for Tipperary last year,' I said. 'When it was needed, ye didn't deliver.'

This was coming from someone who hadn't been seen in a Tipperary dressing-room since our Championship hopes ended five months earlier. Coming from a man who hadn't even considered making himself available for the League.

Truth is, I presumed I had played my last game in the Tipp colours. At least, that's what I kept telling myself.

Maybe a week earlier, the county panel had gathered in Thurles for a fairly heated meeting. In hindsight, the very fact that I went to the meeting suggested that my mind was not yet closed.

Tipp's Munster Championship draw had certainly set me thinking. Only Waterford and Kerry stood between us and a place in the Munster final.

I admitted as much that night in Thurles. 'If it wasn't for the soft draw, I don't think I'd be here,' I said. It was not the most tactful of remarks.

The meeting had developed into a strong, verbal battle between young and old. There was a feeling among the newer players that they weren't getting a fair crack of the whip from management. One of them, Paul Shelly, talked of his frustration at being overlooked for our losing Championship game with Limerick despite the suspensions handed out to Michael Ryan and Paul Delaney.

Tipp always seemed to revert to the older hands and Shelly was frustrated. 'I'm telling ye now that I'm going to be Tipp's full-back in '96,' he vowed bullishly.

Pat Fox spoke for the old guard, arguing, 'I won't apologise to anyone if I make the team.' Fox said he wasn't prepared to hang about as substitute.

In many ways, everyone's intentions looked extremely clear-cut but my own.

And yet now, a week on, Johnny and Declan were being asked to sit and listen as I dismantled their contributions to the previous summer. The conversation, understandably, grew quite heated.

Both of them had played in all of Tipp's pre-Christmas League games. Their commitment was unequivocal. Unlike mine.

At the very least, I harboured doubts as to whether – physically – I had anything left in the tank that could be of use to Tipperary.

Then Declan looked me angrily in the eye. 'Do you expect to be playing for Tipp in the Championship next year?' he asked.

'No,' I responded. 'No, I don't.'

My mind was full of many things. I was due shortly into the Blackrock Clinic for an operation on the ankle injured against Waterford the previous June. And, if anything, I think I was using that injury as a smokescreen.

Being honest, I didn't want to play, I didn't want to train. Physically, I had allowed myself deteriorate like never before. I had turned off the switch, you might say. Because my ankle felt sore, I had a ready-made excuse for doing nothing.

And I felt comfortable with that. Any hurling ambitions that remained were half-hearted. Sure, I wanted to play in another Munster final. But I just didn't have any appetite for the work required to get me there.

It was decided to postpone the operation as the injury wasn't exactly life-threatening. In any event, there was a chance that the problem might 'settle' and allow me run freely without surgery.

So I started to play a few gentle soccer games with friends on an astro-turf pitch in Loughlinstown. And Liam Hennessy got working on my mind.

Even if there was no hurling to be played, Hennessy could never tolerate seeing anybody allow themselves get slovenly. For the last five years, he has been much more than Tipperary's trainer.

In many ways, he has been the spirit of the team.

Almost without knowing, I started to prepare myself for another Championship campaign. I began jogging with my dog, 'Blaze', on a necklace of paths I knew up in the Dublin mountains. I also started doing gym-work.

Then, it seemed like the inevitable happened.

Less than two weeks into the new year, I pulled a calf muscle during one of my runs. It meant not being able to train for a fortnight. Soon after, I went on a skiing holiday to Andorra. Fr Tom Fogarty, I'm sure, was beginning to wonder about my intentions.

The holiday had been arranged long in advance but, given that I was already injured, it probably suggested a lack of commitment on my part to the Tipperary cause. Worse though was to follow.

Maybe two weeks after returning from the holiday, I was picked to play a challenge game for Tipp against Galway in Drombane. It was a game I was anxious to play in given that I had missed the few warm-up matches played so far.

I was also determined to show the selectors that my commitment to the cause was genuine. Doubts, inevitably, linger when someone reports themselves injured during the most inclement time of year. Especially, if they can still find time to go skiing!

On the morning of the game, I got up at about seven thirty to go to the toilet. Incredibly, I could barely walk because of a pain in my left ankle. It was too bizarre for words.

I had gone to bed feeling perfect and now I was a virtual invalid. 'I think I'm after breaking my ankle,' I said to Anne, my mind doing cart-wheels. But how? Had I been sleep-walking? Or was I just imagining the pain?

Anne's look of incredulity mirrored the expressions on virtually every face I would encounter that day.

But the pain was too severe for this to be just a figment of my imagination. It was clear there was something radically wrong yet, for the life of me, I couldn't explain it.

So I got up about ten, put on a track-suit, packed my kit-bag and limped down the stairs, convincing myself that the leg would be fine by the time I got to Drombane. I was wrong. The further I drove, the more the leg seemed to deteriorate. By Thurles, I was barely able to press the clutch.

It was spitting sleet and snow as I reached Upperchurch and Joe Hayes rang me on the car-phone. 'All set for your return?' asked Joe.

'You won't believe this,' I responded. 'I was grand going to bed last night but I can hardly walk with the pain in my ankle now.'

Joe laughed. 'Aah ya,' he said. 'Tis a bit wet and cold out there alright.'

I will never forget the look on Fr Fogarty's face when I got to the pitch and told him of my problem. By now, I was limping badly. Fr Tom is a very honest, genuine man and I could see he had his doubts about my predicament.

With so much scepticism about me, I started wondering if maybe it was all in my head. So I togged out and went to see if I could run it off on the field. But I couldn't walk properly let alone jog.

I remember Pat Fox looking at me and smirking. Nobody was convinced.

The drive home from Drombane proved a real struggle and I actually started to shiver as if I was becoming a bit feverish. So I stopped off in Abbeyleix to get Dr John Keating's verdict.

He suggested it could be a blood infection similar to one I had sustained in 1992. I had collected a little cut on my ankle from skiing boots I had hired while on holiday and, in hindsight, hiring was probably not the most hygienic of arrangements.

That night, back in Dublin, Bill Quinlan came over to the house and confirmed that prognosis. Bill is a Tipperary man from Ardfinnan who actually went to school with 'Babs' Keating.

He had treated me for the previous blood infection and told me, if it worsened overnight, I was to bring myself in to St Vincent's.

Sure enough, by the Monday morning, I was barely able to get out of bed with the pain. I rang by boss and took the day off work.

They admitted me to Blackrock Clinic that night and I spent the next four days on an intravenous course of antibiotics. It was clear that training would be out of the question for at least another two weeks.

On the one hand, I was relieved to have concrete proof for management that my problem in Drombane had been genuine. On the other, I was conscious of how I was now losing out on the groundwork for Tipperary's year.

The League resumed the weekend I got out of hospital and Tipp recorded an impressive win away to Cork.

Ten days on, I returned to training but was not considered for our March 3 meeting with All-Ireland champions, Clare, which Tipp also won. It was disappointing to miss such a game but, at least, I was beginning to become healthy again.

Training had become intense and I remember especially one ferociously tough session on Clonmel Racecourse the following Saturday which I was really pleased to come through. I seemed to be over the worst.

But, to my horror, I could feel the pain returning in my ankle while at work the following Wednesday. The infection had returned.

Two more weeks of oral antibiotics followed and, unable to train, I seemed to be drifting closer to the periphery of Tipp's ambitions for the year. The team was beginning to take shape without me and it looked like Nicky English's time was up.

By now, April had arrived and, in effect, I hadn't trained consistently since January. I felt fragile. The same way I always felt when injured.

Fr Fogarty decided to play me in a challenge game against Galway on the evening of April 21. He needed to assess my fitness but I was amazed a few days later to be picked for our League semi-final against Laois at Nowlan Park.

There was a great deal of hype surrounding the game with 'Babs' now in charge of Laois but I travelled to Kilkenny that day with very mixed feelings. Deep down, I knew I was just not ready for a game of this intensity.

I was conscious too of how unforgiving the Tipperary supporters could be. They wouldn't be gentle on me if I had a stinker, whatever the circumstances.

All my worst fears were realised in the game as I struggled physically from start to finish. I was being marked by Cyril Duggan which didn't help as he never let go of my jersey all day.

I felt so weak out on the field it was unnerving. Being brutally honest, I felt finished. If anything, I didn't really want to be there.

It was clear that I needed a lot more training but more sinister thoughts started to clutter my mind. I had so many doubts about myself, about my physical capacity to survive at this level any longer.

It was the only game I recall ever playing for Tipperary in which I kept looking towards the sideline to see if they were going to replace me.

Tipp came through a tough game without much assistance from their left-corner forward. But now, at least, I had two more weeks of training ahead of me before the final against Galway.

That game was played in Limerick on May 12 and, although I scored a goal when Galway's 'keeper made a bad error, I was still essentially trying to catch up with the others.

Galway won the game with a late flourish and there was a lot of talk afterwards that Tipp's forwards had flunked their responsibilities. As the senior member of the attack, it was obvious that the criticism was being aimed at me as much as anyone.

My fitness was still well short of the requisite standard but that day, for the first time in months, I could actually feel a little strength coming into my legs. It meant I left Limerick thankful in the knowledge that, barring injury, I might still have something to offer Tipperary.

On a disappointing evening for the county, I now – at least – had a little hope to cling to.

It was clear that getting into the Championship team was going to be difficult. Men like the Nenagh brothers, Eddie and Kevin Tucker, had established themselves as regulars during what had been a reasonably encouraging League campaign.

I was also conscious of the fact that Declan Ryan was bound to come back into contention after injury while Pat Fox would come into the equation too. Long gone were the days when Tipp's forward line picked itself.

The more training I did, the more confident I became. We played a challenge against Dublin in Templemore and I scored four points. The progress was slow but definite. I was definitely getting closer to where I needed to be.

A week before the Championship opener with Waterford, we went to the freshly renovated Walsh Park for a training session. In a practice match, I marked Paul Shelly and scored five points. I felt really strong, really comfortable.

Thinking about Walsh Park over the next few days, I couldn't help wonder if it was going to bring a gloomy symmetry to the story of my career. It was here that things had really started to happen for me as a hurler 15 years earlier when Tipp took such plaudits for our All-Ireland under-21 victory.

Now I was going back there as an old hurler, carrying his worries and doubts for company. I didn't want my inter-county career to end in Waterford. But I knew that this was a dangerous game for Tipp.

At our last training session on the Thursday night, I spoke in the dressing-room. I tackled the charge of Tipp's forwards 'shirking responsibility' in the League final. Whatever my own personal worries, I now felt a central member of the team that would carry the county's hopes. I was conscious of the fact that the Paul Shellys and Liam Cahills would be looking to the likes of me for leadership. And it was important that I supplied it.

I said that, never in my life, had I knowingly shirked responsibility for Tipperary and I wouldn't be doing it in Walsh Park.

In many ways, I was trying to fill the role Tadhg O'Connor ('82) and Noel O'Dwyer ('84) had filled when I was a kid. At the time, I considered anything they would say as gospel. I found their words calming, re-assuring.

To me, it was obvious that – above anything – Tipp would need tough men if we were to come safely out of Walsh Park. We had hammered Waterford in the '95 Championship and now, on home soil, they would be a seriously driven team.

Being honest, it was a huge game for both teams and I felt extremely nervous travelling to the ground. I remember thinking 'Why do I do this to myself?'

Walsh Park has always been a difficult place to play in. The field is very tight but maybe, if I'm honest, it now suits me better to have a pitch that way. Nowadays, I'm a better full-forward in places like Walsh Park than I am in Thurles. The play is closer to me and I can dictate things a lot more effectively.

That, at least, is how it seemed to work this time. I scored a couple of early points and played well generally, using my head where once I'd have been depending on my legs. Tipp won the game reasonably comfortably even if there were obvious worries.

Mid-way through the second-half, the team seemed to get really jittery as Waterford rallied. We couldn't pull away from them and there were a few occasions when the full-back line looked in disarray.

Maybe, most significantly, Johnny Leahy didn't play well. Johnny is a vital man to Tipperary now but, in '96, he clearly had other things to concern him.

Truth is, Johnny was having one of the toughest years imaginable. The threat of jail lingered for a good few months and, being fair, it was a wonder he could keep his mind on anything but his troubles.

Personally, I think he's a much better person now. Sometimes, when Johnny drank, he wasn't the nicest guy in the world.

But now that he's got his life sorted, I think he can become a great player for Tipperary again. It's going to take him time to adjust to a new lifestyle but, from what I've seen so far, Johnny will be back.

In '96, I sensed his hurling suffered because he just didn't want the limelight. If you intend playing well in the Championship, you have to want the ball, you have to love it. This summer, Johnny Leahy never looked as if he felt that way.

Still, Tipp did enough to beat Waterford that evening in Walsh Park and the win gave me an immense surge of satisfaction. There is no other buzz like the one you feel at winning a tough Championship match.

On a personal level, it was lovely to be told I had played well after the traumas of the previous few months. The only blot on the day for me was that I didn't score a goal, my first-half shot ricocheting off an upright.

It meant I was still looking for my first Championship goal since 1991.

The night would end back in Pat Fox's pub in Cashel. It felt just like old times. I had hurled well and, barring a calamity, Tipp were headed for the Munster final.

Kerry, evidently, would have considered such sentiments a little insulting but the reality is that our trip to Tralee on June 15 was never going to be anything other than a gentle stepping stone for Tipperary.

The very fact that it was to be played on a Saturday night, enabling us all attend the following day's 'real' semi-final between Clare and Limerick, indicated the general lack of expectation.

It turned out to be a beautiful, sunny evening devoid of any pressure.

In fact, the thought had struck me on the way to Tralee that this might just be the place to score my first Championship goal in five years. It was a definite opportunity to build confidence.

I had been feeling a little soreness in my calf during training and now, in the puckaround before the game, the leg felt pretty tight. So, for reassurance more than anything, I got a rub from Liam Hennessy.

He asked me if I wanted the leg strapped up but I said I thought it would be okay.

Briefly, I considered pulling out of the game but that thought didn't linger long. There was just no way I could drop out five minutes before a Championship game.

Anyway, the pain was in the inside of the calf which had never been the case previously. 'All in your mind,' I told myself.

But, first time I sprinted in the game, the leg felt really tight. Suddenly I didn't want to sprint. My marker easily beat me out to the next ball as I tried to move too gently. It was getting a little stupid.

I scored a nice point but the leg kept getting tighter and tighter. Soon, I was looking towards the touchline, trying to catch Hennessy's eye. I wanted to stay on the field but it soon became clear that that wouldn't be possible.

Mid-way through the half, I tried to spin around my man without the ball and pulled the muscle badly. So I called Liam and just hobbled to the sideline. It was shattering. There were only three weeks to the Munster final.

They put ice on the leg for me but I had to be helped across the field to the dressing-room at half-time. The injury felt a deep one.

Inside, life was carrying on quite efficiently without me.

Tipp were comfortably ahead and I could sense people thinking 'Nicky's gone again, so what's new.' It was strange trying to absorb the general sense of resignation

The others had got used to looking on me as fragile so there was no great commotion about me breaking down again. Quite the contrary.

I could hear the cheers greet them back onto the field as I took off the number fourteen jersey and slapped my gear into a kit-bag. Looking at the jersey, I couldn't help wondering 'Will I ever see it again?'

I had a quick shower and hobbled back out to watch the remainder beside a few Kerry people in the third row of the stand. I was an anonymous face in the crowd.

My self-doubt was compounded the following day when Clare and Limerick locked horns in one of the most gripping Championship matches I've ever witnessed. It was a fantastic contest, won with virtually the last puck of the match from Ciaran Carey.

Sitting in the stand, watching these guys plough into one another resurrected a lot of demons. The game was so fast, so physical in soaring temperatures, I just couldn't see any possibility of me being able to play at that level just three weeks on.

Still, over the next two weeks, I actually put in a great deal of hydrotherapy work in a swimming pool to try and get the leg right. I was desperate to make the team that would play Limerick and now, with every pool and physio session, I could detect tangible improvement in my leg.

Ten days before the Munster final, Tipp played a practice match against the county's under-21s. I knew it was still too early to test my calf muscle so I sat the game out. Ominously for me, Declan Ryan, showed up really well at full-forward.

The following Saturday, there was another full-scale game at training and, again, I didn't participate. I sensed the leg was almost right now but decided it would be silly to risk really testing it until the actual week of the game.

Time would reveal that the selectors adopted a different view.

The European Soccer Championships were on all this time and, every day, I was monitoring the progress of German striker – Jurgen Klinsmann – who was battling to recover from a similar injury to my own.

I couldn't help wondering what kind of treatment he was receiving as most of the speculation suggested that he would be available to Berti Vogt's team inside a week.

'If he can come back in one week,' I kept telling myself, 'surely I can make it in three!'

Anyway, the team to play Limerick in the Munster final was named before I got an opportunity to prove my fitness. It emerged that, if I had played in the Saturday practice match and come through unscathed, I would have been selected.

But not having played, I was now listed among the substitutes.

To put it mildly, I felt angry. Not because I thought I had any divine right to a Tipperary jersey, but simply because I felt I hadn't been given the opportunity to prove my fitness.

Sure, I could have played in the Saturday practice match if the selectors were insistent. But, to me, it would have amounted to an unnecessary gamble.

I know my body well enough after all these years of fighting injury, to pace my recovery with reasonable accuracy. Now I found myself listed as injured when, in my heart, I knew I was perfectly fit to play.

When the team was announced at training on the Monday, I just threw myself into a practice game, determined to show the selectors what I thought of their decision.

Hennessy, realising what I was doing, ran onto the pitch and told me I was being 'stupid', that I ought to protect the leg. He was right, of course, but an angry man is not always a rational one.

At training, the following Wednesday, I felt absolutely perfect. Maybe the selectors were right. Maybe I should have been willing to test the leg a little sooner. But I didn't think so then.

And, being honest, I still don't now.

It felt strange preparing for the Munster final as a substitute. The only previous experience I really had of it had been in '93 but, back then, my mind was so cluttered with other things I didn't really care as much as I should have.

This was different.

I remember sitting down with Pat Fox during the parade before the game and saying that this was probably the last Munster final we'd see as players. In those circumstances, it felt bad to be sitting on the line. Especially given that, deep down, I knew I wasn't injured.

That day in Limerick gave me a whole new perspective on the substitutes' role. It gave me a lot more respect for the guys who sit on the line just waiting in hope, a lot more respect for the commitment they maintain, often without ever reaping any visible rewards.

I wasn't nearly as psyched up for this Munster final as I would have been if I was starting the game. I felt no nervousness, no worry. Just a vague, unsettling detachment.

Mind you, with the way Tipp started the game, I had no difficulty becoming a face in the crowd. The team was frightening in its power and confidence. They just ripped into Limerick with virtually every man dominating his marker. The blue and gold attacks came in majestic waves.

Physically and spiritually, there was only one team on the field.

Declan Ryan and Liam Cahill were ripping Limerick asunder and Tipp were hardly flattered to reach half-time with a ten points lead, Cahill having rifled a great goal.

What followed, even now, is difficult to fathom.

From a position of absolute dominance, Tipp were pushed unceremoniously onto the back foot. Cahill missed a goal-chance that would probably have put us out of reach and Limerick started coming back. Slowly but surely, they began climbing back up the rock-face.

Incredibly, in a 20 minute period, they out-scored Tipperary by 0-10 to 0-0. The cakewalk had crumbled into a nightmare.

With less than 15 minutes remaining, the sides were level and it looked as if Limerick's momentum would swallow us whole. I was dispatched from the bench to full-forward in an effort to win a few balls and, maybe, snatch a score or two.

Soon as I went in, I felt strong. I caught the first few balls that dropped between Mike Nash and me, scored a point and genuinely started to make a bit of a difference.

As the minutes flew, Tipp and Limerick were exchanging points, neither side seemingly capable of putting the other one away. Then, with the game approaching injury time and Tipp leading by a point, I got my chance to be a hero.

Catching a high ball on the edge of the square, I turned and headed for goal. Mike Nash grabbed hold of my jersey and, momentarily, I hesitated in expectation of a whistle.

But the whistle never came, so I went on again. Moving now towards the right of goal, I decided to just take my point but – as I swung – Nash managed to block me down.

As I turned around and realised that the ball was on the ground, I was shattered. I just could not believe he had managed to block me.

After all of my frustrations, someone up there had been actually thinking of me. With time virtually up, I had been given the chance to – effectively – kill the game. To put Tipperary into the All-Ireland semi-final against Antrim. And, now, the ball was on the ground behind me.

In my disgust, I actually turned around and fouled Nash. It was a gesture of desperation. The game had been there for me to win and I couldn't take it.

Without question, I should have been awarded a free as Nash was blatantly pulling my jersey. But, deep down, I was more angry with myself for being blocked down.

Seconds later, Frankie Carroll fired over Limerick's equaliser and one of the most incredible comebacks in Munster Championship history was rewarded with a draw.

The Gaelic Grounds seemed to hum with excitement and relief as both sets of supporters headed away afterwards into a clammy evening. Tipp people were a little incredulous as to how the team could surrender a ten points lead.

Yet neither side could be too downbeat about getting another chance. Because both had, at different junctures, stared despair in the face.

The replay was fixed for the following Sunday at Pairc Uí Chaoimh as part of a live television double-bill with the Leinster final between Wexford and Offaly.

Through the next few days, I couldn't help thinking of how much simpler it could all have been if I had scored with that late opportunity. I was pleased to have come on and played reasonably well but, ultimately, frustrated that Tipp weren't now Munster champions.

Driving down to Cork for the replay, a certain nervousness had returned. I was chosen – at Tommy Dunne's expense – to start the game in the left corner-forward position. This would bring me into direct conflict with Stephen McDonagh, a man I consider one of the best and quickest corner-backs in the country.

We stayed in Cork on the Saturday night and, the following morning, we went for a gentle puckaround at the St. Finbarrs ground. This is the best way of easing nerves and setting free a little pent-up energy.

Instinctively, you find yourself monitoring your touch at such moments. It's naive, of course, but you're trying to get some kind of signal as to how you're likely to play.

Overall, I felt good. Happy to be there.

On the bus-ride to Pairc Uí Chaoimh, the sirens of the Garda out-riders quickened the pulse a little. This has always been the way. The sound of the sirens creates that little edge of tension that might have been missing until you sat on the bus.

Now, the sense of expectancy hits everyone.

It struck me on the journey to the ground that Tipperary's supporters were vastly out-numbered by Limerick's. So much had changed from '87, '88 and '89 when I think it was fair to say that Tipp supporters travelled in far bigger numbers than those backing any of the teams we met.

But not any longer.

In the tight, cramped dressing-room, the usual people made their speeches. The mood was urgent. It was time to prove we hadn't left our hopes behind us on the field in Limerick.

The dressing-rooms in Pairc Uí Chaoimh have always been a disaster. Rumour has it that the architect designed them with eleven soccer players in mind. They're just far too small for the numbers they have to accommodate. Normally, you get to use two connecting rooms. But that day in Cork, we were sharing with the South Tipperary Under-16 team who had just played in a curtain-raiser.

Sitting there, listening to these kids, I couldn't help wonder if a few of them might emerge – with time – as the stars of tomorrow. It was a peculiar feeling, knowing the possibility that this might be the last time either Pat Fox or I inhabited a Tipperary dressing-room.

Cramped for space, most of us couldn't wait to get out into the open spaces of the field. I have always felt that way when stuck in the Pairc Uí Chaoimh dressing-rooms.

As in Limerick, Tipp managed to make the more aggressive start. But, this time, shots that flew over the bar seven days previously, were drifting wide of the target.

Unbelievably, we shot eleven wides in the first eighteen minutes and it was a statistic that would take its toll on us. I actually started the trend, missing a simple scoring opportunity from my first ball.

It was a terrible wide. A free shot basically that I honestly believed I couldn't miss. But the ball drifted right of the posts and it was to be typical of Tipp's day.

Looking back, it would have been a great start – not just for me – for Tipp generally. But, instead, it was followed by a couple more wides and, while having the lion's share of possession, we never once managed to hurl with the fluency of the drawn game.

I got an added little set-back about five minutes into the game when, while challenging Mike Nash for a ball, my hurley broke. It was a hurley I had been really happy with to the extent that I never paid much attention to having a second or third in reserve. Something I would normally have done.

When it snapped in my hand, I could have cried. I walked over to Noel Ryan who has been making and repairing hurleys for the Tipp team for as long as I've been involved and he handed me a replacement.

It felt warped in my hand after the beautiful weapon I had just surrendered. 'How in the name of Christ am I going to play with this?' I asked Noel.

The sides were level at half-time but, with our full-back line looking surprisingly porous, Limerick had already broken through for two goals. Tipp were living on their nerves.

The first seven minutes of the second-half, effectively, ended the game – TJ Ryan and Owen O'Neill charging through for two more Limerick goals. Then, with more than twenty minutes remaining, the selectors decided to substitute Johnny Leahy who was, again, struggling to make an impression.

The roar from the Limerick supporters as Johnny walked off was a massive psychological moment.

Much would be made afterwards of how the selectors substituted three forwards when it was our full-back line that had been in disarray. It was certainly hard to fathom how Noel Sheehy could be left sitting on the bench for 70 minutes.

As the game drifted on, Limerick set about a policy of containment. They did not score in the closing 13 minutes but, in that time, we managed only three points when we needed a minimum of six.

Michael Cleary's confidence had collapsed with the free-taking and he would miss his last three efforts. Watching 'Skippy's' shots go wide, I just knew we weren't going to make it. At one point, Aidan Ryan – who had come in as substitute – carried a ball out over the end-line. The clouds were gathering.

It was like a slow rope-burn torture realising the game was drifting away from us and feeling relatively helpless as it happened. I had scored three points from play and hurled reasonably well against an opponent who could beat me comfortably to any balls played out towards our corner.

All year, I had felt I was no longer fast enough for the corner, that full-forward was now my best position. My touch was good and I was winning balls but, that day in Cork, McDonagh just sprinted past me on any balls we had to run to.

Time was, I used to love seeing balls directed out towards the sideline. Pace, you see, was once my friend. But not any longer.

Now, I prefer a pass delivered inside me towards the goal simply because I can't compete for speed with the flying corner-men.

This was my frustration as the seconds drifted by in Pairc Uí Chaoimh now. That I didn't have the legs to dig Tipperary out of a hole.

The county needed younger, stronger hurlers to be its cornerstone men now. Standing there, watching the life drain from the team, I felt helpless. Helpless and a little melancholy.

Soon, the roars of the Limerick crowd came washing over me. I had reached the end of the line.

Sitting on the bus edging away from Pairc Uí Chaoimh afterwards, I was conscious of my own weariness. Kevin Tucker sat next to me, a young lad who probably feels like he could run forever on a hurling field. The way I used to feel.

Back in Jurys Hotel, I gave my two remaining hurleys to Liam Cahill.

Then John Hayes came over to me. John is known as 'Hotpoint' to the panel because he drives a van for that company.

He is an incredible character who has been carrying hurleys and bottles of water around the sidelines for Tipperary since we made the breakthrough in 1987.

'Hotpoint' never misses a training session either for the seniors, juniors, under-21s or minors. In many ways, he's one of those people we've all taken a bit for granted through the years. Believe me, he'd be missed if he ever stopped helping.

John wanted one of my hurleys so I had to retrieve one from Liam Cahill.

The night then drifted away quickly as we made our way home, settling – ultimately – in Pat Fox's pub in Cashel. Long after the crowd had left, four of us stayed chatting.

Pat and Marita, Anne and me. We talked about how so much had changed in our lives through the time we had been hurling with Tipperary. We both acknowledged that we weren't the players of old anymore, that the game was beginning to drift away from us.

Pat seemed quite resigned to it all. He had been carrying an injury for most of the year and sounded like someone who had made his mind up about the future.

Sitting in the quiet of a deserted bar now, the sadness washed over me in gentle waves.

II
THE TABLE

I HATE this place.

To the naked eye, it's just a room with a table in the middle of the floor. A table with a sheet across it. Looks like you could just lie there and sleep a little if you wanted.

Of course, it's not really one room, but a number of them. Everything keeps changing. Sometimes the voice you hear is male, sometimes female. Pain is the only constant.

Can't imagine how many of these rooms I've been in since the hurling started. Can't imagine how many tables I've been stretched out on, how many physios have tried to knead the trouble from my legs.

You see it's been as much part of my life now as training sessions or late-night journeys home through Urlingford, Abbeyleix and Monasterevin. 'Babs' once said to me, 'Nicky, if I had legs like yours, I'd be wearing nylons.'

Injuries have dictated the rhythm of my career. Recently, I sat at home, re-winding the memories from a decade and a half in the Tipperary jersey. And the thought struck that my history with the county has been almost as much an out-patient's diary as a hurler's scrap-book.

Counting half games I missed as well as full, injury has kept me sidelined for approximately nine of the 40 Championship games Tipp have played in that time. I've also missed three National League semi-finals and two finals.

It gets to a point where you begin to wonder about yourself. A point where doubt contaminates your thinking. I don't know of a worse feeling than sitting watching others play when you're injured. It's as if your own weakness is cruelly amplified

I was conscious this year of how reluctant the younger guys in the panel were to even ask me about the well-being of my legs. When the calf muscle went in Tralee, it was as if everyone around me was saying 'Ah, God love Nicky!'

I suppose I'm getting old.

But you see the mind is such a powerful thing when the body is locked in sick-bay. For me, the first 24 hours after sustaining injury have always been the worst. That's the time despair inflicts its strongest grip.

Then, within two or three days, you're walking better, feeling better. Mind games come into play. You start telling yourself that you've, say, three weeks to get it right. You listen intently to the physiotherapist, buying every ounce of optimism they can sell you.

'Miracles I can do,' one physio liked to joke with me. 'But the impossible takes an extra day!'

People at home in Tipperary say the move to Dublin destroyed my legs. They argue that if I was still in Cullen, my muscles wouldn't be so brittle.

It's hypothetical but I can see the logic.

Today, most of my life is spent either driving a car or sitting at a desk. Seems to me that people's lives, generally, are more sedentary now.

We are asking our bodies to respond to extremes with nothing in between. I sit all day in the office, then drive to Thurles and train as hard as I'm physically capable. It's asking too much.

In the old days, hurlers made more consistent demands of their bodies. Far more of them worked manually and a lot would have cycled the short distances we now slavishly use the car for.

In any event, players just didn't train as hard then as we do now. Hurling matches were nowhere near as fast in the sixties. Thinking about it, I don't suppose any other field games were either.

Sportsmen and women, generally, are moving much faster now and – consequently – placing far greater strain on their bodies. Levels of fitness have soared in the last thirty years. When my legs allowed, I have always preferred to train hard. Maybe that's been my problem. I love the feeling of solidity it brings, that sense of strength and well-being. And I've always liked to train as I intend playing.

Unfortunately, that's probably meant trying to do more than I was able.

I've heard just about every theory imaginable put forward for the sheer volume of my injuries through the years. I've submitted myself to every promised antidote.

I've had hydro-therapy, acupuncture, reflexology, cortisone injections, all manner of massages. Effectively, I've tried everything bar a visit to Lourdes.

The truth is, when summer comes – like any other athlete – I would do virtually anything to get my legs in working order. If someone told me that jumping off O'Connell Bridge and swimming the Liffey would do the trick, I'd almost consider it.

You see, in Championship especially, you get so few chances.

I know – at times – some people have wondered about the sheer regularity with which I seemed to be sidelined. 'Must be in his head,' is a whisper I'm well aware of.

If the injuries had been more visible like broken bones or gaping head wounds, they would probably have been accepted a lot more readily. After all, a calf muscle seems a pretty insignificant little piece of equipment at the back of your leg.

But try running if you pull it.

Evidently, my injuries were caused by a variety of incidents and circumstances.

But physios and doctors alike have all maintained that the most fundamental problem with my body is that I'm flat-footed. You can actually see the problem when I'm in my bare feet. The foot-arches are virtually non-existent.

To compensate for this, I actually run too much on my toes and this – combined with the sheer strain I appear to place on my body – makes for some interesting facial expressions. Sometimes, I look at photographs of myself going for a ball and my face seems grotesquely contorted with the effort.

Still, logic alone doesn't explain the sheer repetition of what my body's been through.

The mind boggles as to what kind of money I've cost the Tipperary county board during the last sixteen years!

What I do know is that hurling has virtually owned my life. If it had just been a question of training and playing, the commitment would have been relatively easy to absorb.

But, so often, injuries have all but tripled the hours I've been obliged to put in. Get up in the morning and go to physio before the office. Skip lunch for another session... Five times a week? Believe me, it gets tiresome.

And yet, perversely, in time I'll look back on these as the happiest days of my life. I've no doubt about that. Hurling was all I ever wanted to do and, for all the bad days, there have been countless good ones.

Funny, but I learnt so much about myself this summer. About how lucky I've been. About how my bad days have really not been so bad at all.

It's not a tragedy when someone loses a game of hurling. It's not a calamity when you pull a muscle or crack a bone.

While I was trying to get my leg right for the Munster final this year, I spent a lot of lunchtimes swimming in a pool at the School for the Blind. Every day at one o'clock, these little kids would come pouring in to have their swim.

One day, especially sticks in my mind now. A beautifully sunny day. I remember looking at the children, these little five and six-year-olds and thinking how they would never get to see that beautiful blue sky or the trees swaying gently in the breeze.

I don't want to sound soppy here. But I have spent so much of my life wrapped up in my own worries – obsessed with injuries and the thought of playing in Munster finals – that I've never stopped to look at things like blue skies and green trees. Never stopped to think of other people's problems.

So much of my time has been spent just staring down that tunnel.

That's the kind of thought that has filled my mind lately when I lie on that table, having the weakness wrung from my legs. I'm a different player today to the one the 'papers trumpeted for giving out 'English lessons' during the League run of '88.

I no longer even try to take opponents on because my legs won't carry me the way I need them to. Compare how I played against Waterford back then and the way I played against them in June of this year.

Damien Byrne played against me both days and I'm sure he'd say he was marking two different players.

Lost pace is a price we all must pay for experience and I can't pin-point exactly when mine deserted me. I'm sure it was still there in 1990 and again in '91 before the hamstring snapped.

But since then? No, it disappeared on me some day while my back was turned!

Strange thing is, you don't feel it go. It's as if you convince yourself that people around you are just getting faster. If I think about it, I haven't run a genuine sprint against anyone in training during the last five years.

Most of the time, because of injury, I've just felt too fragile. I've been trying to save myself for the games.

When you do that, you lose a proper perspective of where you really stand in terms of speed. Within my own mind, I felt physically capable of imposing myself on a Championship game in 1990. But I haven't felt that way since.

You see my head had to become my legs in later years. I had to think my way out of corners rather than sprint, I had to anticipate rather than respond. You might say decline was the mother of invention.

But I've had it with this place now, had it with this table.

I'd love to play forever but I know now that my body just can't do that. It's creaking and I'd be a fool if I didn't start to listen soon.

I could cope with getting another hundred stitches, I could handle all the cuts, grazes and bruises any game could throw at me. But, if I'm honest with myself, I don't think I can give any more time lying on this table, putting the rest of my life on hold for another summer.

I can't do that anymore.

III

THE HEADSTONES ARE WATCHING

IN the closets of a child's mind, there are no dull games.

I grew up in a tiny village called Cullen, just short of the Tipperary border with Limerick. The only son to Donie and Maura English, I learnt early how to improvise.

Some of the most intense and enthralling Munster finals I have known were played out in the little yard at the back of my father's shop. They had to be. There weren't really any other kids of my age in Cullen at the time so the games always followed a similar flight-path.

I was goalkeeper, midfielder and forward rolled into one. A hurling giant in a Tipperary jersey, surging to incredible heights to save the pride of my people.

Every game was played out to a breathless commentary and the winning goal was always scored by Gerry English. Gerry? You see, I just didn't think a name like Nicholas had much credibility in a serious hurling battle, so I would christen myself Gerry for the heroics.

In the early days, it was a tennis ball that rattled around the yard and the most cussed marker I knew was the post holding up my mother's clothes line. God knows how often that line hooked me.

I was known to take liberties too. On days I felt that Tipp needed an extra helping hand, men like Limerick's Eamonn Grimes and Cork's Ray Cummins were miraculously recruited to the cause of the blue and gold.

Basically, any player I admired became a Tipp man whether he liked it or not.

My passion for the game, came from my father and my maternal grandfather, Jackie, who never seemed to miss a Tipperary match. To hear them talk hurling was to understand the depth of emotions it could stir.

So I grew up a kind of junkie to a game I hardly knew. Until I was old enough to go with them, my hurling world revolved around their stories of tense days in Limerick, Thurles and beyond. I loved listening but always resented being left behind.

One of my worst memories is of having to stay home as my father headed to Killarney for the 1971 Munster final. I was eight at the time and would have travelled with him but for the fact that he considered the day too wet to be burdened with a child.

My anger knew no bounds as he left to catch a train from Limerick Junction. We had a small room at the back of the shop and I spent the evening in there – stepping in and out of a wardrobe, imagining it was the train.

I vaguely remember listening to some of the match on radio but, being honest, I don't have much recall of the drama at the end.

By now, I had befriended a few older lads in Cullen and – occasionally – we would play hurling up and down the street with a tennis ball. One of them, Joe Carroll, who lives in Boston now, carved the Liam McCarthy Cup out of a block of timber and covered it in tin-foil.

It's hard to describe the excitement we felt, hurling for that cup in front of Joe's house during the long, summer evenings of '71. To us, it might as well have been the real thing. I remember playing goal-to-goal against Christy Matthews one evening and almost bursting with the will to win that 'trophy'.

Joe and Christy Carroll both worked in my father's shop and my mother often joked that I would wear the two of them out from dragging them into the street for hurling or football.

When they weren't around, the action invariably took place in the backyard where my biggest worry was putting a ball out over the wall into the graveyard behind us. I hated having to search among the headstones and would come racing out of the place as if I was being chased by ghosts.

It's funny how uncomfortable a child can feel walking among the dead. It's like they're watching you and you can almost feel a cold breath on your shoulder.

One of the greatest ordeals I endured was a fruitless search of that graveyard for my very first sliothar. It had been my pride and joy, coming in the post with a small Tipperary jersey from my mother's brother, Sean, who was a post-office worker in Thurles.

To this day, I can remember the green box it came in and the pride I felt at the distinctive sound it made when struck by a hurley. In my heart, I knew I had only been hamming it with tennis balls. Now I was a real hurler.

Losing it in the graveyard, left me almost inconsolable. For years afterwards, I would put aside my hatred for the place and search for my beloved sliothar. But the search was always futile.

Maybe six years later, Christy Matthews and another lad were mitching from school one day. They were sitting on a slab, smoking fags when they found the ball underneath. It was still as white as the day I lost it and, after all my sobbing, they obviously knew it was mine.

But I had my work cut out persuading them that 'finder's keeper's' should not apply in this instance. I think it was a few weeks before they did the decent thing.

While hurling had the strongest hold on me, I mimicked virtually every sport I came across on television. Some days I'd play in an FA Cup final for Leeds United, other days I'd be riding the Derby winner at Epsom or jumping home-made fences for the Aga Khan Cup.

On the afternoon Leeds beat Arsenal in the '72 FA Cup final, I momentarily lost my bearings in the back-yard and launched into a diving header that ended painfully, chin-first on the concrete. The resulting wound required four stitches, the first stitches I ever needed. It was a terrifying experience having Dr John Wallace come to the house and place a sheet over my eyes so I couldn't see what he was doing. It is not so much the pain I remember of that evening, just the feeling of being very afraid.

On more boring days at home, I would employ my sister – Eilish – as a kind of guinea-pig. I loved challenging her to races because I knew she'd never win – even given odds. It was a selfish way of fulfilling my craving for competition. Eilish never had much interest in sport and I suspect I was part of the reason.

In hindsight, there was probably a bit of distance between me and the other kids in Cullen because I didn't go to the local national school. My mother was a teacher in Galbally so it made sense that I travel the ten miles with her every morning.

I do have memories of hunting for rabbits with fellas like Christy Matthews and Joe Carroll around Cullen but they were all a bit older than me. And I can never recall us catching a single rabbit!

Like any sports-mad kid, I was desperate to wear the jersey of a proper team and my big moment came in second class at Galbally. A football challenge was arranged against Aherlow National School and my mother drove me to the game.

I couldn't take my eyes off the black and white Galbally jerseys. This was what I had waited for, to actually wear the colours of a team. But they couldn't get a jersey small enough for me and I cried my eyes out at the injustice.

Eventually, I was allowed act as substitute in a black jumper and, fair play to them, they eventually gave me a run. But I felt tiny amongst the bigger lads, a Lilliputian lost in a forest of Gullivers.

Size was a constant millstone in my early years. It seemed I was always trying to play with taller, older children. Always in the way.

But my fragile confidence got its first boost in 1972. I had begun cycling the three miles to nearby Lattin so that I could get regular games of football in the evenings. Hurling had so few takers, I suspected the biggest prize I'd ever play for was Joe Carroll's McCarthy Cup.

Football was different. Around Lattin, there were always games to play in. In many ways, it wasn't the done thing for a young Cullen boy to make the kind of journey I was making. From my earliest days, I was aware of a certain spite that existed in Gaelic games between the two villages.

It dated back to the fifties and a game between them that had to be abandoned when fighting broke out. I could remember being shown a local newspaper headline of the time observing 'Clontarf-like scenes at Sean Treacy Park.'

The bad blood left over from that game survived for years.

But, to those of us for whom the row meant nothing, the spleen between Lattin and Cullen was simply a thing of curiosity and – often – slagging. In fact – in later years – playing for Lattin-Cullen, those of us from Cullen would blackguard the Lattin fellas by telling them not to worry about getting scores. Us Cullen lads would get enough between us!

Still, back then, I was conscious of a few frowns when I'd take myself off to Lattin. My father never tried to discourage me but it was clear some people considered it a mild betrayal.

The truth was though I couldn't give a damn that night in '72 when – as a ten-year-old – my team won the under-14 league. Captain of that team was a chap called Niall Hassett who – eighteen years later – would be the first person onto the Croke Park pitch to congratulate me after Tipperary won the '89 All-Ireland final.

Winning the under-14 league gave me a genuine sense of self-worth that I hadn't previously experienced on the playing field. There may only have been four teams involved but people were congratulating me for winning something.

Me! Nicholas English, not Gerry.

Going to Lattin, brought me into contact with more people of my own age. I became friendly with guys like Finbar and Stan Walsh, Christy Ryan and Pat O'Halloran. We seemed to play everything except hurling. In fact, for a time, tennis became our main interest.

Playing for the local club, we actually won the Munster under-14 title – the Elvery Cup – on the day Cork beat Wexford in the 1977 All-Ireland hurling final.

I was never a great tennis player, certainly not as good as Finbar or Stan. But I was handy enough. I could give them a game and I once played number seven for Munster in an interprovincial match in Limerick.

But the truth is, no matter what competition I played in, there was always someone who could beat me. Clonmel's Sean Lonergan was the best around and I knew I would never get to his level.

Even back then, I tried desperately to bring hurling into the equation. Finbar, Stan and myself would try scoring goals between two stakes holding up the lettuce wire behind the court. Using the tennis racquet like a hurley, I could always beat them at this bastard game.

In everything I did, I remained – above all – a frustrated hurler.

Lunch-hours at Galbally were filled by frenetic games of Gaelic and soccer in the old school field. For months, I pleaded with my class-mates to try their hands at hurling.

One day, they relented but my tutorials behind the shop had left me too knacky, too handy for those around me. The only fun to be had that day was mine. So hurling was given the thumbs down.

Desperate for recognition, I cherished the days Mick Roche would call to our shop selling cigarettes for Carrolls. One of the greatest Tipperary players of his generation, Roche invariably dwelt a while to talk hurling with my father.

No sooner would he enter the shop than I would have the hurley out and be beating a sliothar against the wall, hoping he would notice me. Praying he might say something complimentary. But the truth is I reached the age of 12, never having hurled for anyone!

Still a dreamer for the crowd's roar.

IV
GROWING PAINS

ONE of the hardest pieces of criticism I ever had to swallow in sport came from my own grandfather.

I was 13 at the time and playing football with Lattin. It was unusual for any members of my family to come see me playing but, on this particular evening, both my father and grandfather (Jackie) came to Emly.

Aherlow were our opponents on a lovely sunny evening and it was one of those futile assignments we were well accustomed to in Lattin. For us, these games – against patently superior opposition – were simply about damage limitation.

Still, it was a big moment for me with my father, Donie, watching. I was desperate to impress him, to convince him that I hadn't been making up stories about being one of Lattin's better players.

Anyway, Aherlow proceeded to hammer us as we more or less expected and I'm afraid I didn't manage to make the explosive impact I had craved.

On the journey home, my worst fears were fulfilled. Jackie and Donie more or less ripped into me, telling me in no uncertain terms how bad I was.

Looking back, I could have lived with that. After all, I had done virtually nothing in the game other than swan around vainly trying to look stylish when the roof was caving in. To some extent, maybe I had invited their criticism.

But I wasn't prepared for what happened when I got home.

My mother was asking them how I played and they weren't being gentle on me. 'Didn't do great now,' Donie said. Then Jackie devastated me with one sentence.

'Bit of a coward,' he shrugged.

At that moment, I would have given anything for the ground to open up and swallow me. The words literally cut through me. I was devastated.

My mother became annoyed that he would say such a thing in front of me. It left me in a state of shock. Of all the criticism that could be thrown in my direction, this one had to be ultimate.

I remember I cried all night afterwards. The thing was I didn't know whether or not he was right.

You see I thought about these things a lot, about being a man on a playing field, about being brave and strong when your team needed you to be.

I certainly suspected I was a coward in hurling alright but again that was only a suspicion. After all, I had only just started playing the game with Abbey CBS in Tipperary Town and couldn't really be judged on that just yet.

But football? Dammit I was well used to wearing the Lattin colours and considered myself a fairly useful player. No. Better than that. I thought I was good, one of their better men.

A coward?

No, that was something I could never tolerate in myself. I couldn't bear the thought of people sitting in a stand watching me play and deciding that I didn't have the stomach for it.

I had been going to school only a year in Tipp Town and this question was now boring a hole in my brain.

From my first day there, I had picked hurling as the game I wanted to play most. I can remember the day vividly. We were called into a room in the school called 'Siberia' and asked which sport did we want to become involved in.

Although I had never played a competitive game in my life, I chose hurling without hesitation.

A Corkman called Nicky Barry, was in charge of the Rice Cup team for that year. The first time he addressed me it was, 'You in the Tipp jersey'. I was so proud to be wearing the county colours (it was the same jersey that my uncle Sean had sent me years earlier), prouder still that he acknowledged them.

My first match for the Abbey was in the local Sean Treacy Park. It was a Rice Cup trial against Doon CBS and, compared to the other lads, I was really very small.

Nicky put me corner-back and my memories of the day are pretty bleak to say the least. There were a few ferocious hail showers and, at one point, I remember the pitch being almost totally white – forcing us all into a little shed until the skies relented.

I was absolutely miserable and can't actually recall touching the ball in the entire game.

I was marking this fella called Richie Quigley who I've often met since. He's a Garda now who went on to play minor hurling for Limerick. Well Richie and I were both 12-year-olds and both small so at least I didn't feel too overwhelmed.

There was a moment in the game when I remember blocking Richie down. But that was the height of my achievement. I certainly never got the ball in my hands.

Hooking and blocking people had become a big thing for me at the time. You see in all my great battles behind the shop in Cullen, I was never required to stop anyone else from scoring, although the clothes-line pole was there to block me down. Heroes were never needed for such menial tasks.

But now, if I was to make it as a corner-back, it would have to become one of the fundamentals of my game.

I remember one day Nicky showing us how to block somebody. He was stressing on us the need to get in really close. That way you were less likely to get hurt.

It was around this time I first started worrying about the possibility of cowardice in my make-up. I was afraid to ask Nicky at team-meetings what would happen if you just weren't able to get in far enough to block the man. Should you stand back or just charge in?

This thing was spinning around in my head and I couldn't summon the courage to ask him. Because I thought by asking, he'd assume I was a coward.

So it just festered there, preying on my mind, deepening my own self-doubt.

Meanwhile, we quickly became accustomed to getting hammered in the Rice Cup. If Lattin were making up the numbers in football, Abbey CBS were doing much the same in hurling. My sporting life, by now, was utterly unromantic.

Losing seemed to have become a way of life.

But my second year on the Rice Cup team gave us the briefest glimpse of glory. We actually cobbled together a decent side and got to the semi-finals. In fact, the truth is we should have won the whole damn thing but didn't.

Lismore were our opponents in Kilsheelan and I can always remember the feeling of actually playing in an important game for the first time. The big crowd provided a real atmosphere and I was picked to play at wing-back.

But a few days before the game, I got a knock while playing at school and all my toes turned black. It was desperately sore and, from memory, I ended up playing at wing-forward.

The good news was that I scored a goal. The bad, that we were beaten narrowly.

By now, I had come under the influence of a teacher in the Abbey called Michael Ryan. As Lattin had no hurling team, Michael knew that my only access to competitive action in the code was through the school.

At the time, Michael was in charge of Arravale Rovers and one day he invited me to travel to Dublin with the club's under-14 team for a tournament game in Croke Park. I was thrilled to be asked and even more elated when I discovered I'd be playing.

They played me at centre-forward and I scored 'a great goal' at the Railway End. I still have the moment frozen in my mind. Knowing immediately how well I had hit the ball, seeing the net shake, feeling the adrenaline explode.

We won the game and I have since kept a photograph at home of me standing in the black and yellow jersey of Arravale. It would probably make a good quiz question. Who was Nicky English playing for when he scored his first goal at Croke Park?

Looking back, that was such a big day in my hurling life.

I remember how proud I felt on the journey home, willing the miles away so I could tell everyone in Cullen about my goal. We stopped in Portlaoise for chips and I could have sworn people were already looking at me differently.

Still, the truth remained that this was no more than a brief respite from the normality of playing on losing teams. At under-14, 15 and 16 levels, I never won anything in hurling or football. In fact, truth to tell, I spent most of the time on teams that were getting hockeyed.

The first thing I ever won was a West Tipperary minor football final in 1976. I was 14 at the time and playing corner-forward for a Lattin-Emly team that beat Arravale Rovers in Bansha.

Playing midfield for us that day was a giant of a man called Mick Leahy. Almost 20 years later, Mick would surge to national prominence with a series of spectacular performances for Kilmacud Crokes in winning the All-Ireland Club Football Championship.

He was in his last year as a minor that day in Bansha, a huge, gangly young fella who must have already been about six foot three in height. I scored a point but we then lost the county semi-final on a miserably wet day in Boherlahan.

My father drove me to that game and, somehow, we managed to get lost along the way. Already nervous, I was practically suffering palpitations by the time we pulled into the ground literally minutes before the throw-in.

Nenagh beat us and it was the first time I could remember a manager really letting rip behind a dressing-room door. Manny Condon was from Emly and he didn't take kindly to anyone shirking their responsibilities.

At half-time, he absolutely exploded and I couldn't believe my ears. A manager who shouted was a new phenomenon to me. That same day, I didn't get a kick of the ball and travelled home thinking I might just have a better picture of why most of my outings with Lattin and Abbey seemed to be losing ones.

We probably didn't want victory as badly as we should have.

By now, I was a handy hurler. But no more than that. There was no game I could ever lay claim to have dominated. My size was constantly against me.

I used to love coming home from matches with real fanatics like Nicky Barry and Michael Ryan. We would argue passionately about the game, balancing the relative merits of great players from one county with another.

Who would you have in your team? Martin Coleman or Noel Skehan? Tadhg O'Connor or Ger Henderson? Ray Cummins or Tony Doran? Jimmy Barry-Murphy or Pat Delaney? To be fair, the two men were more than willing to listen to the often strident opinions of – basically – a snotty-nosed schoolboy.

I may have achieved nothing on the field of play. But boy could I argue a good game.

Soccer was always the sport we played in the Abbey at lunch-time. I would have preferred hurling but Tipp Town had strong soccer ties and the influence of cross-channel action had taken an undeniable hold.

But all changed utterly the day in 1978 that Paddy Kelly walked through our school-gates.

Paddy was a star. Week in, week out, Limerick's main score-getter, his name and photograph were consistently in the national newspapers and on television. I looked up to him as a hurling figure and could hardly contain my excitement when I realised he was now teaching in my school.

Paddy had an aura about him from day one. Always dressed in a track-suit, he moved around with a kind of confident athleticism that was impossible to ignore.

With Paddy's arrival, hurling suddenly became fashionable. It was strange the impact he had on us. For a while, we had known he was coming but no-one even considered the possibility that he would change PE classes so radically.

But Paddy brought a focus, an efficiency to our leisure hours. Guys who had been committed soccer players with the local St. Michael's team were suddenly taking up hurleys in their hands at lunch-time.

Now, suddenly, we had proper PE classes, proper hurling games. Paddy was a godsend and the Abbey would never be quite the same again.

Performances of the school team improved with the increased interest and we actually acquired a certain respectability. We played Croke Cup and Fitzgerald Cup at under-16 and under-17 level respectively and actually won the 1979 Fitzgerald Shield, beating Rockwell College in the final.

If Kelly had become the focus however, Ryan remained the man I confided in most. Michael knew the local hurling scene like few others and was consistently encouraging me to make the very most of what talent I possessed.

Looking back, I think I listened to him without paying too much heed. For me, real hurling heroes just seemed to occupy a different planet to my own.

I was, admittedly, beginning to get an idea of the standard needed. In 1978, Templemore won the Harty Cup with a brilliant young team and then played us in the Croke Cup. The most charitable thing I can say about the game is that they beat us by a cricket score.

But it brought me into contact with young stars of the time like Bobby Ryan, Pat McGrath and Jim Maher. If I ever wanted to wear the Tipperary colours for real, these were the kind of guys I'd be competing against.

That same year, I went to see Templemore beat St. Flannans in the

Harty Cup final in Emly. Now the Emly pitch was one I knew better probably than any other in Tipperary because my Uncle John lived right next door while Uncle Jimmy lived just up the road.

The truth is I had played hurling there for years – most of it with my first cousin, Jenny, who would put many guys I've played alongside to shame with her level of skill. Jenny was a brilliant hurler who went on to play camogie for Tipp.

Anyway, during this game as I stood admiring the talents of guys like Pat McGrath and Bobby Ryan, the ball went out over the stand. No sooner had it left the ground than I was sprinting after it.

I knew, instinctively, where to search.

That evening, I went home with a new sliothar in my pocket – courtesy of the Harty Cup.

Sure I had grander ambitions at the time than feckin balls that went out over stands. I definitely wanted to play in the blue and gold some day. But I just couldn't see it happening. Could never see myself becoming good enough.

My perceptions changed in '79 when Abbey won that Fitzgerald Shield. I was called to a West Tipperary Minor trial in Clonoulty. The game went reasonably well and, soon after, I was told to attend a county trial in Boherlahan on Good Friday.

There was a real buzz about Tipp's minors at the time. It was obvious they were going to have a brilliant team with so many survivors from the '78 side still eligible, guys like Pat Fox and the Templemore brigade. For me, the thought of being part of a potential Munster or All-Ireland winning team covered my skin in goosepimples.

I managed to make it into the final panel of 30 for a further trial game on the back field in Thurles. The tradition at the time was for a chap called Bill

Dwyer to collect all the West players and bring them to the games.

Living in Cullen, I was the first stop on Bill's journey. After me, we went down to collect Pat Fox in Annacarty. I'd never met Fox before and felt a little shy when he got into the car.

Lacking the confidence to say anything, I left the conversation to Bill and Pat for the duration of the journey. They were talking about the panel, Pat moving his finger down a sheet of paper as each unfamiliar name was identified.

Then he came to N. English.

'Who's he?' asked Pat to our grinning driver. That was my introduction to Pat Fox.

It didn't take long for my self-confidence to slip further. Shortly before the commencement of the Munster Championship, Tipp reduced their panel to 24 and yours truly was among those dispensed with.

It fell to Michael Ryan to tell me the dreaded news. He would have known how badly it was going to hurt me. Tipp, effectively, were telling me I was too weak physically. Story of my hurling life.

Michael called me out of class and broke the news as gently as he could. 'Didn't make the final cut,' he whispered, his words trailing off uncomfortably.

I was shattered. Going back into the classroom, I found it hard to stop myself crying. I felt hurt, embarrassed, humiliated almost. Here I was repeating fifth year and imprisoned in a depression few of my class-mates could relate to or understand.

My misery was so private at that moment, I resented the inquisitive eyes that followed me to my desk. I hated myself for caring so much, for wanting a Tipp hurling jersey so badly.

And, in the end, I gave in to my devastation. I finished the class crying quietly.

Public perception at the time would have been that a Lattin-Cullen man had a far better chance of winning a place with the county's minor footballers and I was actually on the team that lost heavily to Cork in the first round of that year's Munster Championship.

Coming from Cullen, football certainly seemed to make more sense. There was a big coaching push on in the county at the time and during, February and March, I can recall famous Kerry footballers like Ger Power, Pat Spillane and Ogie Moran coming to Clonmel to impart their wisdom.

It was thrilling to rub shoulders with such big names but I knew, deep down, that hurling had a special hold on me.

When the minors opened their Championship campaign against Kerry in Nenagh, Brother Perkins – who was manager – spotted me on the way in and invited me to watch the game from the dug-out. He knew I was heartbroken to be on the outside.

Tipp's great team, incredibly, would not get beyond a semi-final with Cork in Limerick that year. The game was played in heavy rain with thunder and lightning providing a vaguely eerie back-drop. I remember sitting on the side of the field and hardly being able to believe my eyes.

It was as if the whole county had been thrown into disbelief. How could such a team be beaten?

Only two of those who played would be eligible again in 1980. Tipp people trooped home that evening, wracking their brains for solutions. I was as confused as anyone.

The bad days looked here to stay.

V

TWO ASPIRINS AND A DEEP BREATH

HURLING dreams had been cleansed from my mind with the dawning of 1980.

The trauma of the previous summer seemed to have subdued an entire county. No-one talked now of Tipp's minor hurlers for the simple fact that there were no longer any faces to focus on. Only Paddy and Jim Maher remained eligible from the team that died in Limerick.

Slowly, reluctantly I began submitting to a feeling that football was where my future lay. I was eligible for the county's minors again and, unusually for Tipp, it looked like we might have a team with serious Championship credentials.

Eight of us were dual players at the time but the truth was we didn't think that we were any good at hurling. So football became the focus. Challenge matches were organised and, with confidence mounting, we triumphed in every single one.

Believe me, we were a decent football team.

We travelled to Dublin and beat Dublin. We travelled to Cork and beat Cork. I remember telling my father that we had a genuine chance in the Munster Championship but – like most Tipp people – he wasn't inclined to believe.

Most pessimism probably seemed justified given the fact that we had been drawn to play Kerry in the first round. It was a daunting prospect but I knew that fellas like Ger O'Neill, Billy Peters, Ian Conroy, Arthur Browne and the rest of us didn't give a damn for the Kingdom's tradition.

The game was played in Clonmel and – to this day – ranks as one of the most wretched disappointments of my entire life. It was, quite simply, a disaster.

With six minutes remaining, Tipp led by seven points and it was obvious to us all that Kerry were mentally beaten. Now this was a Kerry team that included footballers like Ambrose O'Donovan, Tom Spillane and Joe Shannon – guys who went on to make it at senior level.

We had played them off the park. I spent the day moving between centre-back and wing-back.

But incredibly, in the closing minutes, Liam Kearns and Michael McAuliffe plundered goals and Kerry stole the game by two points. The expressions on their faces at the end told us all we needed to know about how relieved they felt.

It surprised no-one that they went on subsequently to win the All-Ireland. They were a fine team with superbly gifted players. But, boy, did we feel cheated.

Dammit, we knew we had a hell of a team too. I think most people who saw us that day would say we were better even than the Tipp team that would get to the All-Ireland final four years later.

But we had nothing to show for it.

In later years, I got to know Joe Shannon really well. We would tour America together with AIB teams and often at night, with a few beers down, the talk inevitably returned to the first round of the Munster Minor Football Championship in 1980.

Joe always admitted he didn't know how Kerry survived that incredible day. I think the entire team were equally bemused.

The September afternoon they beat Derry in the All-Ireland final, I actually pushed my way to the front of the Hogan Stand to get a close view of the presentation. As Joe was coming down the steps, I shouted to him "I bet you thought you'd never get out of Clonmel!"

He just smiled and shook his head.

It took a long time to recover from that failure. There is nothing as bad as lying in bed at night, re-playing games and specific passages of play, wondering if you could have done things differently.

The culpability eats into everyone concerned. If you're on the field of play, you have the power to change things. How Tipp were nine points poorer than Kerry in the last six minutes of a game we utterly dominated was never going to be easily explained.

In our misery, the hurling became a welcome diversion.

Ger O'Neill, Martin McGrath and myself had been the last three players discarded from the 1979 Tipp minor panel. Now we were back and more sure of ourselves. No longer surrounded by big names, we went to the Good Friday trial in Boherlahan unburdened by any real fear.

I was subsequently picked to play midfield in a challenge game against Galway at Nenagh but performed poorly. My father, Donie, watched from the sidelines and – not for the first time – went home disappointed.

Around this time, I was spending a lot of Sundays working as linesman for George Ryan. A Cullen club-mate, George was one of the most respected referees in the country.

At first, I just helped him in club games but – before long – I was patrolling the line in National League finals and provincial finals. Probably not too many people know I was a linesman for the 1978 Munster senior hurling final as well as one of the semi-finals.

It was a job I adored because it brought me into such close proximity with the action. On top of that, I knew I was good at it. I hardly ever made mistakes.

One incident did expose me to the pressures of the big day though. It would happen in the 1981 Munster final when Clare manager, Jackie O'Gorman, thought a ball had gone over the sideline. I didn't think so and waved play on. Limerick kept possession and scored a goal directly from it.

O'Gorman was incensed and let me know in no uncertain terms what he thought of the decision. I knew it was a close call but – even now, fifteen years on – I'd still be inclined to argue the case.

I think it was Jimmy Carroll who hit the ball and Jackie was claiming that he actually threw it out over the line before making contact. It was definitely a pretty close call but it would have been a difficult one to flag back.

The truth is tempers flare in games of that importance and, if a man doesn't contest marginal calls against his county, it means his mind is probably not where it should be.

Jackie was just doing his job.

I also remember doing umpire during a League semi-final between Galway and Wexford in Thurles when Conor Hayes broke Tony Doran's hand. Doran scored a goal in the incident when Conor -- pulling legitimately – made heavy contact with his hand. I was right behind the goal at the time and couldn't believe Doran's toughness in holding onto the ball and scoring.

Thanks to his goal, the game ended in a draw but he was unable to line-out in the replay. Looking back, I think getting close-ups of heroic moments like that one was the attraction for me of working for George.

In 1979, George actually refereed the All-Ireland final between Kilkenny and Galway but Croke Park had a policy of selecting their own linesmen for the big one. It was a hell of a disappointment not to be on duty that day even though George, to be fair, took me up to the match anyway.

But back to 1980 now and the reason for this digression. With George in charge, I was linesman for that year's Harty Cup final between North Mon and St. Colman's of Fermoy. It was a super game that ended in a draw and anyone who saw it would have had to believe that Cork were going to have a brilliant minor team in the Munster Championship.

Fellas like Tomas Mulcahy, Tony O'Sullivan, Paul O'Connor and Joe Noonan were all involved and I couldn't help thinking that day how Tipp had virtually no-one by comparison.

At one point in the game, I actually told O'Connor to move back a 'seventy' he was trying to steal some yards with and he just looked at me disdainfully. There was no way he was going to be told what to do by a little kid his own age.

The 'seventy' was taken from where he chose.

It was a sobering experience given the fact that we were due to meet Cork in the first round of the Championship. Truth is, most of us thought we'd be wasting our time.

We certainly didn't expect to beat Cork that day in Limerick. I was selected at midfield with Joe Hayes while a guy who would one day be 'best man' at my wedding, Ian Conroy, was given the task of marking their main danger-man, O'Sullivan.

Ian was definitely the kind of guy you wanted beside you in the trenches. Maybe not the most stylish of hurlers, he had a level of power and commitment that made a difference when Championship heat was on.

That day, he was like a bull in a china shop – shadowing O'Sullivan's every move, shuddering the air with his ferocious pulling. Ian looked pumped up like never before.

And he managed to break my leg!

How did it happen? Let's just say, the ball got stuck on the ground between Tony and me and Ian intervened without asking questions. Pulling unceremoniously, he made contact with my foot and I knew immediately I was in trouble.

I could feel my foot swelling up inside the boot and, after about five minutes, it was obvious there was serious damage done.

Joe and I had been winning midfield but I was hobbling badly at half-time and it was decided to play me at corner-forward for the remainder. I scored a point and, incredibly, we won the game. It was a turn-up no-one had predicted.

Still, going home on the bus, my leg was in an awful state. I had little appetite for the celebrations as a sharp pain literally brought tears to my eyes. But we had beaten Cork and – among the others – the mood was naturally buoyant.

We went home via Kilcommon, stopping in Rearcross and – eventually – Jacksie's pub in Upperchurch. This was a roundabout way of getting home but TJ Dwyer, one of the selectors, was from Kilcommon club, Sean Treacy's. Needless to say, it was extremely late by the time I got to my bed in Cullen.

The following morning, an x-ray in Cashel confirmed what – in my heart – I had already accepted. The leg was broken. My summer looked to be over.

There was a slight possibility that, if Tipp got to the All-Ireland final, I would have a chance of playing. But it seemed a long way away that morning in Cashel.

Still, I desperately wanted to stay close to the scene. All through that summer, I used to go into Thurles on the minibus to watch the others train.

We had great craic on that West bus, driven by a fella from Bansha called Noel Brown.

Martin McGrath, at the time, was in the army so he would have to be dropped back to the Curragh camp in Kildare every training night. It meant a marathon round-trip for me that started at around four thirty in the evening and finished about one the following morning. But I loved every second of it.

Coming home from the Curragh, we'd go around by Hollyford and into Kilcommon with Gerry Doyle, then down to Cappawhite with Ger O'Neill. The journey would take us over some of the worst roads in Ireland but we were oblivious to the pot-holes

Even though I would be the last to be dropped off, I never minded the length of the journey. It being summer, I was off school and – to be honest – just putting down time until my leg was right.

A great bonus for me was the fact that the Moscow Olympics were on at the time so the boredom factor was actually at a minimum.

Much of our conversation on those round-trips from Thurles to Kildare and back again revolved around what was happening in Moscow. And I was more than happy to show the lads how well informed I had become on Olympic matters.

As it happened, Tipp went on to win the Munster final comfortably against Limerick (a future county colleague, Conor O'Donovan, was their full-back) and that meant we got a bye to the All-Ireland final. Our opponents would be Wexford who beat Galway in the only semi-final. At last, I felt I had something concrete to aim for.

Five weeks in plaster, I returned to training on August 20 with only two weeks to stake my claim. My leg was totally wasted from the inactivity and I remember deciding I would have to hurt myself to make a serious impression.

In many ways, TJ Dwyer got me on the team. Even though the foot was in pain, I kept telling everyone that it felt fine. TJ could see my enthusiasm and, listening to my assurances, reckoned I was ready.

Certainly, I was moving okay and I think I was fairly good at masking my discomfort. But it was very very sore and I was always in a terrible state once training ended.

Still, N. English was named to play at corner-forward for his county on the first Sunday in September. After all my dreaming, I would now play for Tipp in an All-Ireland final.

It was strange trying to absorb that reality. After all, we had gone into the 1980 Championship thinking we were useless. Virtually all of the star names, the Harty Cup winners, were gone from the fold. Essentially, those of us left behind were nobodies.

It was as if we had bluffed our way to the top table.

I went into Limerick the week of the final to buy new boots, telling my mother that the pair I had were too hard for my injured foot. We bought a pair of Pumas in a sports shop but the truth is they made no difference.

Still, I consoled myself, that it was a good way of getting new boots.

On the day before the final, we travelled up to Dublin and stayed in the Grand Hotel, Malahide. I was rooming with Aki Brown from Clogheen and there was a wedding on in the hotel.

We were like children in a sweet shop looking at all the pretty girls around the bar and lobby and two in particular from England had us totally gob-smacked. They were gorgeous and watching them took our minds completely off the game ahead.

It was all just a huge adventure for us and I have no great recollection of feeling nervous. The morning of the game, we walked on the beach and, if we had a preoccupation, it was with the injuries we were carrying.

Apart from myself, Ger O'Neill was nursing a broken wrist and Martin McGrath had ankle ligament damage. In other words, three of our forwards – half of the attack – really had no business playing.

Brother Perkins, who was manager of the team, didn't say much but he must have been concerned.

In the dressing-room beforehand, it was decided to give me some pain-killers for my foot. I was really intrigued to discover what effect they would have.

I mean, this was what you used read about in the papers. Star players needing pain-killers before a big game. I thought to myself that this meant I had truly arrived. You would have given your right arm at the time to be able to say you needed a pain-killing injection to allow you play.

Anyway, the doctor gave me these two white tablets and, after I swallowed them, I remember looking down at the dark, timber floor of the old Cusack Stand dressing-room and wondering if it was about to start spinning. I was actually a bit nervous they might make me feel drunk.

But not alone did the floor not move, the pain in my foot never softened either.

Much later, I discovered that what I had actually been given was basically two Solpadeine. In other words, two aspirins. So much for my introduction to serious drugs!

Still, I went out on the field that day believing I had some powerful concoction bouncing around my bloodstream. We started the game well and, were it not for the heroics of the Wexford goalkeeper, Tipp would possibly have been out of reach by half-time.

We reached the interval 1-10 to 0-5 ahead and I had the satisfaction of scoring the goal.

It was a relatively straight-forward score, described in one newspaper afterwards as an 'old fashioned' goal. Basically, the ball was hit across by Billy Peters from the Hill 16 side and, running towards it with my marker, I pulled on it first time.

I was elated to see the net shiver but, to be perfectly honest, I spent most of the game confined to the fringes. Very little ball was coming into my corner and the guy marking me, Paul Gahan, was entitled to think he hadn't given much away.

No, the heroes for Tipp that day were Joe Hayes, Martin McGrath, our entire half-back line and particularly Ian Conroy. Like myself, Martin was eventually taken off because of his injury but he had done a fantastic job in restricting the influence of Wexford's huge centre-back, Eamonn Cleary.

Conroy, likewise, proved an inspiration. I will never forget one incident when – having lost his own hurley – Conroy just threw his body in front of a Wexford attacker shooting for goal. The shot was blocked and Conroy walked away unscathed. Typical of the man.

Close to the end, Wexford did launch a bit of a rally but nothing to seriously threaten us. We won the game 2-15 to 1-10.

Tipperary were All-Ireland minor champions and Nicky English, not Gerry, had a medal!

Looking back today, I would have to say the celebrations were a hell of an anti-climax. In later years, I would see minor teams celebrate All-Ireland wins like grown men, dressed impeccably in their blazers, drinking their bottles of Budweiser or Bulmers at the bar counter.

But, back then, we were total innocents. Lambs sent up for the day from Tipperary, led around as if we had no minds of our own.

The Tipperary Association had a function organised for us in some big, echoey hall where we were treated to some salad and a few bottles of orange. Nobody was there except our parents and I know most of us found the occasion a little flat, a little boring.

The majority of us would have taken a drink at the time but we had to wait until we got back to the Grand Hotel in the early hours of the morning before we could relax with a few beers. The evening, to put it bluntly, was a bit of a non-event.

It's strange now to realise how oblivious we all were to the fact that Galway had won an historic senior final against Limerick the same day. We watched that game from the Cusack Stand but it meant nothing to us.

I would imagine it is the same with minors every year. You are wrapped up only in your own cause. Sitting in the front row that day, we were only blackguarding, biding our time before taking the Cup home.

We were so innocent compared to 18-year-olds today. At least I was. Nothing Galway or Limerick did that day would have mattered much to me. Even Joe Connolly's famous speech went right over my head.

I was a little more responsive though 24 hours later at the traditional post-All Ireland lunch in the Burlington. We watched a video of the senior game on a bad screen and, suddenly, the McCarthy Cup was there in front of me.

I couldn't help myself but reach out and touch it. I also said hello to Joe Connolly but, then, I suppose virtually everyone in the hotel did that the same day.

That evening, we travelled home on the bus and I remember what seemed a big crowd coming out to greet us in Thurles. But that was it. Basically, we arrived, showed off the Cup and bade our farewells.

Then, those of us from the West, got into Noel Browne's bus and just headed home.

VI

'IF I HAD A SCISSORS, I'D CUT IT OFF!'

SOME people saw it as betrayal.

The evening in 1990 that Cork dethroned Tipperary as Munster hurling champions, I had a couple of brandies in Thurles Sarsfields' clubhouse with Fr Michael O'Brien. As Cork manager, O'Brien had just been responsible for breaking Tipp hearts everywhere, including my own.

I knew many of my own countymen watched me that evening, wondering how on earth I could fraternise with the 'enemy'. The answer was simple.

O'Brien was a man who had imposed an immense influence on my development as a hurler. With his wit, his anger, his almost demented passion for the game, he left an indelible mark on any young man who hurled under his tutelage.

And, for five years, I was one of those.

You see, within a month of winning an All-Ireland minor medal in 1980, I was on my way to University College Cork, supposedly to pursue a degree in electrical engineering. It was a naive academic choice, dictated solely by the fact that the 24 points I had gained in my Leaving Certificate corresponded exactly with the requirements for engineering.

The truth is, within two years of moving to Cork, a few failed exams confirmed the glaring reality that I had little interest in the course. So I opted instead to do a BA on the brutally simple reasoning that it would allow me more time for hurling.

Going to UCC, I had little awareness of the Fitzgibbon Cup and certainly no suspicion of the hold it would have on me for the next five years of my life. I had gone to Cork primarily because of course selection and the fact that a few others from Abbey CBS were going too.

Linking up with Pat Donovan, Tommy O'Brien and Pat O'Neill was a convenient step given that we could all share digs and – in truth – have a ball on the university social scene.

Other Tipp men like Donal Morrissey and PJ Shanahan were down there too so there was never going to be much threat of loneliness. If anything, in our first year, the craic would prove too good.

Fitzgibbon Cup hurling is played in March so the preparation begins in the months leading into Christmas. Now, in 1980, UCC were one of the poor relations in university hurling, not having won the Cup for more than ten years.

It was decided that an outsider was needed to coach the team and Fr O'Brien got the vote. He had achieved great success with Farranferris previously so the word was that – at the very least – he would shake things up.

To say I had never met anyone like O'Brien in my life before would be a ludicrous understatement. He arrived at the college like a whirlwind.

Tipp people often ask me what kind of a man O'Brien is behind a dressing-room door. There is a certain fascination there after what happened in 1990 and his perceived ruthless twisting of the 'donkeys for derbies' remark.

My answer to them is that he is like a mad man. Not in the bad sense you understand. At the time we were hurling Fitzgibbon for UCC, we developed an incredible respect and affection for the ploys he adopted to get our minds focused on battle.

But, if you didn't know him, if you didn't understand exactly what he was trying to achieve, you would definitely come to one conclusion and one conclusion only. That the man was certifiably insane.

To this day, I maintain that he is a wonderful actor. In my first year, admittedly, I thought he was completely cracked. But, as time went by, you saw the effect he could have on a team and its supporters, the way he could whip people into a frenzy.

If you did something wrong in a game, he would look you in the eye and say, 'What are you doing to me?' Always, the focus was on playing for him, on not letting him down. He took defeat more personally than any man I knew.

I didn't know him from Adam when he arrived at UCC. For a few weeks, I had been playing with the Freshers' team and Fr O'Brien was only involved with the seniors. But, on a lovely mild, dry day, in October 1980 UCC travelled up to play Queens University at Santry in a preliminary round game for the Fitzgibbon Cup.

For some reason, Danny Buckley – a Cork senior hurler at the time – couldn't travel and, without much warning, I was thrown in at right-half forward. We won the game well and I scored something like 2-8 – Queens were very poor at the time.

On the journey home, we stopped off in the Talk of the Town restaurant in Newbridge for a mixed grill and chips. I can still remember O'Brien calling me over to his table and asking me if I was related to Theo English. I told him I wasn't but, from that day on, he always took a big interest in my career.

UCC were due to play a challenge game the following morning but all

I wanted to do was get off the bus in Cashel and get home for the weekend. In many ways, the fact that I had played well against Queens made my position easier.

If I had played poorly and insisted on going home for the weekend, I knew in my heart and soul I wouldn't make the Fitzgibbon panel. That would have killed me.

But I had done better than expected and now knew I was in Fr O'Brien's plans. Anyway, my mother was sick at the time so I bade my farewells in Cashel.

No questions were asked.

Over the coming months, we were to become virtually professional hurlers, our whole lives geared to what I believe O'Brien saw as his new vocation, bringing the Fitzgibbon Cup to UCC.

I had never come across anyone like him before. We would train ferociously in the Mardyke where he barked his instructions like an army officer. Everyone had to do precisely what he preached or risk his wrath.

Those training sessions were Heaven for me as – physically – I started to become much stronger and I loved the drills he would have us perform, making us think a little deeper about how to unlock defences. You could have your fun with him, so long as he could see that you were working.

Needless to say, my engineering suffered as hurling became the unquestionable priority. The fact is I didn't study at all. Hurling was all I lived for.

People who have never come in contact with the Fitzgibbon Cup can never quite understand the emotions it stirs in those who have. It is like the players become family. You eat, drink and sleep hurling for the duration.

O'Brien's use of psychology, his capacity to bring the best out of young players at this time had to be seen to be believed.

I remember for our first Fitzgibbon final he put in Tadhg Coakley to do a marking job on Tipperary senior player, Eamon O'Shea. Now O'Shea was a star at the time, having played in the National League final of 1979.

Even though Tadhg was on the Cork minor team of '79, not many of us would have fancied his chances against O'Shea. Tadhg was a 'boot boy' from Mallow, a skinhead with a donkey jacket who adopted a very nonchalant attitude to life.

To all of us, he was one of the nicest fellas in the panel and a well respected corner-forward, but hardly the man to wear down an inter-county star at wing-back.

Anyway, Fr O'Brien picked Tadhg at wing-back and he never gave O'Shea a puck of the ball.

What he managed was no accident. O'Brien had been trainer to the Cork minors in '79 and he knew precisely what Tadhg Coakley was capable of. Maybe even more so than Tadhg himself.

That year's Fitzgibbon tournament was being hosted by UCD and we stayed in the Clarence Hotel on the quays. On the Saturday, we won our semi-final comfortably against UCG in miserable rain and muck.

The match is memorable to me only for the fact that I had long hair at the time and it kept going in my eyes. O'Brien was becoming incensed on the sideline and, eventually, stormed out towards me with this headband which he tied around my forehead.

'If I had a scissors, I'd cut it off,' he bellowed.

I remember too that our centre-back, Noel Leonard, got a bad belt on the back of his hand the same day. After the game, Noel put ice on his hand and left it there. He had never heard of ice-burn!

When he took the ice off, all his skin came with it. The poor man was in terrible agony and had to have a special glove made up so he could play in the final the following afternoon. To this day, I don't know how he managed to get through that game.

Anyway, the morning of the final, we all went to Mass in this big church on the quays. There was a small balcony in the church and Fr O'Brien gave a private Mass for us up there.

It was to be my first experience of how he could turn a sermon around to tie in with that afternoon's game. It would become his Fitzgibbon party-piece, delivering some kind of message to us from the pulpit.

But this was my first time hearing an O'Brien sermon and I will never forget how he finished it. 'Enjoy the game,' he told us. 'Play it in a sporting way.

'AND WIN!'

Without even taking a breath, he then entered into 'I believe in God, the Almighty...' At no point did he smile, look left or right. Just glared straight ahead and continued with the Mass.

That evening, we beat a very fancied UCD team at Croke Park by seven points. They were probably the better team but goalkeeper, Johnny Farrell, made some incredible saves. I played centre forward and got a goal which effectively put us clear.

It was a big moment for me.

In a matter of just six months, I had now won All-Ireland minor and Fitzgibbon Cup medals. But, more than that, I had come from being a real bit-part player to being one of the mainstays of the team.

If I was truthful, the minor victory hadn't given me any intense satisfaction. Even though I had the excuse of injury, I was taken off in the All-Ireland final. Truth is, I knew Tipp would have won that game with or without me.

No, make no mistake, the Fitzgibbon was what made me as a hurler.

Over the next five years, UCC would not lose a game in the competition and the bonds between those of us on the team and Fr O'Brien became intense.

Coleraine hosted the competition in 1983 when we were going for three-in-a-row. We played UCD in the semi-final and I can always remember this vaguely surreal experience of watching an enormous ship slide by on a river maybe 150 yards from the pitch.

Our centre-back, John O'Connell, got a bad eye injury in that game and, although we were leading well at half-time, there would be a ferocious gale in Dublin's favour for the second-half. I told O'Brien that I played centre-back for my club so he agreed to put me in John's position.

The move went well, I hurled out of my skin and we held on to make the final against UCG.

That was to be a game played on a windy day in Bellaghy as curtain-raiser to a National Football League clash between Dublin and Derry. I remember that fact purely and simply because I subsequently discovered that Charlie Redmond made his inter-county debut that same day.

The truth is we didn't give a damn who was going on after us. They might as well have been holding the World Cup final in Bellaghy that day and it would have gone completely over our heads.

We annihilated UCG in the final – full-forward, Mick Quaide, scoring 3-2 – but, having marked Michael Coleman from centre-back, I was named 'Man of the Tournament'.

Looking back, I would have to say it was my best Fitzgibbon ever. I was physically strong, full of confidence and totally comfortable with the people around me.

Anyway, we went straight to the bar when it was over and I made the mistake of starting to drink brandy. That night, about an hour after the presentation, I was talking to Professor Willie Smith – one of our selectors – when I just collapsed off my seat onto the floor.

Willie had the good grace to put it down to pure fatigue. The bus journey home the following day was a nightmare. I lay down at the back for most of the way, sleeping off the excesses of the night before. It took us almost two hours just to get as far as Belfast and, while everyone else got off for coffee, I couldn't bring myself to move.

Just outside of Cahir, the bus broke down and we had to sit there waiting for a replacement to come from Cork. In all, it took us thirteen hours to complete the journey from Coleraine. We got to Cork at two in the morning.

Around this time, Mick O'Dwyer had taken charge of the college footballers for Sigerson and I remember a fairly strong internal rivalry building up between himself and Fr O'Brien. Certainly, we were made aware that it would not be acceptable for us to be seen losing if the footballers were going well.

I always maintained that Fr O'Brien was never as tough as he liked people to believe. Everything was image for him. He was generally limping during training, suffering pain from hips that needed replacing.

When I think of him now, I see him standing on the sideline beneath a peak cap, wearing this old blue anorak with its woolly hood, his socks pulled up outside his trousers.

A man of habit you might say, in every sense. And superstitious too.

The first year we won the Fitzgibbon, he got the peak cap from a guy called Frank Ryan who was from Doon in Limerick and doing dentistry. Frank was a sub that year and Fr O'Brien took his cap one day when it was teeming rain.

We won and he wore it for every Fitzgibbon after that.

There were certain, crucial rituals to our hurling lives back then. On the coach ride to a game, Fr O'Brien had his favourite songs that he reckoned would get us going. 'The Lonely Woods of Upton' was a popular choice or 'The Banks of My Own Lovely Lee'.

Admittedly, the UCC versions did not always tie in too accurately with what you might hear on the radio. If the conventional version followed polite, romantic lines, our one went something like 'Where we sported and trained, in the shit and the rain...'

Always, Fr O'Brien would get us incredibly pumped up for those games.

During my second year in UCC, the Fitzgibbon was played in the Mardyke. We were playing UCG in the semi-final and, although far superior on paper, we just couldn't shake them off. We were leaking goals and Fr O'Brien was almost beside himself with rage.

In the dressing-room at half-time, he turned on us. Now the Fitzgibbon Cup is a huge cup but he had it in one hand, shaking it at us furiously as if it weighed no more than a rolled up newspaper.

At such moments, his language could be colourful.

'Ye want to f......g give it to them, ye can f......g give it to them, but I'm not,' he bellowed. 'If they want it, they can f......g follow me up the Marina for it.'

Sitting there in the dressing-room, this bizarre image stuck in your head of the whole Galway team chasing Fr O'Brien up the Marina to get the Cup off him.

'Who are we?' he would roar then. 'Do we want it?' And he would show us the Cup.

It may sound over the top but to be there, behind that closed door, was to go to the very edge of emotion. We knew so much of what he was doing was no more than an exuberant act, but it worked on us. Set the blood racing.

The more we won, the more we learnt to celebrate. In fact, I think it's fair to say that, by then, Fitzgibbon dinners were beginning to get a little out of hand.

That year's dinner was held in the Metropole Hotel and we warmed up for it in Dan Lowry's pub nearby. The two beaten semi-finalists tended to spend the day of the final drinking so – come dinner-time – they were invariably in rowdy form.

Suffice to say, food tended to travel from table to table and I hope it was merely coincidence but, the year after I left UCC, they decided to do away with Fitzgibbon dinners.

My old mate, Ian Conroy, came to the university in September of '84 and immediately hit it off with Fr O'Brien. Ostensibly, he came to do an arts degree but everyone knew he had come to hurl.

Ian was no genius with a hurley, 'a good man to cut down a ditch' as one Tipperary selector of our era described him. But he was a fantastic competitor with the heart of a lion. Give Ian a job to do on a hurling field and he was one of those guys you never had to think about again. A man you could depend upon100%.

That year we played UCD in the final, a titanic game played in appalling conditions in Maynooth. Entering injury-time, the sides were level when a UCD player, Gerry Drennan, struck a brilliant shot for goal.

The ball hit the inside of a post, spun along the goal-line but never crossed it. Had it gone in, I have no doubt our reign was over.

But we got away with it and Conroy got the next ball. He would exaggerate it and say he was no more than twenty yards out from his own goal. I would say he was at least twenty five!

But, anyway, he took possession and soloed his way up along the sideline to UCD's twenty one. Conroy was bouncing off fellas, losing the ball, getting it back and somehow managing to keep going. When he got to the twenty one, he hit the ball.

Unbelievably, it flew over the bar and he had won his place in Fitzgibbon folklore.

I would say it was the one Fitzgibbon tournament we had played in and not really deserved to win. In hindsight, it was just pure heart that won it for us. Ian Conroy's heart.

For years after, he would never let us forget the day he won the Fitzgibbon 'single-handedly'. I'd swear I've heard him saying he actually got the ball on his own goal-line.

Anyone who was there that day though will know exactly where he got it. Because what he did was just incredible.

Fr O'Brien liked to have a team going out on the field believing that the whole world is against them. He would tell you how your opponents didn't respect you. He'd get you riled up to the last, get your back up, get you angry.

That's what he did with Cork in 1990. I could see his hand on every move they made that day, their mood, their almost demonic need to put Tipperary down. I'm sure I could nearly have given the speech he made before that game.

O'Brien was written all over Cork in 1990 and Tipp paid a heavy price.

Motivation was his forte and Ian Conroy had long been one of his favourite pupils. O'Brien liked him as a person, liked the way he played, his character, his courage.

Conroy was always on his wavelength and they had an intense, mutual respect.

On the eve of that game in '90, I remember chatting to Ian on the phone. He had stopped playing for Tipp by then but we still talked a lot about where the county was heading.

I wasn't particularly happy with the way the team had been picked. Truth is, I couldn't make a lot of sense out of some of the decisions taken. Still, I was reasonably hopeful that we'd win. Tipp were in their prime whereas Cork – being honest – looked no better than average.

Conroy said he thought we'd win too but added a numbing caveat. It has stuck with me ever since.

'Remember Nicky', he said. 'O'Brien is a dangerous man!'

I always remember a League final match we played against UCG in Mountrath I think and one of the Galway players was abusive towards Fr O'Brien.

Typically, he made a big thing out of it. You see he saw it only as a potential weapon, something to be used as part of our psychology.

He wanted all of us to react, to know that he had been abused by one of the Galway players. 'See, they have no respect for me,' he'd roar and we'd all feel personally slighted by what had just occurred.

One of our easiest Fitzgibbon victories was the one that completed our five-in-a-row. It being my last year, I was captain and from a very early stage we reckoned we were close to being unbeatable.

Fr O'Brien was also manager of Cork at the time and I remember we played them in a challenge. Now this was the full Cork team, Jimmy Barry-Murphy, the whole lot.

We played them in the 'Farm which is out in Bishopstown and we beat them well. The frightening thing is that it didn't really surprise us. We were a virtual inter-county team ourselves. Without a shadow of a doubt, that was the best college team I ever played on.

Sometimes, I wondered what a total stranger would have made of our team talks in a dressing-room or on a bus. He would probably have thought we were lunatics on a day-pass.

It was like we occupied another planet. We were all utterly consumed by the need to keep UCC winning, to fight for the honour of each other. Over the years I was there, that unity was our greatest weapon.

Sure we had some wonderfully gifted hurlers. But I doubt if any of our opponents ever wanted victory more than we did. And that was O'Brien's genius.

He was larger than life, an eccentric who warmed to non-conformists like himself. Around this time, he was the navy chaplain in Haulbowline and he was always into flash cars. I remember especially a white Opel Manta that caught the eye.

Sometimes, I look back to those days and marvel at how much I grew as a hurler at UCC. Maybe it was purely coincidental, something that would have happened anyway in the fullness of time.

But the truth is that, under the management of Fr Michael O'Brien, my game came on in leaps and bounds. I acquired enormous respect and admiration for the man. Something that has survived to this day.

People who know him only vaguely probably don't realise that so much of his aggression, his taciturn appearance is actually put on. We adored his training sessions because he was always poking fun at somebody or some thing.

O'Brien, I know, loves Cork and he loves UCC. He never liked to be beaten and anything he could do to win he would.

He was having one of his hips done during our five-in-a-row bid so he wasn't around as much as previously.

One day we were playing a League game in the Mardyke and the reality is that our lads didn't give a damn about the League because we knew we could win it at will.

In my team-talk before the game, I found myself saying to the lads 'You know you can see the Mardyke from the hospital above in Shanakiel.

'Fr O'Brien's probably above there watching us at this very moment!'

It was a ridiculous thing to say, but that's the kind of effect he could have on you. Somehow, even if he wasn't there, you sensed he had a way of knowing if you weren't putting it in.

On that evening in Thurles Sarsfields' clubhouse six years ago, where Tipp people wore the blank expressions of the bereaved, I did not feel remotely guilty for drinking with Cork's manager.

To me, it was the most natural gesture in the world, given all the past battles I had fought with Fr O'Brien.

Of course, I was devastated that Tipp's Munster and All-Ireland crowns were gone. In fact, I wasn't in much of a mood for talking hurling.

O'Brien knew that too and the reality is we talked about everything bar the game. We didn't talk about the 'donkeys' business or anything like that. It was just about old times, mutual friends, forgotten battles.

I was happy for him when Cork went on to win that year's All-Ireland final. Happy because I always knew deep down that that was Fr O'Brien's ultimate ambition.

When Cork beat Galway in the 1990 final, he was left with nothing else to prove. And I felt he was entitled to that.

Tipp people might never feel comfortable about welcoming an All-Ireland win for Cork. But I made an exception for my old friend.

VII
'I'M GOING TO PUT HIM INTO THE STAND'

ONE of the greatest hurlers I ever played alongside was a man called Ger O'Neill.

Outside of Tipperary, maybe not many people would know who I'm talking about. Ger was virtually unstoppable as an under-age player but his inter-county career at senior level never quite had the longitude it should have done.

To me, that was a tragedy for Tipperary.

Although very slight in his prime, O'Neill was a hurler with everything. Speed, touch, vision, accuracy...I saw him destroy more teams single-handedly than any other man I've known. A native of Cappawhite, he was a good friend too, the kind who never took himself too seriously. In hindsight, maybe that became Ger's problem.

By the time Tipperary's under-21 trials were held in Holycross at the beginning of 1981, Ger's hurling was incredible. The two of us had come off the same All-Ireland winning minor team and we didn't harbour too many insecurities.

That was saying something given that Tipp were bidding for their third All-Ireland Under-21 title in a row. The reality was that, to get on the team of '81, was going to be quite a challenge.

Needless to say, star names like Bobby Ryan, Pat McGrath, Peter Brennan and Pat Fox weren't expected to submit themselves to trials. So that day in Holycross, Ger and myself could see nobody to unnerve us.

I was full of the confidence acquired from six months in UCC and the truth is that this was to be the first day Ger and myself really gelled on a hurling field. Physically, I had developed to such an extent that Danny Morrissey – a selector for the under-21s – told me he could not believe the change in my condition from the previous September.

Tipp's first Championship match of '81 was down for April 22 against Kerry. It meant I was coming straight off my first Fitzgibbon Cup win – a fact, to be honest, that made little impact on Tipp people.

The Fitzgibbon meant nothing where I came from. In fact, to this day, I think a lot of the people I grew up with are a little bit bemused by the intensity of emotion I feel for UCC. It's as if they wonder how any Tipp man could feel such affection for a Cork institution.

But I think Morrissey's comments reflected just how emphatically I had grown as a player during my first six months on Leeside. Now I was superbly fit and far stronger than ever before.

For the first time, I could mark a man like Cormac Bonner and not be shunted aside like a rag-doll. The change in me during those six months was nothing short of staggering.

Despite the big names available, I wasn't hugely surprised to be picked at midfield for the game against Kerry. The surprise lay in how confident I had felt in the Holycross trial.

For a young lad, midfield was the romantic place to play, the glamour spot. It meant you were there for the throw-in, right at the centre of the action.

In kids' teams, the best players always seemed to man midfield.

But presumption quickly went out the window when I played poorly against Kerry and was left to absorb the reality that, whatever else Nicky

English was going to be in hurling, it wouldn't be a midfielder.

I wondered if they'd retain me for our Munster semi-final against Waterford. All the brashness, the sense of certainty was gone as I waited to see the team-sheet for that game. Luckily, I made it.

Named at right-half forward, I felt far more comfortable on a wet evening in Thurles and enjoyed the game, scoring four points from play and – generally – making up for the ground lost against Kerry.

That victory – on a resounding 6-14 to 1-3 scoreline – assured us of a Munster final date with Cork, the kind of assignment I used dream about during those childhood days behind the shop in Cullen.

This was big for me. In Tipp, hurlers were measured generally on Championship performances, specifically on how they could deal with the challenge presented by Cork. I had followed the under-21s the previous year and seen the huge crowds they drew.

Tipp, at the time, were playing a really attractive brand of hurling and people wanted to see them. When they won the All-Ireland in 1980, the Munster final had been played in Fermoy and the size of the attendance there had to be seen to be believed.

At that time, I would never have dreamt I could get a place on such a team. But here I was twelve months on and, maybe for the first time in my hurling life, feeling an excitement bordering on fear.

The game was to be played in Thurles and, while we had our share of star names, Cork had fellas like Ger Cunningham and Kevin Hennessy. It was easy to be apprehensive.

I remember being at home the evening of the match and going to bed for an hour or two, just to get a bit of sleep. Afterwards, it seemed like a bad idea. Because it left me feeling really tired.

In hindsight, nervousness was taking its toll.

Still, I got into the game nice and early and two first-half points helped settle the butterflies. I was playing well and my confidence began to grow.

It's funny but the better you play, the higher your dander rises.

Early in the second-half, John Hartnett – a brother of Pat – went to rise the ball about 50 yards from goal and missed it. Now he was bigger than me, but I just came and hit him with a shoulder.

The impact knocked him backwards and I just picked the ball up and put it over the bar. To this day, I can remember the cheer that erupted. It was as if the whole of Semple Stadium shook and I felt goosepimples sprout all over my body.

At that precise moment, I knew no fear. I didn't give a damn for personal safety, I would have run through a wall for the blue and gold.

At another juncture, I submitted to one of my worst habits and lost my hurley just under the new stand. It was something I was prone to doing – possibly because so many of my instincts were still those of a footballer.

I think it was John Hodgins who got the ball at left-half back and, moving in to block him, I suddenly realised I had nothing to block him with. But I remember thinking 'F... it, I'm not going to let him clear this.'

So I just dived in and blocked him down with my hand. The ball actually broke out over the line and it was our line-ball. A big thing was made of it in the papers afterwards, of how I had risked my own personal safety to stop Hodgins from clearing.

And that was important to me.

A lot of people would have looked on me until then as being a bit casual, the kind who didn't really get involved and just waited around for scoring opportunities. Maybe even a bit of a 'coward' as my own grandfather once so cuttingly put it.

But, as a wing-forward, I was actually covering a lot of ground, working really hard. And I wanted people to know that.

We beat Cork 1-15 to 0-10. I had come a long way in twelve short months.

Galway were to be our opponents in the All-Ireland semi-final and, as part of our preparation, we played Glen Rovers in Thurles seven days before the game. I was marked that night by Denis Coughlan which, to me, was an intimidating prospect given his fame throughout the country.

But I did well and apparently Coughlan went to Danny Morrissey afterwards and said he couldn't imagine any other under-21 team living with us. We were playing fantastic hurling with Ger O'Neill at right corner forward and Martin McGrath beginning to come through on the wing.

The truth is, we couldn't see ourselves being beaten either.

It was to no-one's surprise that we went on to hammer Galway in the semi-final. This was an absolute cakewalk. The score was 3-17 to 0-7 and O'Neill, especially, was just out of this world.

The backs were brilliant too, specifically Pat Fox in the corner. We had gone to Ennis that day feeling virtually invincible and the performance confirmed everything we believed.

Even though I played relatively poorly myself, a realisation was beginning to dawn that this Tipp team was something out of the ordinary.

Football-wise, my career had been following more familiar lines. After the heartbreak of losing to Kerry's minors twelve months earlier, I was now on the under-21 team that lost to Cork.

My job for the day was marking Dave Barry and we lost the game 1-6 to 0-10. Truly, the Gods were not on the side of Tipp's footballers.

Elsewhere, I had – predictably – abandoned my engineering course at UCC. The obvious alternative was to go to Thomond College for PE but

I had been bitten by the bug of Fitzgibbon hurling and chose to stay in Cork.

Technically, I would stay to do a BA. In reality, I was staying to hurl.

There was to be a huge build-up to our All-Ireland final confrontation with Kilkenny. It seemed the whole country was talking about this game due to be played in Walsh Park, Waterford. Tipp were favourites but we knew that Kilkenny were not in the habit of lying down.

We had a well-packed car driving to Waterford that morning with Ger O'Neill, Pat Fox, Austin Buckley and myself all travelling together. Anyone who saw us would have thought we were just another car load of supporters.

We had a huge Tipperary flag out the back window and I don't think any of us had even contemplated losing.

Getting to Walsh Park, two things made an immediate impact. Firstly, the crowd was enormous. Secondly, the dressing-rooms were incredibly shabby. Time would reveal that 25,000 turned up for that game and I recall almost losing my breath at the sight of the throngs packed tight around the pitch.

But the dressing-rooms were the kind to bring you back down to earth. This may have been an All-Ireland final, but we togged off in the kind of room you might have expected for a junior club game. Luxurious it was not.

As the new jerseys were taken from their cellophane wrappers, I couldn't help wondering if we would be allowed keep them when the game was over. After all, this was an All-Ireland final and I wanted a memento.

The man assigned to mark me that day was Mick Cleere, whose father had played senior for Kilkenny. That thought unnerved me a little. Even though I didn't know anything about him, I reasoned that – with a famous father – he would have to be something special.

But I got a couple of points in the first-half and then there was a disputed goal between myself and Donie O'Connell. Both of us were actually in on the act of putting the ball over the line but the reality was that Donie scored it.

Not that I would ever admit that to him!

Yet again, my abiding memory of this game was the performance of Ger O'Neill. To put it mildly, he was sensational.

Ger was marked that day by Bill O'Hara – a brother of the bearded Dick, who was one of Kilkenny's great corner backs at the time. Now the O'Haras were uncompromising men who didn't stand on ceremony when the opportunity to make a hit presented itself.

I recall Bill coming out at one stage, having conceded a couple of points to O'Neill, and the look in his eyes told you he meant business. Ger was bending to rise a ball on the sideline and, if you could read O'Hara's mind, it would almost certainly have been saying, 'I'm going to put him into the stand.'

Well, as Bill arrived, Ger just flicked the ball past him, lifted it into his hand and put it straight over the bar. It was unbelievable, absolutely unbelievable. As the roar went up, Bill O'Hara was still going full pelt for the wire.

That day, O'Neill was star of the show, scoring six points from play. He broke Kilkenny's hearts and we ended up winning the game with reasonable comfort (2-16 to 1-10). Our performance was lauded afterwards in the national newspapers.

Most argued that, with our third successive under-21 crown safely gathered, Tipp's fortunes at senior level surely had to improve soon. For this was a serious team and most of us felt ready to make the step up.

I remember the *Kilkenny People* newspaper carried a glowing report of our victory, highlighting especially the performances of Ger O'Neill and Pat Fox. Donie O'Connell, Bobby Ryan and myself had done enough to get our names in the senior hat too. It seemed our time had come.

Quite rightly, it was decided that – after their three-in-row – the under-21 selectors should now be given the management duties of Tipp's seniors as well. So Mick Minogue, Billy Carroll, Danny Morrissey, Mick Ryan and Paddy O'Meara became the five wise men of Tipperary.

They were appointed to the job on the evening of September 20, 1981 and – maybe two weeks later – I made my senior debut for Tipperary.

It meant being sent to Coventry!

VIII

'THAT'S WHAT YOU GET FROM HURLING WHEN YOU SHOULD BE STUDYING'

NAIVETY imprisoned Tipperary hurling through the early eighties.

The county had not won a senior Munster Championship match since 1973 and, for one of the supposed super powers of the game, that was nothing short of belittling.

It grated hugely with Tipp people that Cork and Limerick could get to All-Ireland finals when we couldn't win a game. So, when the under-21s went on their glory run, it was human nature that the imaginations of an entire county would ride with them.

We were a genuinely exceptional young team in '81 and no-one could reasonably have argued against the decision to promote us almost *en bloc* to senior level.

That said, we were merely in the puberty of our hurling lives and, as everyone knows, puberty can be painful.

The experiment of putting boys in against men was destined to fail. And some of us would learn a few harsh lessons along the way.

The supposed new dawn commenced in late September of '81 when we travelled to Coventry in the English midlands for a challenge game against reigning All-Ireland champions, Offaly. At home, the senior club championship was in full swing so the new selectors were severely limited in their options.

I was named at right-half forward where I would be marked by Brendan

Keeshan.

Naturally, Offaly weren't in much of a mood for hardship. They were All-Ireland champions for whom the celebrations were in full swing. I remember standing beside Keeshan thinking how we were on two very different missions.

I wanted desperately to play well, to take the first step towards a regular spot in the Tipp colours. Brendan, I think, was more interested in the craic that was certain to follow.

We beat Offaly that day but it didn't mean a thing.

Three weeks later, nine of the under-21 team were picked for our opening National League Game against Waterford in Thurles. There was Johnny Farrell, Peter Brennan, Pat Fox, Pat McGrath, Alan Kinsella, Martin McGrath, Ger O'Neill, Philip Kennedy and myself.

We waltzed into Semple Stadium, ready to pick up where we had left off with the beautiful, expansive game of summer. And Waterford promptly kicked us in the teeth.

Physically, the match was very tough. Men against urchins in many ways. Waterford were well seasoned by then, a team destined to win its way into successive Munster finals, albeit both being games they would lose heavily to Cork.

That day, they simply cuffed us aside with something bordering on disdain. I was being marked by John Galvin who was a huge man and he had little difficulty in keeping me quiet. I can remember doing a few half decent things but the bottom line was I didn't score.

Losing came as a terrible shock to the system. I think we felt we would just pick up where we had left off in the under-21 final and clean off Waterford. But they gave us a sharp dose of reality.

To some extent, that game was a godsend. Because, between that and

Christmas, a certain sanity took over and we got a run going – beating Galway, Offaly and Clare.

By now, the selectors' taste for revolution had softened a little and the use of under-21s became a little more circumspect.

I was one of those who held my place though, my best day coming against Offaly when I had a good game on Ger Coughlan.

The three pre-Christmas wins re-generated optimism in the county. People started talking about us again, saying that Tipp were genuinely on the move. Looking back now, it was naivety bordering on madness.

Sometimes, I recall those days and wonder how on earth we thought a team of 18 and 19-year-olds could go and impose their game on hard, often ruthless hurling men almost twice our age. When you think about it, by the time we eventually made the breakthrough in 1987, we had undergone a pretty thorough education.

The problem for us in '81 was that we weren't being beaten so it was hard not to surrender realism. Everything that was being put in front of us, we were taking care of. What we didn't absorb at the time was that the likes of Offaly were simply trundling through the motions.

As I would discover myself in later years, people don't give a tuppenny damn about the League if they've just won the Liam McCarthy Cup.

Reality dawned beneath big, black clouds in the post-Christmas muck of Semple Stadium when Cork beat us easily. But we then scrambled a play-off place by overcoming Laois on one of my least favourite pitches in Ireland, Rathdowney.

In reality, we were running just to stand still.

What we had qualified for was a play-off game with Cork, the loser of which would get a quarter-final berth, the winner going straight through to the semi-finals. That game was played in Limerick and I felt physically tired beforehand after the exertions of that year's Fitzgibbon Cup.

Masseur, Ossie Bennett, gave me a fairly hard rub in the dressing-room to get me right but, maybe 20 minutes in, I had nothing left in my legs. It was a horrible feeling. There was a big crowd, it was a nice day and I was a spent force almost before the game had even warmed up.

Cork gave us an absolute trimming the same day (0-16 to 1-4) and – given the fact that we were due to play them again in the first round of the Munster Championship – the result represented a demoralising blow.

Even if we couldn't admit it, the writing was on the wall.

Our 'reward' for losing to Cork was a quarter-final game with Wexford in Walsh Park played out in arguably the worst conditions I've ever faced on a hurling pitch. Stronger than us physically, Wexford had little difficulty in disposing of the Tipperary threat.

As it happened, I played quite well even if the arrival of Colm Doran as a Wexford substitute eventually put a halt to my gallop.

Still, it was now the end of April and Tipp's Championship campaign was an ominous six weeks away. A League campaign that had opened to a fanfare of ambitious promise, was now well and truly buried.

It was clear we had our problems.

The mind, though, is capable of wondrous tricks and it was surprisingly easy to dip back into our giant well of self-delusion. I thought, personally, that once the ground dried up we might start flying again.

Certainly, there was no hint of despair or helplessness in our minds for the Championship game with Cork. Although, they had already beaten us comfortably twice that year, we genuinely thought we might catch them.

The selectors, though, clearly harboured worries and, after we went out of the League, 30-plus players were told to report for a Thursday night trial game in Thurles after which the Championship panel would be named.

Exam pressure was beginning to bear down on me at the time. Having failed and subsequently abandoned engineering, I was now doing a BA which I quite definitely could not afford to mess up.

I came up from Cork for the trial but, quite early in the game, attempted to hook a guy and he broke my right thumb with his hurley. The main bone was left sticking sideways and I knew instinctively it was bad.

An x-ray in Cashel that night confirmed the bad news and it looked like my ambition of playing for Tipperary in the Championship lay in tatters. My mother was more concerned about my exams than any impending game and told me sensitively, 'That's what you get from hurling when you should be studying!'

A temporary cast was put on my hand that Friday and I remained in terrible agony until the Sunday night when the thumb was finally set. Over the next few weeks, all I could do was run and hope to God the selectors did not forget me.

Ten days before the Championship game, I returned to training and it emerged I had made a surprisingly good recovery. Contrary to what I expected, my touch was good and certainly my appetite was not in question.

When the team was named, AN Other was selected at right-half forward. And I knew that man was me.

With the game being played in Pairc Uí Chaoimh, it meant I could relax and have a bit of a lie-in on the morning of my senior Championship debut. Four of us were renting a house up in the Farranlea area of Cork which is off Model Farm Road and I can remember walking down the hill on a real roaster of a morning to get a double-decker bus into the Metropole Hotel.

Looking back, I think I was more nervous of my thumb than of the impending ordeal of facing Cork. But, as I met up with the rest of the Tipp team, the butterflies certainly started kicking in.

Mick Minogue did most of the talking in the dressing-room before we went out that day but my most abiding image of the field is one of confusion.

I was playing on one wing and 'Bomber' Carroll, who had previously hurled for Limerick, was on the other. The plan was that 'Bomber' would go with Dermot MacCurtain and I would pick up Cork's other wing-back. Only trouble was, Cork weren't inclined to accommodate us.

MacCurtain refused to go with 'Bomber' and it meant that the four of us were left eye-balling one another in a little muddled ball right, smack centre of the field. I couldn't believe that this was happening. 'Bomber' started giving MacCurtain dog's abuse, telling him that he wasn't 'man enough' to come across and mark him. It was incredible.

I've always said that I'd love to see those early moments of my Championship debut on television because this argument seemed to go on forever. In my own mind, I thought the situation was becoming ludicrous. At the end of the day, we were forwards, they were backs. It was up to them to mark us. We were just making it easy for them by huddling together.

Deep down, I wanted to play right-half forward, the position I had been picked in. So, eventually, I just said 'F..k this. I'm going over to my wing and whoever wants to come and mark me can'.

Over I went only to be followed by MacCurtain. And he proceeded to destroy me.

It all started well enough admittedly. I won the first couple of balls that came my way but, with confidence growing, then made an error that would haunt me for weeks after.

Bobby Ryan was playing full-forward for us that day and, as most people know, Bobby is not the tallest man for such a task. He was being marked by Martin Doherty who was, effectively, the king of full-backs at the time.

Cork had flown Doherty back from America especially for this game and – if anything – that made him an even bigger man in our minds.

Naturally, the instruction given to us that day was to hit low ball in towards Bobby. Anything else would amount to just giving away possession.

Anyway I caught a ball out near the touchline and lost the run of myself totally. Winding myself up, I drove it back into the clouds in an attempt for a point but immediately realised it was dropping short. Dropping right down between Doherty and Bobby.

To this day, I can see Bobby being blown out of the way as Doherty met it on the run and drove it maybe 90 yards down the field where a Cork forward collected and immediately dispatched it to the Tipp net.

That put Cork in front and the roar would have sent a chill down any young hurler's spine. I had never heard anything like it in my life.

Tipp had been going well right up to that moment. Now, suddenly, we were behind and – being honest – it was a real struggle for the rest of the day.

Cork went on to win pretty easily with Tony O'Sullivan, who was known at the time as a bit of a god in North Mon, having a magnificent game on his Championship debut. I had known Tony from his minor days but this game emphasised just how far ahead of me he now stood.

I ended the game scoreless and a little chastened. Bobby often reminded me afterwards of my moment of stupidity that effectively turned the game in Cork's favour. That evening, I left Pairc Uí Chaoimh knowing I had a lot to learn.

I've often thought since that we were incredibly naive thinking we could go down to Cork and beat a team that had already demolished us twice in the League. But the human mind is an incredibly resilient thing when it comes to sport. New days always bring new possibilities, new hopes.

I had a few drinks that night in the Metropole with 'Bomber' Carroll. We talked about our own innocence and about the error – in hindsight – of putting so much trust in youth when experienced and respected inter-county men like Jim Kehoe and Noel O'Dwyer were left sitting on the bench.

There had been huge changes made to the team in 12 months and now, again, further major surgery was required. If anything, Tipperary hurling was just spinning around in circles.

Two weeks after losing to Cork, we re-grouped to try and defend our under-21 crown. Something like twelve or thirteen of us had survived from the year before and most people considered us overwhelming favourites to bring a fourth consecutive under-21 All-Ireland crown to Tipperary. Pat Fox, too, was bidding for his fourth medal to equal the record held by Mick Malone of Cork.

But things had been neglected a little because of the senior campaign. Maybe, too, there was an element of over-confidence. Whatever our excuses, Limerick got hold of us in the first round of the Munster Championship and won easily.

We were back on the merry-go-round. Spinning aimlessly.

Little boy dreaming – Posing in my first Tipperary jersey

Whip on it – Battling with Mossy Carroll in the '84 Munster Semi-Final

Eyes on the Ball – Shooting for goal in the '85 Ford Open Draw Final

After you Donie! – A celebratory drink with Donie O'Connell after the '85 Ford Open Draw Final

Watch out Maradona – That goal in the drawn '87 Munster Final

Who needs a hurley? – That celebration in the draw '87 Munster Final

The Famine is nearly over! – Richie Stakelum leading us in the parade before the '87 Munster Final replay

Watch the top–spin! – Scoring a goal despite Aidan Fogarty's attentions in the '88 National League Final

Oh Captain my Captain! – Leading Tipperary out for the '88 All-Ireland Final

Never look back – Going for goal in the '89 All-Ireland Semi-Final

High Fives – Celebrating a goal with Cormac Bonnar in the '89 All-Ireland Final

Happiness is... – Being chaired off the field after the '89 All-Ireland Final

Brothers in Arms – Soaking it all up with Pat Fox after the '89 victory

Fair play Johnny! – Embracing Johnny Leahy after the '89 West Tipperary Junior Hurling Final

Unlucky my boy! – Commiserations from Fr O'Brien after the '90 Munster Final

Ouch! – Colliding with John Considine in the '90 Munster Final

You tell them Joe! – Joe Hayes defending my honour to some abusive Galway supporters during the '91 All-Ireland Semi-Final

Happy Days – A training ground joke shared with Donie Nealon and the lads

In the bag! – Celebrating the '91 All-Ireland Final win with county chairman, Mick Maguire

Elephant Man – Making 'Babs' look handsome in April '93

IX

'WHATEVER YOU DO, DON'T LOOK IN THE MIRROR!'

HURLING has never been the game for a man sensitive about his looks.

Elsewhere in this book, you will see a photograph of me taken after one opponent's stickwork went some way towards re-designing the shape of my face. All over my body, I have the scars and little skin creases to remind me of past battles.

For those of us who chose not to wear helmets through our hurling careers, there has never been much likelihood of being asked to appear in toothpaste commercials.

I have no idea how many stitches I've collected over the years. They are part and parcel of the game we play. Truth is, you often don't even realise you've been cut until someone brings your attention to it in the dressing-room.

Whatever ambitions I may have had for a career on the catwalk were certainly well and truly buried in the summer of '83.

This was, in many ways, a momentous summer for Tipperary given that the county would win its first Championship game in ten years. But my own personal recollections are almost entirely of blood and broken teeth.

Len Gaynor had taken over as team-manager but the new regime endured a miserable League campaign that offered little apparent hope for summer. Our first round Championship opponents were to be Clare at the

Gaelic Grounds in Limerick and, having gone a decade without a solitary victory, Tipp supporters were fairly muted in their expectations.

I was just back from my first Allstars tour (as a replacement), having visited New York and San Francisco in the company of men like Limerick's Leonard Enright and Kilkenny's Billy Fitzpatrick. It was a fantastic trip and a wonderful experience getting to know hurlers I had only observed previously from a distance.

No matter what anyone liked to say about Allstars trips, they were first and foremost about craic. Sure, you took the games seriously when they came. But, by and large, we were there primarily to enjoy ourselves. And, in '83, we did.

Being truthful, I wasn't in the best shape for Championship hurling by the time I got home. I was tired, very tired. A mixture of jet-lag and late nights had taken its toll. On top of this, the selectors had picked me at right-corner forward where Tommy Keane would mark me. And I knew it wasn't my best position.

There was a fair amount of expectation on my shoulders that year because I had dominated the Fitzgibbon Cup with UCC. I was conscious of that fact, aware that people were looking upon me as a potential match-winner.

But I started poorly in the right corner before they moved me to the left where I was marked by an old UCC team-mate, John Minogue. Again I didn't do great there so, eventually, the selectors moved me to centre-forward on Sean Stack for the last quarter.

Now Stack was a hero to me, a great player who would have won a hat-ful of All-Irelands had he been born in Cork or Kilkenny. But, as a Clareman, his career amounted to a long list of heroic Championship performances on losing teams.

That day, to my surprise, I started winning balls in front of him. One, two, three balls came in towards us and I caught every one. Slowly, right through the field, Tipp began to grow more confident in a tight, nerve-wracking game.

Cormac Bonnar had come on to make a difference at midfield and, with the game on a knife-edge, he instigated the move that freed Tipp from a black hole.

Big Bonnar broke the ball to Michael Doyle who found Tom Waters with a 30-yard hand-pass. Waters took off on an incredible solo-run down the right wing without ever looking like he had the ball totally under his control.

It seemed to be running away from him all the time but Tom kept going before unleashing an unstoppable shot past Seamus Durack. Almost immediately, Enda O'Connor goaled for Clare at the other end but now, with about ten minutes remaining, you could sense the difference in Tipp's mood.

Paul Dooley, John Grogan and myself put over three unanswered points in those closing minutes to secure Tipp's victory and ignite the most extraordinary outburst of emotion from our followers. Blue and gold hordes invaded the pitch from all sides and we were swept off our feet more like men who had won the McCarthy Cup than players who had scraped over a first round hurdle.

I would have liked nothing better than to submit myself to the celebrations. Ten years had been a long, lonesome wait for such a proud hurling county.

But I had an exam the following morning in UCC and a friend from Cork, Stephen Ryan, had promised my mother he would bring me straight back down as soon as the game was over. And Stephen was true to his word.

I was actually back in Cork before the 'Sunday Game' even started. Theoretically, I was supposed to spend the night studying but, with Tipp having won, I was desperate to see the highlights.

A friend, Pat Donovan, had a small little portable TV so I went over to his place to watch them. Jim Carney singled me out for special mention on tv that evening, doing a little feature on me and suggesting that I'd be in the Tipp jersey for a while to come.

It meant a lot because I had never really been singled out in such a way before.

There was one specific incident that seemed to catch everyone's eye that evening. In fact, maybe even a year later, John Minogue asked me how I had done it. Basically, a ball had come in and I killed it dead on the bas of my hurley. A ball has to bounce at least an inch when it makes contact with the ash. Doesn't it?

To this day, I'm not sure what it was I did that killed that ball.

When the programme ended, I went back to my text-books and studied maths long into the night for the following day's exam. I remember thinking that the guy who would mark my paper would be absolutely oblivious to the kind of day I had put in. That Tipperary was ending a ten-year drought meant nothing in the exam hall.

And I couldn't help envying the lads at home and the craic they were now certain to be enjoying.

Three weeks later, my exam safely passed, we met Waterford in Pairc Uí Chaoimh. Now this was a whole new ball game. On even their worst days, Waterford have always been physically tough opponents. For sure, there have been days when they've over-stepped the mark in that regard.

But, being fair, '83 was not one of them.

That said, it was still one of the hardest, most uncompromising battles you could imagine when we locked horns with them that day in Cork. And it was to leave me feeling pretty sorry for myself.

I had taken to wearing a gum-shield that summer because of an accident my girlfriend (and future wife) Anne and I had had the previous November. We had been cycling down the Glasheen Road in Cork – Anne perched on the crossbar – when her foot got caught in the spokes of the front wheel.

I was catapulted out, head over heels, landing face-first on the road, breaking two of my front teeth. Anne came away without a scratch but I was absolutely destroyed.

I had to have my front teeth crowned and my face was just red-raw from scraping along the road. I remember it vividly because around that time I was getting myself organised for flying out to America where I would play in the New York Championship with Tipperary.

I had to go to the American embassy in Ballsbridge in order to get a visa. Now I will never forget the look on their faces when I walked into the room, this red line of raw skin stretching from my forehead, down across my nose, lips and chin.

Looking back, it's a wonder they were ever willing to let me leave the country.

Anyway, that was the reason I wore a gumshield for the first time in the summer of '83. And, to this day, I'm thankful that I did.

Like I said, the Waterford game was a real man's game with no quarters asked or given. Scores were tight all through and the match was still alive with two minutes remaining when my Championship came to an abrupt end.

What happened? I remember Seamie Hannon, who was a real tough corner-back at the time, throwing up the ball to clear it. I charged in completely open to block him down, stopping the ball but forgetting that the hurley would be behind it. Seamie, I'm sure, was trying to drive the ball into the next parish, and – unfortunately – his follow-through caught me smack in the face.

It was completely accidental. My own fault really.

The impact split my lip in two just under my nose. I went to spit out my gum-shield and a few teeth fell out with it. I had taken an awful slap and I knew it. I can remember lying down on the ground in absolute agony and Len Gaynor coming over.

'Get up,' he was roaring. 'C'mon, get up it's nearly over.' Tipp, you see, had already used three substitutes and, without me, we'd be down to fourteen men.

Then Len turned me around and I will never forget his words. 'Oh, sweet Jesus Christ,' he said. It was all I needed to know,

They carried me off and put me into a Garda squad car for the journey to the Regional Hospital. By putting my hand up to my mouth, I could feel how badly my lip was broken.

The match was already over as we edged our way out through the crowds, sirens blaring. Tipp had been beaten by four points.

The car was full, Anne sitting with a few other people in the back, Martin McGrath squashed beside me in the front. I put my hand up to the vanity mirror, to grab a glimpse of what I looked like.

Martin stopped me immediately, 'Jesus, don't look in the mirror,' he said. 'You're in an awful mess.'

From memory, they put twenty stitches both on the inside and outside of my lip that evening. But my teeth were the real problem. They were absolutely mangled. And the specialist in charge of dentistry was out 'on call'.

If I went away without seeing him, I was obviously going to lose a lot of teeth, so I had no choice but to sit and wait for him in casualty. Sit there in my Tipp jersey and togs, caked in mud, blood and perspiration.

After about three hours, Martin McGrath headed away and Anne went off to get me a yoghurt. For a while, I felt incredibly alone. Tipp had been beaten but I knew all the other lads were now away somewhere drowning their sorrows. I wondered did they think of me at all. Were they even curious about my condition?

The wait just seemed to go on forever until, eventually, the dental specialist materialised.

He took one look at me and said it was a job that ought to be performed under general anaesthetic. Effectively, he was going to put a wire around my gums to hold the teeth in place. But, as he was going on holidays the following morning, he could either do it now under local anaesthetic or I could look elsewhere tomorrow.

It was a pretty stark choice.

So we agreed that I'd have it done under local anaesthetic and I will never forget the hour or so that followed. Most of the stitches that had been inserted in my lip came away again as he did the major excavation work required.

It was a nightmare that I know I'll never forget.

Anne sat with me while it was all being done and it's fair to say it was the worst thing I have ever endured in my entire life. I was actually crying the pain was so severe.

To be fair, he was more than aware of the agony I was in. He kept telling me 'We're nearly done now, nearly done. Just hang in there for another little bit.'

A kind of plaster of paris was inserted basically like a gum-shield to protect the teeth and it was going to have to remain in place for six weeks. I was wrecked by the end of it, absolutely wasted.

It must have been close to ten o'clock by the time he was finished and there was nothing left to do but to walk back to the flat I was staying in in Cork. That's how my Championship ended then in '83. Feeling sorry for myself, walking home in darkness nearly six hours after the game with Waterford had finished. I remember lying in bed that night, unable to sleep with the pain in my mouth. Thinking to myself that the world had more or less forgotten me.

Next day, we went into the city, to a pub called Clancy's where I attempted drinking a bowl of soup but I just couldn't manage it because it was a little bit too hot for my gums.

So I just had a pint of Guinness and went down to the railway station to get a train back home to Tipperary.

I looked like someone who had been in a bad car accident. My whole face was swollen and my teeth ached as if they had gone twelve rounds with Muhammad Ali.

That evening I knew a hurler's looks could never be his fortune.

X

'DRIVE AROUND THE SQUARE AGAIN'

YOU get to know your real friends in a losing dressing-room.

The very same people who crowd around you on a good day are the first to turn their backs when the bottom falls out of your ambitions. And, in the Championship, that can happen with jarring ferocity.

Looking back, I can say with certainty that I have never been in a more desolate room than that which housed the Tipperary team after the 1984 Munster final. This was Centenary Year, the year the All-Ireland hurling final was to be staged in our own Semple Stadium.

There was an almost religious fervour in Tipperary regarding the impending plot for summer. It was like the script had already been written. This had to be our year.

From the players' viewpoint, I think we were slightly incredulous at the talk in the county. After all, although we had managed to win our first Championship match in ten years the previous summer, it scarcely entitled us to serious consideration as potential All-Ireland champions in '84.

Still, when enough people start peddling optimism, it is hard not to absorb some of it yourself. And there was certainly a sense that Tipp were not going to be easy meat for anyone in Centenary Year.

The season began encouragingly when we won promotion from Division Two of the National Hurling League and we followed that up with a quarter-final victory over Laois which was shown on TV.

Limerick then took care of us in the semi-final, courtesy of a last minute Paddy Kelly point and, to my disgust, I played poorly. Over the years, I was always anxious to do well against Limerick, coming as I do from a village so close to the Limerick border.

It amounted to something personal. I couldn't bear the thought of near-neighbours having reason to put me down.

Still, League defeats have never been too crushing, given that the Championship is everyone's priority and – in '84 – we also had the small matter of the Centenary Cup to contend with.

About two weeks after losing to Limerick, we played Laois again in what turned out to be an absolute war in Nowlan Park. Tipp had three players sent off, Laois had two. Effectively, it was twelve players against fourteen for most of the game.

Don't ask me how it started. All I remember is it being a fairly robust contest – as it invariably was against Laois. There were only about ten minutes gone when Tom Waters and John Bohane of Laois got their marching orders.

I scored one of Tipp's goals to put us into a reasonably comfortable lead but, just before half-time, our centre-back – Gerry Stapleton – got the line for tangling with Martin Cuddy.

That kept the fuse lit and, on a beautifully, sunny day in Kilkenny, Tipp and Laois proceeded to tear into each other with a fair degree of abandon. Incredibly, despite the anger, it turned out to be an absorbing game with the teams never more than a goal apart right to the very end.

I played really well on the day, scoring 2-1 and giving their defence a reasonably awkward time. At one point, I remember their full-back, Christy Flynn, come sprinting towards me, determined to put me away with his shoulder.

Christy, I could see, wanted to demolish me. He wanted to bury me. But, just as he arrived, I jinked past him and Christy slipped awkwardly. I can still hear the horrible crack from his knee as he went down.

It was a bad injury and I don't think he ever played for Laois again.

I always felt sad afterwards when I thought that, however inadvertently, I was actually involved in an incident that – to all intents and purposes – ended a player's inter-county career. But the other side of the coin was that, had Christy made the contact he intended, I mightn't have played for a long time myself.

I actually scored a goal in the incident and we were leading right up to the end when just at the death, Joe O'Dwyer was sent off and Billy Bohane popped over the winning free.

Laois won the game by a point although, because of an inaccurate scoreboard, they had to check with referee John Denton before being confirmed as 1-17 to 4-7 winners.

Any analyses of the result or performance were rendered redundant by the four sending-offs. We were actually disgusted that the game didn't go to extra-time in which case we would have been allowed field 15 players again.

As it happened, we finished the game with just four forwards and our heads far from down. Progress made in the League had clearly been sustained and we were beginning to feel like a coming team.

This was to be the year I won my first Railway Cup medal for Munster and that was something that meant a great deal to me.

People like Joe McKenna were on the Munster team and I considered it such an honour to be playing in the same forward line.

Bobby Ryan and myself were Munster's wing-forwards for the semi-final played in Limerick and, in his television commentary, Micheal O'Hehir made a point of suggesting that we were two men to look out for in the future. I couldn't imagine a bigger compliment.

To me, O'Hehir was literally the voice of the GAA. If he went to the trouble of mentioning you in a commentary, it surely meant that you were good. That, at least, was my reasoning.

The night before the semi-final, we were staying in Ennis and – naturally enough – I was rooming with Bobby. Now, for me, playing Railway Cup was a deadly serious business and I was almost preoccupied with the need for a decent sleep.

Bobby had a more relaxed approach to the challenge and took himself away for a few pints. Then, to my absolute disgust, he got up in the middle of the night to have a fag.

Jesus it was four in the morning and here he was sitting on the end of the bed puffing away merrily. I was almost incoherent with rage. I just couldn't understand his mentality. This was too much for me to handle.

I was wired into making a big impression in the Railway Cup. At the time, I was trying to build myself a reputation and I couldn't accept Bobby's seeming indifference. To say the least, we exchanged a few choice words and he went off to the loo to finish his fag. The following day, Bobby played out of his skin in a Munster victory.

Typical Bobby Ryan!

As the Championship grew closer, Tipp seemed to be on the right road to a reasonable balance. Jim Keogh came out of retirement to play full-back. A real gentleman, who had been an Allstar, he definitely strengthened us in that department.

Then we had people like Dinny Cahill, John McIntyre, Ralph Callaghan, Donie O'Connell, Philip Kennedy, Seamus Power and an experienced old hand like Noel O'Dwyer who had also decided to come back.

There was a significant change at management level too where Donie Nealon had been brought in to work on the motivation of the team.

In training, you could detect a new intensity, a new resolve about the way we were doing things. There was a great deal of talk about it being Centenary year, about the need for Tipp to make a decent Championship bid.

Clare were our opponents in the first round and it turned out to be a titanic battle in Semple Stadium. I hurled really well throughout, being constantly involved in the game and scoring four points from play off none other than Ger Loughnane.

It was to be a game that earned me a certain notoriety, mind you for something a little different from my hurling ability.

On the morning after the game, the *Cork Examiner* front page carried a photograph of me with – shall we say – more than my tongue hanging out as I raced through on goal. I couldn't believe my eyes when I saw it.

There I was, in all my glory, the side of my shorts opening just sufficiently for the family jewels to protrude. Incredibly, to my knowledge, it got through every edition.

Anyway, we won the game by the narrowest of margins. Two points behind in the dying seconds, I was brought down for a penalty and Seamus Power stepped up to take it.

There was an almost eerie hush in the ground as Seamus prepared to strike. Standing next to me, Noel O'Dwyer told me to be ready, to watch the break. I looked at Noel and groaned, 'He can f...ing score it now or that's that.'

The voice of inexperience.

It just so happened that the ball was saved but Liam Maher reacted quickest and poked the rebound to the net. O'Dwyer knew what he was saying.

So, after much huffing and puffing, we had made it to the Munster final. The Centenary dream was still alive.

Now that was something...Munster final day '84 in Thurles.

We came up in Jackie Glasheen's minibus and had some tea and sandwiches in the college. The atmosphere in the town was like nothing any of us had known before. There was an electricity, a raw tension in the air.

Driving to the ground, we saw the huge crowds in Liberty Square and the effect on us was spellbinding. 'Drive us around the Square again,' roared Donie O'Connell.

He was speaking for every one of us.

Sitting on the bus, most of us were speechless. Nervous of the game itself, but awe-struck by the throngs. This, we told ourselves for the thousandth time, just had to be our year.

I will never forget the roar that greeted us as we ran onto the pitch. It was an explosion in the air, a deafening cry from our own people for the ending of the famine.

It's been exhaustively documented what followed. Tipp hurled themselves to a standstill and we looked to have it won when Noel O'Dwyer put us four points clear with just six minutes remaining. Noel's little jig of delight encapsulated what every one of us was thinking.

'It's over. It's over. It's over. The longest wait is over'.

I can remember looking at Dermot McCurtain's face and knowing he was a beaten man. All of the Cork players looked ashen, almost nauseous. It was as if they could not believe what they were seeing.

The crowd were going bananas, we were thumping each other, our hearts laughing, our minds ticking over frantically. Counting chickens...

For years afterwards, I found myself re-playing the events that followed. Heartbreakingly, we allowed Cork take advantage of our naivety. In effect, they mugged us while we celebrated.

John Fenton pointed a free and then Tony O'Sullivan goaled after a Pat Hartnett shot was deflected directly into his path. Without us having time to catch our breaths, the sides were level.

One subsequent moment forever stands frozen in time. Michael Doyle made a run up the left and passed it in across the edge of the square. It was a pass I never expected and – to my despair – Denis Mulcahy intercepted in front of me and made a huge clearance.

The ball went to Tony O'Sullivan and he tried for a point, his effort dropping just over the crossbar. Goalkeeper, John Sheedy, tried to block it down but succeeded only in batting the ball out to a lurking Seanie O'Leary.

And that was it. Another goal for Cork. Game over.

We were absolutely numb when the final whistle went. It was like living a bad dream. I've always felt angry with myself for not getting to that pass from Michael Doyle. Sure I thought he would go for a score himself but, with a Munster final at stake, I should have got to the ball somehow.

That's what I've kept telling myself ever since Mulcahy made that fateful clearance. If it ever happened again, nothing would stop me reaching the ball.

But hindsight is a dubious ally when you're out of the Championship and I don't think I've ever experienced scenes of devastation like those that littered in the Tipperary dressing-room after that game.

Grown men cried, people everywhere looked like they'd just seen a ghost. One minute, the Championship was ours. The next, we were back out in the wilderness.

There is little talk in dressing-rooms when defeats are that traumatic. You just shower, pull on your clothes and yearn for a quiet pub somewhere, far away from the scene of battle.

What had happened to us was unbelievable. The silence of the dressing-room reflected our confusion. It was like being at a funeral for someone who had died suddenly.

I remember a few of us walked back down into the square and, despite their devastation, you could tell that Tipp people felt genuinely proud at the way we had played. What had happened in the last two minutes or so, obviously left us all bewildered.

But Tipp, for the first time in many years, had shown they could play Championship hurling with the best again. So, if on the one hand, we felt despair, there was also hope and no little pride that we were on our way back as a hurling power.

If anything, bad luck had stalked us throughout the day. Bobby had to go off injured, Dinny Cahill and Pat Fitzelle went off early too. The team was actually decimated even though Johnny Doyle and Brian Heffernan, who came on as subs, both hurled brilliantly.

It had been a long time since Tipp played with so much fire. Scoreline apart, we had delivered on what the mentors asked.

I will never forget the speech Donie Nealon gave us in Hayes' Hotel the night before the game. Donie could send shivers down your spine he talked with such passion about the game.

And, on the night in question, the effect he had on us was just unreal. I remember coming out of the room afterwards and saying to somebody, 'I wish the match was on this minute!'

Basically, he had talked about Tipperary and what hurling meant to the people. He went into the history of the county, gave us a sense of perspective on what we were trying to achieve.

Donie told us that everyone expected Tipp to be beaten and it was up to us to prove them wrong. Looking back, we came desperately close to doing that.

My own performance had disappointed me, not for the first time Dermot McCurtain managing to keep me relatively quiet. From a personal viewpoint, that put an extra shadow on the day.

That evening, a few of us made our way down to Moriarty's pub just beyond the Cathedral and watched the 'Sunday Game'. It was the day Frank McGuigan had scored an incredible 0-11 from play for Tyrone in the Ulster football final against Armagh.

I remember being hugely envious of Frank's smile as he was interviewed afterwards.

That summer I worked as a labourer at Limerick Junction Racecourse, just doing a variety of maintenance jobs around the track. They had recently put new drains in and there was renovation work to be done. To put it mildly, I was distracted by thoughts of what might have been.

The truth is, no end of optimistic words for the future could cushion the reality that – despite coming so close to beating Cork – the Centenary final in Thurles would now go ahead without Tipperary. Losing in the Championship is a bleak, unforgiving ordeal.

'Next year' might as well belong to another millennium.

It was no shuddering surprise to see Cork go on and take the Liam McCarthy Cup. Once they escape from the heat of Munster, Cork teams invariably acquire a certain swagger.

As it happened, they played Offaly in the final and I made a weekend of it in Thurles, going into the town on Saturday, coming home on Monday.

But, to be truthful, the weekend served only to get me down.

Cork won the final with something to spare and, all through, the image of Noel O'Dwyer doing his little jig of delight with six minutes of the Munster final remaining played on my mind. Watching Cork collect the Cup, it was impossible not to believe that it could so easily have been Tipp's year.

After the match, I met Bobby Ryan, Pat Fox and Jim Maher for a few pints, Bobby still being in plaster. Tipp people everywhere were locked into the same, frustrating mind-set. Could have been us lads. Could have been us.

Still, there was no point in becoming morbid about the occasion. Obviously, I knew some of the Cork lads from UCC and they were having their celebrations in Dundrum. So I dropped out just to shake a few hands and warn them unconvincingly about what Tipp would do with them 'next year.'

Life now was changing fast. For the second successive year, I won an Allstar award and my name was becoming pretty well known throughout the country. Hurling aside, I was also in the process of doing my Dip, teaching maths in North Monastery.

At the start of '85, I captained UCC to our fifth consecutive Fitzgibbon Cup win and also managed to win a Railway Cup medal with Munster in Thurles. The latter should have been a happy experience but our team-manager, Justin McCarthy, succeeded in leaving me with very mixed emotions.

We were playing Connacht in the final and, for some reason, I almost missed the game by sleeping it out. Looking back, I'm convinced I must have had some kind of a bug at the time. The game was on at two o'clock but, at twelve thirty, I was still asleep in my bed in Cullen.

My father woke me to take me to the match and I was actually falling asleep in the car along the way. I felt weak and tired, in no fit condition really to play a serious game of hurling.

Galway's Tony Kilkenny was marking me that day and, in the first-half, he beat me up a stick. I just couldn't get into the game, my batteries seeming totally flat.

I was moved in to corner-forward during the second-half and, slowly but surely, things started to happen in my favour. I scored two goals in quick succession, the first one being a cracker even if I say so myself. But, as soon as the second goal went in, McCarthy took me off without a word.

It was the first and only time in my entire career that I was ever substituted without being injured.

I have to admit, that angered me. He never said a word to me, just made the decision and left me sitting in the dug-out feeling pretty much humiliated.

You have to understand that, with the game being played in Thurles and me being one of just two Tipp men in the starting line-up (Donie O'Connell was the other), it was terribly embarrassing to be substituted. Don't get me wrong, it's not as if the crowd was huge or that my ego just couldn't absorb it.

Truth is, it was a bitterly cold day with a hopeless attendance of no more than maybe 300 in place. But, having scored the goals, I felt I was just beginning to get into the game. My confidence was up and I felt capable of doing a bit more damage.

As it happened, Munster were lucky enough to go on and win the match by the narrowest margin. Afterwards, I went for a few pints in the Park Avenue with Limerick's Jimmy Carroll who I always found good company. Jimmy was from Hospital and, years earlier, my sisters and I would often have played tennis for Lattin against Hospital.

The pints were going down nicely but, that evening, I had to get the train back down to Cork alone. On the way, I couldn't help thinking about McCarthy's decision to take me off, couldn't help wondering if he was trying to tell me something.

I would have had no argument had he replaced me while I was struggling so badly during the first-half. But where is the logic of substituting a man immediately after he scores two goals? I don't have the answer to that one and, unfortunately, Justin never bothered to give me his either.

From Tipp's viewpoint, momentum was slow to gather at the start of '85 as we endured a pitiful League campaign that culminated in relegation. But a great run in the Ford Open Draw competition, climaxing with a final victory over Galway in Pairc Uí Chaoimh, got the show back on the rails.

That triumph was a watershed for all of us on the Tipp team. It was the first inter-county trophy we had ever won as seniors and the style of execution hinted at a brighter future. Ominously, it meant we would now be going into our first-round Championship match with Clare as favourites but that was a price we all felt happy to accept.

Beating Galway, we finally managed to hurl with the mix of venom and fluency that had eluded us through our League campaign. Seamus Power was man-of-the-match but most of us played our part. Things, we told ourselves, were 'different' this time.

The Clare game was played in Ennis and, sadly, brought us back to earth with a heavy thud.

We were atrocious, a mix of confusion and incompetence that must have left the supporters shaking their heads in despair. On a personal level, the game proved an unremitting nightmare.

Clare placed veteran, Johnny Callinan, on me and he proceeded to put me in his pocket. I was dreadful, useless, a waste of space. The first ball I got, I carried it out over the sideline and – from there – things just went from bad to worse.

It was a galling experience. Johnny was noted as a wing-forward, but here he was now – a surrogate defender – marking Tipp's Allstar into oblivion. The worst part of it all was that we were convinced we had a better team in every aspect than the one so narrowly pipped by Cork the previous summer.

Ian Conroy had made it to the team by now and there was a definite sense that we were going into the Championship extremely well prepared. So much though for the best-laid plans...

Perhaps the only constructive thing I did in the entire game came with the very last ball when I managed to score a point from close to the end-line to secure us a draw we scarcely deserved. The score was 1-8 to 1-8. Talk about getting out of jail.

That evening, myself and Conroy ended up in a disco at the Two Mile Inn just outside Limerick. We were both in bad form. Ian had been taken off in the game and the two of us just sat there brooding about how on earth all the hard work had seemed to go to waste.

In our misery, we neglected to work out exactly how we were going to get home that night. Next thing, we realised night had given way to early morning and we were stranded.

Eventually, we met a chap called Leo Cunningham who was still wearing his furry blue and gold Tipp hat. Leo was our only hope of getting home and, despite the poverty of our performance against Clare, I think he was delighted to help out two players in distress.

So Leo came to our rescue. It had been that kind of day, a day when someone had to.

Curiously, we destroyed Clare in the replay and I managed to take some semblance of revenge on Callinan, scoring 2-0. The show was back on the road, or so we thought.

Victory meant we would have our chance of vengeance on Cork. The flip side was that we had to face them in Pairc Uí Chaoimh. But it was a complication we were certain we could deal with.

This was to be the one and only time Tipp travelled to a match by train. I can remember dressing up for the occasion, believing that – if you were playing in a Munster final – you ought really wear a shirt and tie. The sense of expectancy was palpable. We truly believed our time had come.

But, of course, it hadn't.

In many ways, the '85 Munster final proved an incredible game. Dermot McCurtain was marking me again and, after cleaning me out the year before, I really felt I had to regain some kind of respect this time. Starting at wing-forward, I went wandering over to the far side of the pitch but he wasn't inclined to follow me.

Next thing, a ball flew perfectly out to the wing I should have been manning, McCurtain collected it and returned it 80 yards. I could see Len, Donie and the selectors glaring at me, wondering what my game was. My mind was doing cartwheels. I could either walk across like a sheep now and effectively start marking him or I could hold my ground.

So I decided, damn it, I'll take my chance and drift. Luckily, the next ball arrived perfectly to me unmarked and I had little difficulty in putting it over the bar. McCurtain immediately came running across to pick me up. It was a massive moment psychologically.

Had that ball not come my way, I would almost certainly have had to swallow my pride. Now I felt the advantage was with me.

I've always loved playing in Pairc Uí Chaoimh. Somehow, it's as if you are never quite as far away from the posts as you are in a ground like Semple Stadium. Maybe it's my imagination, but it always seems that you don't have to hit the ball as hard to score.

That first-half in '85 was raining goals. I scored 1-3, Ger O'Neill – who was giving John Blake a torrid time – managed 1-2. Tipp's total at half-time was 2-7 and, between us, Ger and myself contributed all but two points of it.

To my delight, Cork had moved McCurtain off me, giving the job to Tom Cashman instead. But we were having serious problems in defence where I sensed a return to the traditional Tipp style of fire and brimstone was backfiring badly. Some of the lads just seemed to get carried away. They wanted to hammer into Cork, soften them up in any way they could.

Now that may work against some counties but it was never likely to cut much ice with a Cork forward line built around Jimmy Barry-Murphy. One thing Barry-Murphy could never be accused of was being afraid.

So here we were in the Munster final, slowly digging our own graves. The defenders just seemed desperate to hit someone, anyone. We were leaking goals, conceding frees. Too ragged for our own good.

Exploiting our stupidity to the full, Cork pulled away to win comfortably in the end. The scoreline was a remarkable one. Cork 4-17 Tipperary 4-11. It was a huge score to accumulate for a losing team. My own contribution was 2-3. But, as a team, we seemed to be going nowhere. Just not good enough when the heat came on.

It looked like we could take on and beat everyone but Cork. Against them, we had a mental block, an insecurity that continually brought us down. But there were more fundamental flaws too. Here was a day I believed the selectors didn't help us.

For some reason best known to themselves, they took off Conroy and Gerry Stapleton who were both hurling really well in midfield. Conroy, especially, was destroying Pat Hartnett who had an awesome reputation at the time. Now Hartnett was a vital cog in the Cork machine back then, a super player who tended to influence the team hugely.

But both Ian and myself were familiar with him from UCC and I knew Conroy had the upper hand on him from their duels in training. But, incredibly, the Tipp selectors took him off with about quarter of an hour remaining and that was it. Ian never played for the county team again.

I've always said that taking him off that day, while certainly not helping Tipp's cause, made Conroy a very successful businessman. All he ever wanted to do was play for Tipperary and win All-Irelands. But the week after that Munster final, he emigrated to New York and now has a couple of thriving bars there.

The day Conroy flew to America was the day Tipp lost a hell of a midfielder.

Naturally, I'm biased. I've always considered Ian one of my closest friends and he was 'best man' at my wedding. But, truly, he was some hurler too. At UCC, he became a hero in Fitzgibbon hurling, a legend. Savagely competitive, incredibly fit, ferociously strong, he would go through a wall for his team.

After that game in Cork, Ian and I didn't manage to get home until the Tuesday. It was a strange kind of experience. Both of us decided to go to America that week, Conroy to New York, me to Boston. But, for now, we were in no hurry to leave Leeside.

Knowing a lot of the Cork lads from our time in UCC, we met up and ended up going to a nightclub somewhere in the city. Conquerors and conquered seeing the night out together. Ian and I stayed in Pat

O'Donovan's house on College Road with the intention of heading for home the following evening but we never quite made it.

By the Tuesday evening, I was still wearing the shirt I had gone to Cork in and I imagine the two of us must have been looking pretty rough.

We were actually hitching a lift out of Cork when Johnny Crowley beeped as he drove past us. A sales-rep, Johnny had played against us on the Sunday and was now back in the real world, making a living. We were only starting to make our way home. A sorry sight, no doubt, the pair of us.

Five or six lifts later, including a cattle truck, we arrived in Cullen absolutely starving. Low on funds, all we had been able to afford was a couple of orange ice pops in Fermoy.

Home at last, we had a fry and chips before I drove Ian to Borrisokane. The next day, he flew to New York.

Twenty four hours later, I boarded a flight to Boston, the ultimate Irish greenhorn heading for new pastures. A fella called Gerry McGrath from Clonmel had set me up out there with a building job and I was destined to play for the newly formed Tipperary team in the local championship, a championship we went on to win.

This would be one of the most enjoyable summers I would ever spend but, like a lot of the best experiences, it was a little slow to start.

Looking back, it all seems a little comical this image of me going to America with a big bag of hurleys packed in my suitcase. I had never actually met Gerry McGrath, just spoken to him on the telephone. Now, here I was arriving at Boston airport and there wasn't a sinner to greet me.

For over an hour, I sat in the arrivals hall feeling like the loneliest man on the planet. One part of me wishing to hell I was back home in Cullen. The other part getting agitated that I would even start thinking that way.

Eventually, a chap arrived to collect me and he needn't have worried about being late. With no money in my pocket, I was going nowhere.

That summer turned out to be a wonderful experience in every aspect. Three months of hard work on the building sites, success on the playing pitches and great craic in the pubs. I stayed until the end of August, right to the time I was due to start my new teaching job in Abbey CBS.

Despite the disappointment of having lost to Cork again, the same selectors were in place as we faced into a new League campaign with Tipp. Now finished with UCC, I trained extremely hard through that winter with Lattin footballers, harder perhaps than I had ever trained before.

Tired of disappointments, I was determined that the summer of '86 would leave me with something tangible.

A mediocre Division Two League campaign which culminated in a crushing fourteen points defeat against Wexford hinted at lingering insecurities in the Tipp camp. Midway through the campaign, a peculiar alteration to the team's management structure had taken place. About two months before the Championship, Tony Wall was brought in as manager. I remember it as a strange appointment. Wall was based in Dublin and knew few if any of the players on the panel.

Yet here he was being brought in, effectively, over Len Gaynor's head. I felt sorry for Len when it happened. He was doing a good job at the time and, looking back, would have made a better fist of things in the Championship than Wall managed. At least, Len knew the players.

If anything, the move was unfair on Tony Wall too. He just wasn't the right man for the job and, to Tipp's detriment, I felt Len lost a lot of interest when it happened.

Still, players are – by and large – selfish individuals and we were never inclined to examine or question the politics that brought about Len's apparent demotion. All I do know is that it was a bad move for Tipperary.

From a personal viewpoint, I would argue I was in the best condition of my life as we prepared for the Munster Championship of '86. Little did I know that I wouldn't hit a ball in anger for Tipperary that summer.

My world fell apart on the evening of May 4, about a month before we were due to play Clare in Ennis. Lattin were playing their fiercest rivals, Emly, in a football match. It was a big occasion for us. Emly had a more talented team than us at the time but, having trained Lattin, I knew we were in great shape to give them a hell of battle.

With about fifteen minutes of the game to go, I took a punch in the ribs that really winded me. I kept playing away afterwards but I could sense there was something wrong. After the match – which we won – I went to Cashel Hospital for an x-ray, convinced that I must have a couple of broken ribs.

But nothing showed up on the x-ray, so I drove back to Lattin where a major session had begun. That night, we all went to a disco at the Golden Thatch in Emly to rub our victory in a bit for the Emly lads. At the disco, I still found I couldn't catch my breath properly. There was something seriously wrong.

Eating a bag of chips outside the disco afterwards, I remember saying to the lads that I felt dreadful. I was convinced, despite the x-ray, that my ribs just weren't right.

Anyway, I went home, got up the following morning and went to work. It was customary for me on a Monday evening to go delivering coal but – between the ribs and a whopper of a hang-over – I was in no form for lifting sacks. Trying to dodge the task, I told my father I'd just have a cup of tea to let a shower of rain pass.

While I was in the house having my tea, a nurse from Cashel Hospital phoned, telling me to get over there immediately. Someone had looked at the x-ray again and noticed that I had a partially punctured lung. I was out of the Championship match with Clare and had to just hope that Tipp got out of Ennis with a victory.

Ian Conroy came home from America for the game and we went for a few pints in the West County Hotel that morning. Someone with us made the point that there would be as good a Tipp team in the stand that afternoon as there would be on the field. Apart from Conroy and myself, Pat Fox and Gerry Stapleton would be among those on the line too.

Anyway, the game was an unmitigated disaster for Tipperary.

Leading comfortably by seven points at half-time, the team dramatically surrendered all shape and focus in the second-half to lose a game they should have wrapped up with comfort. I am on record as saying that that particular defeat by Clare is the low-point of my time with Tipperary. It's a comment that got me into some hot water with certain Clare people who considered it an insult to their players.

But I never meant any disrespect to Clare. It was just that in '84 and '85 we had the look of a coming team, a team that might just win an All-Ireland.

In '86, we looked as if we had come to the end of the road.

Leaving the ground that evening, I just couldn't see any light at the end of the tunnel. I felt we were going nowhere. All the progress of the last two summers had, apparently, come to nought. I remember thinking that evening that I was never going to win anything with Tipperary.

Tony Wall had said to me the week before that, if I wasn't fit enough to start, I wasn't fit enough to be a substitute. And, being honest, I don't think I would have changed anything had I gone on as a sub that day.

Maybe I'm wrong but, being honest, I was still a long way from 100%

fitness. If anything, I had become a little conscious of minding myself until the lung was fully recovered. So he was probably right to leave me in the stand.

Still, the memory of the day is one of shambles. For me, it was the limit. I will never forget walking up the road from Cusack Park that evening, the sense of abject depression among Tipp people. All the progress of the previous two years had disappeared.

To me, it looked like we were back at square one. Or maybe even worse.

XI

'DON'T ANYONE BE LOOKING AT THE CEILING TONIGHT!'

IN Tipperary, the name 'Babs' has always inspired a special reverence.

Right from my childhood in Cullen, there was something different about Michael Keating that appealed to a kid with dreams. It was as if he brought glamour to hurling, a sense of theatre where others were merely grafting.

Everyone talked about the All-Ireland final of '71, of how he had thrown off his boots against Kilkenny and played on in his bare feet. I had been there to see it with my own eyes and it seemed to me that only a special kind of player, a special person would have done such a thing in the most important game of the year.

The lads at home often called me 'Babs' in our little street games, wearying no doubt of the way I prattled on endlessly about my hero. Keating was the main man of that Tipp team, a natural star who just captured the eye almost without trying.

Living in Dublin, he had drifted well away from hurling in the county by the mid-Eighties. But, having by now almost exhausted the list of former players who might manage Tipperary, I suppose it was inevitable that 'Babs' would eventually get a call.

Tony Wall's tenure had, predictably, ended that evening in Ennis when – to me and many others – it seemed as if we had taken a hundred steps backwards from the progress of the previous two years.

I was in Boston for the summer as speculation gathered about 'Babs' taking the reins. The prospect excited me. Although I had only met him once before, my admiration and respect for the man were always apparent to those who knew me.

That meeting had taken place on a Sunday morning in 1985. I received an Allstar award the previous Friday night and went out to the Commercials pitch in Rathcoole to watch Tipp play Dublin in a challenge. When I saw 'Babs' at the match, I was desperately keen to talk to him but too shy to make my own approach.

I think it was Liz Howard who eventually introduced us but the conversation didn't really go much beyond a polite hello.

Anyway, 'Babs' appointment in the Autumn of '86 seemed like a positive move now to everyone concerned. He just had an incredible air of confidence about him from the first moment he walked into our dressing-room. It's impossible to pinpoint exactly what it was he brought with him, but – instinctively – I think we all sensed that hurling for Tipp would never be the same again.

His first match in charge was a challenge game against Waterford in Clonmel and, straight away, he made an impression. There was something about the way he spoke, the way he carried himself. He was a track-suit manager, a hands-on kind of person.

We won that day and, in the ten years since, I have never been on a losing Tipp team against Waterford.

'Babs' first League game was against Antrim in Dunloy and, here again, the new regime was immediately making its presence felt. As his fellow selectors, Keating had appointed Donie Nealon and Theo English, two men who were hugely respected in Tipperary hurling.

We stayed overnight in Dublin the night before the Antrim game and, while it might not sound much now, they took us to the Jurys cabaret where we enjoyed a few pints. I had never been away with Tipperary before and the sense now of a real effort being made to treat us well was unmistakable.

The game with Antrim proved a tough, hard-fought battle watched reputedly by only five Tipperary supporters. But we won and, on the bus home, 'Babs' jumped to his feet and started singing 'Slievenamon'. It was an amazing thing to do, the sort of gesture I had come to expect from Fr O'Brien during our travels with UCC.

But we had never seen anything like it with Tipperary. It smacked of a camaraderie that we weren't accustomed to.

Hype built quickly with 'Babs' in the hot-seat. Playing in Division Two, there was a sense that the only way for Tipp to go was up. 'Babs' set about starting up a supporters' club, he wanted money collected throughout the county to help ensure Tipperary hurlers were given every chance to start winning again.

It felt like the whole thing was really taking off until Laois came to Thurles for a League match and demolished us by eight points. We could hardly look ourselves in the mirror that evening. I remember going for a drink with Anne and saying, 'Jesus, we're going nowhere again.

'All this hype and all this enthusiasm when, at the end of the day, there's just nothing there.'

The remainder of the League campaign was pretty non-descript as we accounted for teams like Kerry, Meath and Dublin without finding out much about ourselves. The key game was to be against Waterford at Walsh Park in February of '87, a match we simply had to win to retain any hopes of winning promotion.

A massive crowd watched us come out on top in that game, me scoring

2-5 – one of the goals a bit of a fluke. The result offered a glimmer of hope and, after that, we went through the formality of beating Mayo to guarantee a quarter-final tilt at Limerick.

Now this was to be the first serious test for 'Babs' as manager. In my time hurling with Tipperary, we had never beaten Limerick in a game of any significance. Fact is, Tipp hadn't beaten them in a knock-out game since the 1971 Munster final in Killarney.

In many ways, 'Babs' credibility was about to come under scrutiny. His supporters' club had already gathered in excess of £100,000 throughout the county, selling raffle tickets for the chance to win a race-horse. For years, the county board hadn't been able to raise a shilling for a Tipp team. Now, suddenly, the money was simply flowing in.

Apart from the supporters' club, 'Babs' seemed to have men all over the county scouting for new talent. He was talking about the team going away for weekends, about wearing blazers, about getting hurleys, boots, sliothars, anything we wanted.

In essence, he was pushing the belief that playing for Tipperary meant something. That it was a big deal. He was heightening the desire in everyone to wear the blue and gold. And it was working.

He had also put the right men in the right places within the team. None more so than Richie Stakelum, a great motivator and natural leader, who had been brought in as captain.

The game with Limerick proved a tremendous physical battle that had to go to extra-time to find a winner. In normal time, Jimmy Carroll was sent off for a bad foul on Michael Scully who had to go off injured himself. But, as we had already used our quota of three substitutes, it just meant that both teams were left with fourteen men.

Tipp were a point behind going into injury-time when I managed to get the equaliser and ensure another 30 minutes of battle.

But I was struggling badly at that stage, having torn ankle ligaments when Limerick's Leonard Enright clipped me as I ran in front of him. I can always remember that the ankle swelled up so badly, it had come well out over the side of the boot.

Although I played out the whole game, extra-time was especially notable for the arrival of one Pat Fox in at corner-forward. Now Fox was a man who had practically vanished off the scene in Tipperary hurling. Having damaged his knee at the end of '82, he missed all of '83 and '84, came back in '85 but then missed all of '86 again.

I knew he was a genius of a player but, like everyone else, could hardly believe my eyes when 'Babs' threw him in out of the blue against Limerick. Especially at corner-forward. It turned out he had been doing a bit of training himself and was determined to make the most of his second chance. And Fox did, in typical style.

Pat scored 1-1 in extra-time, the goal a brilliantly taken effort that would become his hallmark over the next decade. Then, with the game on a real knife-edge in the dying seconds, he grabbed a puck-out and put over the winning point. It was the crowning moment of an extraordinary comeback.

Beating Limerick in such a tight battle was greeted with incredible joy in Tipperary. It was almost as though people didn't really care what happened us in the semi-final. This was the first tangible signal that there was actually something there, something more than bluff.

From a personal viewpoint, the match lingers in my mind for a slightly embarrassing reason. Having scored a good goal, I made a point of running to the crowd behind the net and making a gesture at them. I was trying to get them going.

Some days later, Mick Roche called to the family shop on his travels for Carrolls and said to my father that I should never react to a goal like that again. Tipp players should never be seen to do that sort of thing. And Mick's advice touched a certain nerve. I always had tremendous respect for him and took anything he said on board.

So there would be no more running to the crowd.

Clare were to be our opponents in the semi-final and with Scully, Richie Stakelum and myself all ruled out because of injury, expectations in the county were reasonably subdued. Having contested the previous year's Munster final (a game they should have won), Clare were well known to have a decent team.

Looking back, I honestly don't believe Tipp people were too pushed as to how we fared against them. 'Babs' made a point after the Limerick game of stressing that the Championship remained our priority and that seemed to be the feeling throughout the county.

I was pretty exasperated as my ankle went in plaster. It was the second year in a row I had picked up a serious injury going into May. I remember expressing my frustration to Fr Jack O'Neill who was chaplain in Tipperary Town at the time. He told me just to be patient.

Tipp lost to Clare by a goal 1-11 to 2-11 in the semi-final and the defeat was considered almost a good thing, given that it would now focus minds for our likely Championship confrontation with them later in the summer.

As training resumed, there was a definite buzz of anticipation in the camp. Although still in plaster, I travelled in to all of the sessions so that I could still feel part of everything. Anyway, living at home, I really had nothing else to do. The players were being measured up for blazers, filled with a sense of real expectancy. It felt good being part of it.

We opened our Championship campaign against supposed no-hopers

Kerry in Killarney and I've often found it sobering to think that the whole '87 thing almost died there and then. Unable to play, I was driven to a beach on the morning of the game by Theo English so that I could have a run on the sand.

Now Killarney isn't exactly close to too many beaches and the fact that Theo was willing to drive me on a round-trip of something close to seventy miles just emphasised how thorough, how professional the whole Tipperary approach had become.

We had arrived in the Aghadoe Heights Hotel on the Saturday night, had a team talk and, generally, relaxed in each other's company. Training had gone really well. The line has often been thrown at me since that, 'You'd think that Tipp had never trained before' the way so many of us mention the quality of training in '87.

But the whole thing genuinely felt different. To be honest, I think the supporters realised it as well. They just seemed a bit more enthusiastic about supporting us with a man like 'Babs' at the helm. It was as if they saw us in our blazers and thought to themselves 'This is being done properly at last'.

And yet, incredibly, Kerry almost beat us.

I remember sitting on the subs' bench at one point and feeling certain that we were gone. Tipp kept missing chances while Kerry just seemed to be growing stronger and stronger. When you are overwhelming favourites in a game and you're just not able to pull away, it becomes harder and harder to keep your composure. It's like sinking into quick sand.

Before that game with Kerry, 'Babs' was pushing the fact that Tipp had never been beaten in Killarney and we liked to hear it. All going well, our semi-final with Clare was due to be played there as well. We felt good about the field.

Still, but for Pat Fox, we wouldn't have got out of there in one piece that day. Fox was brilliant – scoring 1-10 – as we won eventually by fifteen points. But it was nowhere near as convincing as the scoreline implied.

Three weeks later, we returned to face Clare and almost blew it again.

Back in the team, I proceeded to play rubbish that day. John Russell, a very good player, was marking me and succeeded in the job comfortably. Although fully fit again, my touch was terrible and – looking at it on television afterwards – I seemed to swagger around the place like a cocky fool.

Short of match practice, I was definitely a yard off the pace. I got a goal in the first-half but only because the goalkeeper made a hash of my first attempt, batting the ball straight back out to me so that I could have a second chance. Maybe I *was* a bit cocky. After all, I had won three Allstar awards and it might just have started affecting my temperament. I don't honestly know. Towards the end of the game, I remember distinctly getting one last ball and knowing, in my heart, that it was a goal chance.

But I decided instead just to tip the ball nonchalantly over the bar and John Moroney arrived from nowhere to block me down. I felt sick when I saw it afterwards on television, the cut of me trying to look casual when I had all the time in the world to drive it over.

It was unforgivable carelessness. At the very death, Gerry McInerney blasted home a goal for Clare to give them a draw. And I couldn't help thinking we might just as easily have been leading by only two points when he scored it. That would have been the end of our Championship.

That night, one of 'Babs' sayings kept repeating itself in my head. 'I don't want any of you looking up at the ceiling at home tonight, thinking I should have done this or I should have done that' he always told us. Well that night,

I was looking at the ceiling.

The management's reaction to our performance caught a lot of us off guard. Four lads were dropped straight off the panel. It was a ruthless response that had us all a little wary. We knew that we had played rubbish, that we hadn't done ourselves justice. But we didn't think anyone would be discarded.

But this was 'Babs' way of telling us that no-one could take their place for granted. To see people like Philip Kennedy jettisoned came as a serious shock to the system.

Still, the replay proved a repeat of '85. Given the second chance, we blew Clare away. But I felt there was something more pleasing about the way we did it this time. There was actually method to the way Tipp were playing. We used the ball cleverly, playing it in front of the full-forward line.

Bobby Ryan scored an early goal for us that day. Now Bobby would be the first to admit that he was never a natural forward. He was just back from an Allstars trip at the time, having been honoured as the country's finest left-half back but now, with the arrival of Richie Stakelum (his cousin) and Paul Delaney, Bobby couldn't get his place at wing-back.

So, instead, he was named at full-forward where he was never going to get a sympathetic ride from Fox and me. When he asked us in typically earnest fashion beforehand what we wanted him to do, I joked 'Just keep out of the way Bobby'.

Bobby was a real man on the hurling field, someone we all looked up to in the heat of battle. The tougher the game, the more Bobby seemed to thrive. Definitely a guy you wanted with you. But not at full-forward!

Anyway, just two minutes into the game, Bobby got his goal. Donie O'Connell fed the ball through to him and, as he went to hit it, the Clare goalkeeper – Owen McMahon – seemed to turn away. I couldn't really blame him, given the fact Bobby was only about three yards out and ready to unleash a pile-driver. McMahon must have thought he was going to end up in the back of the net with the sliothar.

Only trouble is, Bobby completely mis-hit his shot and the ball barely crept over the goal-line. A vintage Ryan goal you might say.

Still, it set us on the road to a resounding win, yours truly scoring 2-4 but the performance of the day coming from Bobby's younger brother, Aidan, who was absolutely unbelievable. Joe Hayes, too, had a wonderful game in midfield. All in all, Tipp were right back on the rails. Into the Munster final, waiting to discover the identity of our opponents.

Cork and Limerick had drawn in the other semi-final and, a week after our victory over Clare, we travelled *en bloc* to Thurles to see the replay. Again it was a reflection of 'Babs' style that stand seats had been reserved for the entire panel.

Cork won that replay in a canter, the game being most notable for John Fenton's wonder goal – pulled on from about 50 yards out. It was a fantastic goal, the best I think I've ever seen. We were sitting just in line with it and the ball definitely swerved in mid-air. Limerick's Tommy Quaid was a great goalkeeper but he never had a chance of saving it.

The goal was the icing on an easy victory for the Corkmen, setting up another Tipp-Cork Munster final in Thurles. I left the ground that evening with a certain degree of trepidation. Cork had looked absolutely devastating and, in my time on the Tipp team, we had yet to beat them in a game of any real importance.

It was still hard to see the famine ending.

XII

'JESUS, THE ONE GOOD BALL I GET AND I'VE NO HURLEY'

THERE are days that are made for Munster finals.

Hot, sticky, breathless days when the air is so thick, so heavy you feel you could cut it with a knife. Summer days of perfect blue skies, of melting road tar, of heat shimmering off the traffic jams. July 12, 1987 was just such a day in Thurles.

I can never remember the town as packed, the atmosphere so suffocating. If we thought '84 was something special, this quadrupled it for tension. The build-up had been massive, much being made of the fact that Cork were going for their sixth Munster title in a row while Tipp had not won one for sixteen years. There was a desperation in the air. We all felt it.

By the time our bus came down through the town from St. Patrick's College *en route* to the ground beforehand, the sirens of the garda outsiders squealing, most people had already taken their places inside Semple Stadium. Where, normally, pubs would be packed until maybe twenty minutes from throw-in, it was as if the supporters couldn't bear the waiting.

Once in the stadium, we strolled down the tunnel and out into what felt like an oven. I remember the Cork players standing there, looking at us in our blazers. And I couldn't help suspect they were thinking, 'Look at these eejits. We'll show them you need more than blazers to win Munster

Championships'.

This is the strangest of times for a player. You're standing just a few yards from guys you've maybe played alongside at colleges level but there's a distinct distance, a tension between you now. Personally, I've always been quite comfortable with talking to opponents before a big game but it's probably fair to say that most people aren't.

It's as if an unwritten law decrees that you keep your distance until the 'hostilities' are over. So players often find themselves just staring at one another in these moments, looking for glimpses of confidence or nervousness.

I think there was something like 62,000 people packed into the ground and I'll always remember a big Cork flag that someone had managed to erect at the very top of the new stand.

'Babs' was noticeably calm in the dressing-room, given the sense of occasion. It was if he now found himself exactly where he wanted to be. Always a man for the big occasion, he seemed to be revelling in the excitement.

From a player's viewpoint, it's always a little hard to recall exactly how you felt on that kind of day. There is such a mixture of anticipation, resolve, relish and even dread welling about inside you, it's often difficult to articulate exactly what you feel.

But, as long as I live, I will never forget the emotion that charged through me as we ran onto the pitch that day in Thurles. The roar of the crowd was like nothing I had ever heard before. It was simply ferocious, incredible. The place just lifted.

I remember saying to myself 'Jesus Christ almighty, we'll win here today. There's no team will beat us with that support.'

The momentous events that followed have been well documented in the years since. So I'm not going to re-hash a score-by-score account of the happenings that led to Tipp finally breaking from the shadows. Suffice to say, people who cared that day – Tipp people everywhere – could probably recite it all to the smallest detail.

My own personal memory is that I started really poorly that day in Thurles. Denis Mulcahy was marking me and I have to say I think he's the most difficult opponent I've ever faced. Incredibly strong and fast, he seemed to have the hurley in there all the time. I just couldn't shake him off.

After a while, the selectors moved me out to wing-forward where I managed to make a point for Donie O'Connell. But, typically, the pass I gave him had to be kicked along the ground as my old habit of losing the hurley returned with a vengeance.

We reached half-time with a four point lead but it was poor enough reward for the possession we had enjoyed. Being truthful, I had contributed virtually nothing to that advantage, failing to make much of an impression no matter where I moved to.

Early in the second-half, out of sheer frustration, I asked Bobby Ryan to switch with me so that I could have a little shot at full-forward. I said I'd try it just for a few minutes because I wasn't getting much change anywhere else.

I remember almost immediately after the resumption, Ken Hogan had made an incredible save away to his right from Kieran Kingston that seemed to rise the whole team. We were hurling our hearts out to keep Cork at safe distance when – suddenly – I struck for a goal that, to my amazement, is still talked about to this day.

How did it come about?

Well Joe Hayes got the ball in midfield and Joe had a fine delivery. As he would say himself, he could 'gift-wrap' a ball for a full-forward. But this particular pass actually carried a lot further than either myself or Richard Browne, who was marking me, anticipated. As the ball came in over our heads, I realised that – if he missed it – I'd have a big advantage on him.

Back to goal, he would have to turn 360 degrees to chase while I was already facing goalwards. And that's exactly what happened. Richard failed to reach the ball and, in a split second, I was clean through behind the full-back line with only Ger Cunningham to beat.

Just one snag. I arrived in there without my hurley. 'Jesus,' I thought. 'The one good ball I get all day and I have no hurley. What in the name of God am I going to do here?'

People might imagine that what followed was an act of wonderfully calm, instinctive finishing. Nothing could be further from the truth. As I closed in on Cunningham's goal, the sliothar at my feet, I honestly hadn't a clue what I was going to do next.

With my first touch, I brought the ball on a little bit but I was actually waiting for a team-mate to get up to me so I could pass it to them. Looking back, it seems like it took almost ten seconds for the whole thing to occur but, obviously, it happened much quicker.

Anyway, no-one came and Cunningham had started to advance a little bit. So, effectively, I was left with no real option but to have a go. 'I'll just have to try to flick it past him,' I thought to myself.

To this day, I still can't believe what the ball did. It actually swerved around him, just like you would kick a soccer ball from right to left. Some people wrote subsequently that I often practised controlling a sliothar with my foot and the goal was a product of that practice. That's really not the case.

The truth is I liked to mess around with a sliothar, juggling it on my foot but that's all it was if I'm truly honest. Messing.

All I can say is that I wanted to kick the ball to the right of the goalkeeper and that's where it went. But I could never have imagined I'd make such a perfect connection. You could try that kind of thing a hundred times in training and it wouldn't happen. The 'Maradona goal' – as they called it – was down to luck.

It did, of course, have a real novelty value. I couldn't believe afterwards that it looked so well on television. After scoring, I remember coming running out (we were now seven points up) and just catching Bobby's eye. He was laughing at me and I was laughing back at him. Behind the goal, Theo English must have jumped up and down five or six times. The crowd was going berserk. It looked like we had won the game.

And, of course, by the time we stopped patting ourselves on the back, Cork had almost stolen the game from under our noses.

Scoring 1-6 without reply, they moved into a two points lead with only a minute remaining. It was '84 revisited. Surely we weren't leaving it behind us again.

With that minute to go, Colm Bonnar was fouled about sixty yards out from goal and, as Pat Fox lined up the free, he was asking what he should do with it. I told him to put it over the bar and, on the sideline, Donie Nealon was signalling for him to take the point as well.

Fox didn't even wait for the referee's whistle, didn't allow himself time to get nervous before lifting the ball and putting it straight between the posts. Thinking about it now, that wasn't an easy free. Maybe sixty yards out, in front of the old stand. Truth is, it was a great free in the circumstances.

Then Ger Cunningham took the puck-out and everyone knew this was the last chance Tipp would get. There was a mad scramble for possession around midfield and Bobby, typical of the man, was the one to get the ball in his hands. I caught Bobby's eye and he hit a good low ball in towards me which I managed to control ahead of Richard Browne. At least, I kind of controlled it.

I actually had it wedged between my arm and my chest but couldn't manoeuvre it down into my hand because I reckoned it would fall to the ground. So my only chance was to hold it there and see if I could engineer a free.

I went to turn around Browne and he did exactly what I had hoped he'd do, pulling me back when I was never really getting away from him in the first place. If I'm brutally honest, I didn't actually have the ball in my possession but the referee and most of the crowd clearly thought that I did.

The free was awarded to us maybe 50 yards out, straight in front of goal. A reasonably straightforward chance? Hardly. To this day, I often wonder how I would have reacted to the pressure of taking that free. But, when Fox placed the ball, not one of us even considered the possibility of him missing. Bobby came up and tapped me on the back. As far as the two of us were concerned, we had the draw. There was just no way Fox would miss.

In later years, Tipperary would come to fully appreciate the value of having a man like Fox absorbing the responsibility of taking frees. That day, a free being awarded to us in a scoreable position amounted to a point. We really were that confident in him,

And, sure enough, Fox delivered the second chance we craved. Having stared at the nightmare of '84 again, we thus survived. An enormous roar greeted the final whistle. Glancing at the faces of the Cork players, there was no question they looked upon it as a chance squandered.

For us, drawing was almost as good as a win. We were on our way back to Killarney, a home from home. Now, for sure, we knew that Tipp were coming good. We knew too that a lot of us could play much better than we had done this time.

For maybe the first time in my Championship life, Cork no longer looked invincible.

XIII

'CHRIST DOYLE, DID YOU GET TWO GOALS OUT THERE?'

NO game, no day could ever better this one.

People outside of Tipperary must have found it difficult to relate to the madness that erupted in Killarney that hot, July Sunday. If ever a game of hurling transcended mere sport, this was the one. The blue and gold battalions who flocked to Kerry that day, didn't travel in any gentle hope. They went with a demonic certainty that this had to be their day.

This was our fourth trip to Fitzgerald Stadium of the summer. It was the ground we wanted to play on more than any other, surpassing even Thurles in our affections. The whole thing had a comforting sense of routine for us now. Back to Killarney, back to the Aghadoe Heights. It felt good, reassuring.

I've often found it hard to believe in hindsight how that game almost got away from us before we had even warmed up.

We were so sure of ourselves going to the ground that day. Our supporters too. It was as if we all knew our way around this place, as if it was alien territory only for the Corkmen. History was in the making and maybe, just maybe, we were forgetting whose responsibility it was to make it.

Anyway, Cork started with a whirlwind of scores while we looked stuck to the ground. After twenty minutes, they led by 0-7 to 0-1 and you could sense a sickly feeling of panic creep across the Tipp supporters.

The game, in truth, was threatening to deteriorate into a rout.

Around that time, Tom Cashman flashed a ball against the Tipperary upright and Kieran Kingston's shot from the rebound was blocked on his knees by Ken Hogan. Not for the first time, Ken had rescued us from near oblivion. But it was getting pretty hairy.

Being honest, Tipp were really on the brink. A few more Cork scores would, almost certainly, have buried us without trace.

Pat Fox had been missing frees and we needed a signal from Cork that they too were feeling the tension. Then, mercifully, we stepped back from the edge with a goal.

My memory of it is a long ball coming in towards Bobby Ryan. Having started badly in the game again, I was – effectively – operating in a no-man's land. Denis Mulcahy had been destroying me in the corner so I had moved out to the wing on Jim Cashman.

But, even there, I was beginning to get a little lost. So when the ball came towards Bobby and Richard Browne, I had already managed to sneak in behind them. "Leave it Bobby, leave it" I yelled as he went to take it and Bobby – fair play – just let it run through his legs.

Unmarked, I rose the ball, hit it first-time and knew immediately that it was going in unless it actually hit Ger Cunningham. I had connected so sweetly, there was just no way he was going to save it. And he didn't.

The goal brought us right back into the game and, even though, we were still five points down at the interval – 1-5 to 1-10 – there was a different, far more focused feeling about us as we headed for the dressing-room.

Inside, Donie Nealon erupted. I will never forget his anger. He brought us back to '71, reminded us of how Tipp had beaten Limerick here in Killarney after trailing by six points at half-way. 'This is it lads,' he bellowed. 'Ye have a great chance of winning this game if ye want it bad enough. Ye haven't hurled at all and it's still there waiting for ye.'

Now people have often talked about the drawn game in Thurles, about how you could almost reach out and touch the tension with your fingers. They're not exaggerating. But I think the atmosphere was even worse that day in Killarney. It was just savage. Unbelievable.

Put it this way, if we had lost I'm not sure if any of us would have been able to bear the pain. We were on a road with no turning and we just had to keep running flat out.

People might have thought the signals weren't great for us coming out for the second-half. But we were fit, young and ferociously strong. And we were ready to die for the victory.

Martin McGrath, who hadn't even been on the panel the previous Sunday, was now on as substitute and we went at Cork with everything we had. Martin was to contribute three fabulous points as we slowly but steadily closed the gap.

Then, mid-way through the second-half, Fox got a brilliant goal that was disallowed. I hand-passed it to him and he smashed the ball against the stanchion behind Ger Cunningham. To this day, I can still hear the ping of the ball.

Terence Murray's umpires – who would almost cost Tipp the '91 Munster Championship with another error – heard it too but they weren't sure what it had hit. As the ball flew straight back into play, they obviously presumed it had just come back off the post. It went straight to Pat Fitzelle who, not realising there was any confusion, just popped it over the bar for a point.

Fox and myself were furious. We knew it had been a perfect goal and, at the time, Fitzelle's point seemed little compensation. But, in fairness,

Tony O'Sullivan had a goal disallowed soon after at the other end – for an infringement in the square – and it seemed to me afterwards that television evidence showed it to be a perfectly legitimate score too.

Looking back, I suppose the two incidents cancelled out one another.

With about twelve minutes remaining, Fox put us level for the first time since the opening throw-in and – from there to the end of normal time – the match just blazed on wildly. It was fantastic hurling, end-to-end drama played out at a ferocious pace. Munster Championship stuff at its very best.

Right at the death, with Cork leading by a point, Paul Delaney missed a '65' and it looked as if all our efforts might come to nought.

Now what followed is another one of those moments that seem frozen in time. Afterwards, people made a major thing out of my so-called 'maturity' in taking a point when a shot for goal might have been saved. Being honest, I could never see it that way.

With the game in injury-time, the ball had broken to me from a ruck of players and I took off instinctively towards goal. The truth is I was certain someone was right behind me, that if I tried for a goal they'd hook me and the chance would be gone. So I was never going to take that chance.

It just so happens there wasn't anyone close enough to hook me. When I saw it on television afterwards, I couldn't believe it. A goal was definitely on. Hindsight acclaimed it as a brilliant decision but, if we had been beaten, make no mistake it would have gone down as a bad one.

But what followed coloured forever the way everything was to be seen that famous day. And I wasn't about to argue.

Still I found it just a little strange to hear people say things like 'what great thinking' and 'no-one else would have thought of that.' Believe me, it was no act of genius.

In the dressing-room, at the end of normal time, Nealon went to work on us again. The same tirade, the same message. The game was there for us if we wanted it bad enough. This time, though, I don't think we needed any more words of fire and brimstone. We knew ourselves how close we were to history.

Coming out the door, I can remember a Clareman called Pat McCarthy – a detective in Tipperary Town – standing by the wire. 'They're gone,' he shouted to me. 'Cork are absolutely f....d, they're gone'.

Pat had just observed their faces, their body-language as they left their dressing-room for the last time. He had seen a tiredness in them that we didn't have.

It took us a while to realise it but, when John Fenton – playing at corner-forward with his socks around his ankles – missed his first free of the day having scored thirteen in a row, the signs were finally there for all to see. It was from about fifty yards out, well within his normal range and the huge Tipp roar which greeted his miss carried 16 years of pent-up anger.

That happened about two minutes into the second-period of extra-time and was followed by a Donie O'Connell point which gave us the lead for the first time in the day. Cork, we knew, were ready to go under.

The goals that followed are, even now, just a blur of exhilaration.

Michael Doyle got two, O'Connell got the other. It was, in one sense, poetic justice. Doyle had taken so much abuse in Tipperary since '84 which was desperately unfair. He was a fine, intelligent player and personally I was thrilled for him that now, at last, people were talking about him for all the right reasons.

We were like a team with a tailwind in those closing flurries, demolishing Cork with a vengeance, burying all our bad days.

At one point I was thinking, 'Jesus, we're nine points clear, surely there's no way they'll catch us now'. You see we still had this awful fear of Cork. We had never beaten them in anything, let alone a Munster final. Now that the monkey was finally coming off our back, we could hardly believe it.

Those closing minutes were just a blue and gold carnival. Tipp supporters came spilling in over the wire in their hundreds. Now the wire in Killarney is pretty high and I remember seeing this old man – in his seventies at least – clambering to the top of it and swinging clumsily over. I genuinely thought he was going to kill himself. He was wearing a Tipperary bandana but, if he fell, I don't think he'd have felt any pain.

Like everyone, he was grinning from ear to ear. As if in a beautiful trance.

We were swallowed up at the final whistle. Just manic stuff. A whole county bouncing around this field in Kerry as if some terrible weight had been lifted. Swept off our feet in the throng, most of us never even reached the stand for the presentation.

I don't remember much of Richie Stakelum's speech apart from the immortal opening salvo, 'The famine is over!' After that, it was just a case of battling your way to the dressing-room, taking the back-slaps, the bear-hugs, the kisses along the way.

Inside, the emotion was beginning to spill over. I think most of us still found it hard to grasp that we were finally Munster champions. Standing in one corner of the room, Michael Doyle was puffing a fag and grinning like a madman. Everyone seemed to be congratulating him on his goals.

'Christ Doyle did you get two goals out there?' someone asked him. 'I did,' he roared. 'I went feckin mad.'

Of all the games I would ever play in my career, this was to be the one

I'd cherish most. The emotion of the day, the drama, the sense of sheer ecstasy when it ended, could never be surpassed again. I think I even sensed it as we left Fitzgerald Stadium that evening. Something special had just taken place. Something that would never be forgotten.

Looking back, our hunger had been unbearable. You just had to look at Colm Bonnar coming up the field during the second-half of extra-time and literally running through Johnny Crowley. Johnny had to go off and I was sorry to hear afterwards that he had sustained a broken nose.

But Colm, with the ball in hand, just ploughed through him. He, like the rest of us, was just ready to go.

The traffic that evening in Killarney, as we headed back to the Aghadoe Heights, was horrific. A few of us were in Donie O'Connell's car and it took us ages to get through the town. On our way, we met Martin McGrath's sister – Anne – and she asked us where the session was going to be. Whatever way Donie answered her, she thought he said 'Aherlow House' and told us she would see us there.

Back in the hotel, everyone wanted to see the game again. There was a feeling of having been witness to something truly special. So much energy had been spent, be it physically in the players' case or mentally in the supporters', a certain tiredness had set in too.

Some of the lads went up to 'Babs' room to watch the 'Sunday Game', while the rest of us watched it on a television in the bar. Every Tipp score was greeted with the kind of roar that could crack pint glasses. Having watched it, confirmed for ourselves that it wasn't just a dream, we headed down the town to celebrate for real.

First the Laurels, then the Danny Mann Inn and, finally, a disco. My abiding memory of that disco is of Pat Fox and a few other players being chaired around the place on supporters' shoulders at about two in the morning. Killarney had been good to us.

We had a bit of a session on the way home the following day, stopping for a few in Punch's of Patrickswell before ending up eventually in Borrisoleigh. There was a homecoming party for us there where we were all introduced to what seemed like a massive crowd.

Then, on the Tuesday, I played golf in Tipp Town and was amazed when I got home to see the whole of Cullen draped out in flags and bunting. I remember the outside of our house was being plastered at the time and the scaffolding was covered in blue and gold.

That night they lit a bonfire in the village and, with a crowd gathered, some speeches were made. It was all done for my benefit and I found it a bit embarrassing to be honest.

The whole county was on an incredible high and, in time, the celebrations would be blamed on our loss to Galway in the All-Ireland semi-final. People probably looked at us that couple of days immediately after Killarney, downing pints, listening to speeches, crowding around bonfires and presumed we had lost the run of ourselves.

It was a myth that was allowed develop. That Tipp celebrated so wildly after beating Cork, we were in no fit state to take on Galway. Nothing could have been further from the truth.

For us, the drinking had stopped that Tuesday. Sure the supporters kept celebrating and why not? The feel-good factor was intense in Tipp around that time and there was immense pleasure to be had from talking hurling over a good pint.

But the notion that players were out toasting themselves and their achievements for weeks after Killarney was, to say the least, mischievous.

We knew we faced another mountain.

XIV
GALWAY AND THE MYSTERY OF THE McGRATHS

YOU could call it the Tipperary 'sting'.

A Saturday afternoon and we're sitting on a bus, making our way to Dublin for the All-Ireland semi-final against Galway, minds whirling at what lay ahead. For all the hype that had attached itself to Tipperary, we couldn't escape the reality that we were a team coming from Division Two.

Galway were League champions, had played in the last two All-Ireland finals and – having lost both – were an intensely driven team. Breaking the tension, 'Babs' announced to all and sundry that he had a sure thing of a horse running that afternoon.

Now, when 'Babs' says he has a tip, you listen sometimes. I know few men who have as many or better contacts in the racing game. You might say he gets information directly from the horse's mouth.

Anyway, we all took his advice that afternoon, stopping off at a bookies' on the journey to put our few quid on some piece of horse flesh none of us had ever heard of. True to form, the tip was a good one. Our horse cantered in at odds of 6/1 and we arrived in Dublin convincing ourselves that it was a happy omen.

That night, we stayed at the Royal Marine Hotel in Dun Laoghaire, killing the threat of boredom by finding a local snooker hall. The mood was upbeat.

Many of the weekend's newspapers focused on the fact that 'Babs' had been part of Galway's management team when they got to the All-Ireland final of 1979. It was implied that this game would be a personal battle between himself and Galway manager, Cyril Farrell, given the fact that they had sat in the same dug-out eight years previously.

Being honest, it was an angle few of us could relate to. If 'Babs' saw the game as a personal battle of wits between himself and an old colleague, there was little evidence of it in his team talks.

I've no doubt, looking back, that there was a certain edge between the two of them. The cult of manager was very much in vogue at the time and so much attention was focused on their achievements as distinct from those of their teams, it was only natural that a distinct competitiveness grew between them.

But the reality is that Keating and Farrell were actually good friends too, hurling men who had much the same ideas about how the game should be played. Both, admittedly, were brilliant at manipulating the media and – in many ways – the hype surrounding that '87 semi-final offered concrete proof of their talents here.

Looking back now, we lost the game purely and simply because Galway were too good for us.

It galls me the way defeat, for some people, always needs to be packaged in the worthless twine of excuses. The truth of '87 is that we had none. Galway won the game because, at the time, they were the best team in the country.

It had nothing to do with Tipp indulging in wild, reckless celebrations on the weight of a first Munster title win in 16 years. Our supporters might have seen fit to burn the midnight oil and, if so, they were fully entitled to it. But we didn't. That's the truth, end of story.

That semi-final was, arguably, the finest game of hurling I ever played in. It had a relentless tempo from start to finish and some of the scores were breathtaking.

On the day, I felt good every time the ball came near me. So much so, that my final tally of 0-6 from play actually disappointed me. Two of the points literally skimmed the crossbar as they went over and I often thought afterwards that I might easily have wound up with 3-3 on the day.

Within nine seconds of the throw-in, I had given Tipp the lead and that's just the kind of start any forward dreams of. But Galway had been around long enough not to be dispirited by such moments and the truth is they had recovered almost before the cheering even died.

Now a lot of Tipp people blamed Richie Stakelum, not just for Martin Naughton's quick-fire goal, but for our defeat generally. I didn't go along with that. Not then. Not now.

The truth is that, for the early goal, Richie was dragged in to cover the centre as Brendan Lynskey thundered through and Lynskey, typically, flicked a brilliant pass to Naughton. Even then, no-one really expected Naughton to go for a goal – least of all Ken Hogan I'd say. But Naughton shot and the ball ended up in the back of the net.

Galway, thus, were up and running before we even knew what hit us and, in reality, we spent the rest of the day playing catch-up. That said, there was still well over an hour of hurling still to play so how anyone could blame Richie for our subsequent defeat is just beyond me.

Contentious incidents peppered the game from there to the final whistle. Coming up to half-time, I drove low over the bar from an acute angle only to see the umpire – incredibly – wave the shot wide. But then, on another occasion, I actually drove a shot inches off target but the white flag went up immediately. Ultimately, I couldn't really complain.

Just a minute from the interval, I had the ball in John Commins's net but the whistle had already gone for a foul on me. Pat Fox took the penalty and he'd be the first to admit himself that he actually made a mess of it but, thankfully, it still went in.

That meant we were just four points down at half-time and Tipp reappeared with a vengeance. I've often wondered how Martin McGrath's career might have gone afterwards had fate been just a little kinder to him early in the second-half.

With Tipp having reduced the deficit to a single point, Martin made a great run in from under the Hogan Stand and unleashed a stinging drop-shot which rebounded to safety off the post with Commins seemingly beaten. He was in unbelievably hard luck. That would have been one of the goals of the year.

Martin was taken off shortly after that in a move most Tipp people remain adamant amounted to a breakdown in communication from the dug-out.

I am not so sure.

Popular legend has it that the selectors actually intended taking off John McGrath but ended up taking off the wrong man. Admittedly John hadn't been having the best of times that day whereas Martin did seem a strange choice for replacing.

But 'Babs' always liked the notion of bringing someone off the bench to win a game. He had managed it with Michael Doyle in the replayed Munster final and I suspect that, in this instance, he was just looking for some new spark on the field.

Obviously, after his performance in Killarney, Michael was going to come on at some point in the semi-final and – let's be honest – no-one was about to argue. In that sense, I think, at the time, it was more a case of who was coming on rather than who was being taken off.

It may well be that the wrong McGrath was taken off but, personally, I suspect that theory of the incorrect substitution to be rubbish. Look at it this way. If you are a selector and the wrong guy is coming off the field it's not exactly difficult to rectify the situation, is it?

No, I just can't go along with that claim.

There was, of course, another incident involving John McGrath that was to exercise the minds and tongues of Tipperary people for many months after. It happened eight minutes from the end of the game and was, unquestionably, the moment that killed us.

Pat Fox had scored a brilliant goal to put us ahead for the first time and, although Galway had come back to level, we genuinely felt the game was ours for the taking. Then Commins collected a ball to the right of his goal from Donie O'Connell and cleared the ball straight out to me, which I returned over for a simple point.

But referee, Gerry Kirwan, whistled from precisely where I had taken the shot, signalling a free out to Galway. It emerged that he was penalising John McGrath for what he saw as a late challenge on Commins immediately after the ball was cleared.

Eanna Ryan got possession from the subsequent free and hand-passed beyond Ken Hogan for a Galway goal that absolutely knocked the stuffing out of us. In an instant, there had been a devastating four points swing. Instead of us leading 2-16 to 1-18, we now trailed by 2-15 to 2-18.

Thereafter, we ran ourselves to a standstill but Galway had that critical bit of breathing space and it was no huge surprise when veteran Noel Lane, who had come on as a substitute, whipped home a killer goal with two minutes remaining to confirm that our great adventure was over.

Joe Cooney quickly added a point to leave the score at 3-20 to 2-17 in Galway's favour. It had been an unbelievable game in which, to my mind, the standard of hurling had been incredibly high. On a personal note, I had played really well – scoring 0-5 off Conor Hayes at full-forward and 0-1 off Gerry McInerney on the wing.

But that refereeing decision left us all wondering what might-have-been.

It may surprise people that I never asked John McGrath about the incident afterwards. But, when a team is beaten, the last thing you want to do is clog the aftermath with post-mortems. Players tend to just break into little groups and go their separate ways.

There was a rumour in Tipperary that, having refereed the All-Ireland Club final of that same year which McGrath's club – Borrisoleigh – won, Gerry Kirwan might have gone into the game with some pre-conceived ideas about the player.

Certainly, if you study the video, Commins was back in goal extremely quickly, something he'd hardly have managed if John had deliberately charged into him after the clearance had been made. What can certainly be said is that whatever (if any) contact was made with the goalkeeper, did not interfere with play in any way.

Personally, I don't believe John McGrath fouled John Commins that day in Croke Park. But then you'd expect me to say that wouldn't you? Make no mistake, it was the moment that game was lost for Tipperary.

Still, looking back, it was disappointing but hardly heartbreaking.

While people busied themselves with analysis and counter-analysis of what had happened, I think – deep down – the players knew they had been beaten by a superb team. In hindsight, we had neither their experience nor – probably – their hunger. Here was a team that had lost the last two All-Ireland finals. Defeat against these new boys from Tipp was surely, for them, unthinkable.

Wherever you turned, different theories were doing the circuit. If it wasn't that we had been celebrating too much, it was that we were all simply jaded after having to play five hard games to escape from Munster.

All I can say to that is – personally – I didn't feel tired. In fact, I felt better that day than I had in either of the two Munster final games with Cork and I think my performance reflected that.

More logically, I think you could make the point that it was Tipp's first big Championship day in Croke Park since the All-Ireland final of 1971. It was a nerve-wracking responsibility, one I think reflected in the fact that we were five points behind really before the game had even started.

Galway must have relished seeing all the hype we were bringing with us from Munster, they must have been chomping at the bit to cut us down to size. We were the fancy team, the team the media had all but adopted as their favourites.

And yet here were Galway with forwards like Joe Cooney, Eanna Ryan, 'Hopper' McGrath, Martin Naughton, Brendan Lynskey and Noel Lane to call upon. They were streets ahead of us in terms of cuteness.

I always believed that Lynskey never got the credit he deserved. Hugely strong and powerful, he had a great brain on the field. Look at the old videos and you will never see him wasting a ball. All these little flicks and passes, often when hemmed in by opponents. Lynskey was a supremely intelligent hurler who kept Galway motoring in those days.

Losing the semi-final, thus, was never going to dismantle what Tipp had achieved that summer. If you look at it honestly, we were involved probably in three of the greatest games ever played. For me, the standard that day against Galway even surpassed the two games with Cork. It was a wonderful, open contest so different from later clashes between the two counties as familiarity gradually bred a certain mutual contempt.

Don't get me wrong. Disappointment did strike home with some intensity that night as we drowned our sorrows in the Loch and Quay pub. I remember a crowd of us ended up going back to Anne's flat in Harold's Cross, still grappling with the realisation that we had come so close to reaching the All-Ireland final.

The following day, Richie Stakelum was getting a B&I Player of the Month award in the Gresham Hotel, so Aidan Ryan, Martin McGrath and myself decided to make our way in and offer some 'moral support'. To say the least, we must have been fairly rough looking, wandering down O'Connell Street in our blazers from the previous day, hurleys under the arm.

By the time we managed to get the bus in from Terenure, Richie's function was already over. But we stayed around for a few pints, had a Chinese meal and then went down to Heuston Station to get the train home to Thurles.

Being honest, I think we were all pretty certain we'd be back hurling in Croke Park again sooner rather than later.

I did come up to Dublin for the final between Galway and Kilkenny but never managed to get any further than Corbetts' pub in Camden Street. Borrisoleigh had just won the All-Ireland Sevens out in Kilmacud the night before and I met up with a few of the players.

The pints were good, the day was foul. So we watched Galway collect the Cup on television.

XV
THE ROAD TO DUBLIN

THESE were the best of times and the worst of times.

Never again, in my years playing, would Tipperary's hurling pedigree dwindle to the extent it had in the late Seventies and early Eighties. 'Babs' arrival had transformed ambition and expectation within the county. After the heroics of '87, it was now accepted that we were back in the Big League. And the onus was on us, the players, to stay there.

Four of us had won Allstar awards – Ken Hogan, Aidan Ryan, Pat Fox and myself – Tipp's biggest representation in the awards scheme since '71.

Yet, still, we couldn't avoid our hiccups.

None of us will ever forget that horrendous March day in '88 when we went to Nowlan Park for a National League game against Kilkenny. Already safely through to the quarter-finals, we brought huge support with us to face the beaten All-Ireland finalists.

Now, as bad days go, this took some beating. Kilkenny, themselves trying to stave off relegation, absolutely annihilated us to a scoreline of 2-12 to 0-4. It was embarrassing, humiliating even.

We had an extremely tough training session the previous Thursday and I know my own legs certainly felt tired. But, in reality, we had no excuses for a performance of such mediocrity that the crowd were actually laughing at us.

I remember in the second-half, Tipp were playing up into the town goal and we could actually hear the jibes and laughter in the crowd. It was an absolute joke. At one point, I looked over to Pat Fox and he was looking at me, throwing his eyes to the heavens at something I had just done.

Joe Hennessy was marking me and he won just about every contest we had that day. Joe, to be fair, was an excellent player but he absolutely destroyed me that day in Kilkenny. As players, Tipp were literally falling around the place. A total mess.

'Babs', naturally, reacted pretty badly to the performance. I remember him telling us that he didn't really know what to make of us anymore. Whether we were going forward or backward.

'Babs' was a notoriously bad loser. At the worst of times, he was never inclined to attribute any blame towards himself. Always, a scapegoat would be located elsewhere in the dressing-room.

This would be seen most brutally later in the year when he went on television after the All-Ireland final and, effectively, blamed Pat Fox for our defeat. It was a side to him that was often pretty difficult to digest.

Two weeks after the Kilkenny game, we were a chastened team facing Antrim in the quarter-finals.

On a personal level, I was hugely determined to regain lost ground. The sound of Kilkenny people laughing at me had touched a nerve. It was as if I felt I needed to prove myself all over again at the highest level.

Going back to Croke Park and performing well there seemed the perfect antidote to my depression. And that's precisely how it worked out.

We beat Antrim comfortably (2-20 to 2-9) and, having been given the responsibility of taking frees, I managed a personal tally of 2-7. Now, being honest, I was never a particularly good free-taker. At the time, I had this way of just leaving the sliothar on the bas of the hurl for a split second to get a little balance before striking it. Later, it actually became a little controversial as some people maintained I was committing a foul.

For the next couple of years, I would take frees for Tipp but at no point did I ever feel entirely comfortable in the role.

Still, my general play was excellent that day against Antrim. I think I was fitter and stronger than at any previous stage of my career. Terence 'Sambo' McNaughton was Antrim's full-back that day and I think it's fair to say I gave him a difficult afternoon.

After the collapse in Nowlan Park, it was immensely reassuring to be back on the winning trail and, maybe more to the point, playing the kind of hurling that had won us so much praise the previous summer. And, over the next few weeks, travelling to Croke Park was to become a glorious routine we came to find addictive.

The way it worked was that five of us travelled together. Seamie Grogan would collect Pat Fox, Andy Lacey, Michael Corcoran and myself for the trip to Dublin. On arrival in the city, we'd go to St. Brigid's in Blanchardstown for the pre-match puckaround, followed by tea and sandwiches.

It worked like that for the quarter-final against Antrim, the semi-final against Waterford and again for the final against Offaly.

Of all the games I've played for Tipp these past 15 years, I suspect that one with Waterford was my best. On the day, I literally felt that I could do anything I wanted. It was an incredible feeling. Everything just seemed to come to me so easily.

We destroyed Waterford (4-19 to 1-8) and my personal tally was 2-11. Looking back, Waterford weren't that bad a team. They were physically tough but, if anything, a little bit rash in the challenge. There was an amount of rash pulling and they paid for it by the concession of needless frees.

On the day, I don't think I actually missed a free and the hype in the papers afterwards really went overboard. The popular headline seemed to be 'Waterford given an English lesson.' It was flattering of course but I couldn't help thinking I was being set up for a big fall.

After all, the League final would now be my first appearance in a national final and these headlines could easily become a dangerous distraction.

That night, we stopped at Whites in Portlaoise on the journey home to catch the highlights on television and I remember being disgusted that they showed only about two minutes in total. Like anyone, having played well, I was hoping to see more.

Funny, looking back now, to think how my emotions were almost the complete opposite maybe twelve hours later when I got my first glimpse of the morning newspapers. It really was a little over-the-top the way they reported my performance.

By now, I was teaching in Abbey CBS and I recall going into an early morning maths class feeling uncomfortable. In Tipp Town, everyone was treating me perfectly normally and, yet, the papers were writing about me as if I had become some kind of super-human.

I would be on a hiding to nothing in the final against Offaly.

You know it's funny the way my life, at the time, seemed split onto two separate levels. In class, the kids never really brought up my hurling and that's the way I wanted it. I can still remember the normality of that Monday, the sense of detachment from the hype exploding in the Dublin newspapers.

As usual, having finished school, I went delivering coal with my father, our run taking us into Limerick Junction where – again as usual – I stopped for about fifteen minutes to play soccer with the local kids. It was just a routine I had developed. Something I really enjoyed.

Training continued over the next couple of weeks without any real hitches so I went to Dublin on April 24 in Seamie's Merc, fit yet apprehensive. Aidan Fogarty was the man who would be marking me that day and I think it's fair to say there were, at the time, few more difficult assignments for a hurling forward.

Fogarty was, in my opinion, a great player – intelligent, skilful and a genuinely tough man. He was actually still hurling with St Rynagh's up to a couple of years ago which says everything about his quality.

Having played so well against Antrim and Waterford, I went into that League final terrified that I would now resort to the kind of form that had stoked ridicule from the terraces of Nowlan Park just seven weeks earlier. Put it this way, I knew I wasn't going to be able repeat the form of the Waterford game.

As it happened, I managed to play just reasonably – scoring 1-3 in a final we ended up winning by nine points thanks to two fine poacher's goals from team-captain, Pa O'Neill. My own goal, being honest, was no great classic.

I was always messing around in training, putting top-spin on the ball and that's what I did on this occasion, shooting off my right-hand side into the Canal End. I don't know whether the top-spin deceived Jim Troy or not but the ball seemed to slip under his hurl. Now Jim was a hell of a goalkeeper and I could see he was angry at not stopping the shot.

Again, it just seemed a further reflection of how all the luck was going with me at that time.

Every time the ball came near me that day, I was conscious of the expectancy in the crowd. Nicky English was very much the centre of attention and, while I found that intensely exciting, it also brought its pressures. To say the least, I was not a dominant player in that final.

Still we pulled away in the end, winning the final reasonably comfortably and it was a great thrill to see Pa going up to collect the League trophy. After all, I had been hurling with Tipp effectively since September of '81 and this was the first major title we had won in those seven years.

We had unbelievable support at the time too. It was all so new to Tipperary people and here they were flocking to Dublin virtually every two weeks for another big match.

Winning the League was confirmation that Tipp were genuinely back in the big time. And back to stay.

As the celebrations erupted that night though at the Embankment in Tallaght, I was conscious of having felt a peculiar twinge in my hamstring while chasing a ball in the first-half. Never having had a hamstring injury before, I really didn't know what to make of it.

That Monday evening, as usual, I played soccer with the kids in Limerick Junction and the feeling in my leg just wasn't right. I knew there was something wrong with me.

But the following Thursday, the Allstars were leaving for America so I convinced myself there was nothing to worry about, that I should just forget about it and enjoy the tour. Which is what I tried to do.

Galway being the All-Ireland champions, we were due to play them twice out there, first in Boston, then in San Francisco. Now those matches, being honest, were harmless enough affairs in which the players were not always in the best of shape for combat after the activities of the night before. I had been in Boston myself for the summers of '85 and '86, so there was no shortage of old acquaintances to look up.

With a big local support behind them, Galway beat us comfortably in the Boston game – Pat Fox and myself being the Allstar corner-forwards. Again I knew my leg just didn't feel right but, in a gentle game, it didn't amount to a serious problem.

The San Francisco contest proved a little different.

I got a rub on the leg beforehand but it was obvious to me that there was a problem. Anyway, the extent of it was soon to dawn. Getting a ball early in the game, I went to accelerate past Conor Hayes for goal when – all of a sudden – BANG. The hamstring just snapped.

Now it was a beautifully sunny day and all the Meath footballers – All-Ireland champions at the time – were sitting watching the game from a bank behind one of the goals. Their team-manager, Sean Boylan, would be a big help to me that evening.

When your hamstring snaps, the pain is unbelievable. It's like being shot, like having a spear plunged into the back of your leg. David Beggy, one of the Meath players, told me afterwards that I was actually flipped upside down as the injury occurred. Running flat out, it is like your leg just exploding under you.

I couldn't get to the ground quick enough with the pain. Lying there in agony on a field in San Francisco, I had no idea what the extent of the problem was. Nor of the implications for the remainder of my hurling career.

It was the first time I had ever pulled a muscle so severely. The first but not the last. This was to become the story of my hurling life.

XVI
'NICKY, YOU'LL BE CAPTAIN!'

CONSPIRACY theories are the lifeblood of small minds.

This I discovered with some discomfort in the autumn of '88 when I was named Tipperary captain for the All-Ireland final against Galway. It ought to have been one of the most pleasing experiences of a lifetime. Instead it became a nightmare.

Now I have heard all the whispered rumours, about how that team selection was supposedly hatched in Tipperary Golf Club.

The word was that 'Babs' and the Supporters Club wanted the team's glamour boy (me) to lead the team against Galway. Naturally, I was not exactly seen as a passive figure in the arrangement. 'A grabber' in the eyes of some, it was said I was already preparing my victory speech.

As with all the best stories, the reality is decidedly less colourful.

Tipp got to the final by way of victories over Limerick, Cork and Antrim. My damaged hamstring kept me out of the Limerick game which Tipp made heavy weather of winning. It was a forgettable game, made notable on a personal level for just one factor.

This was to be Johnny Leahy's first Championship game.

The Munster final against Cork at the Gaelic Grounds was one of the strangest I've been involved in. Tipp eventually won by nine points but, having led 1-14 to 0-5 a minute into the second-half, we completely lost concentration – allowing Cork back to within a two point margin – with maybe ten minutes remaining.

One of the more bizarre memories I have of those nervous moments is of Tipp being awarded a free maybe 60 yards from the Cork goal. Now this was my first Munster final as a free-taker and I will never forget looking at the ball as I went to place it only to discover that it was completely out of shape.

The Cork supporters were jeering, a sure sign that the free was an important one. I had scored a few beforehand but, with Tipp cruising at the time, they hadn't exposed me to any degree of pressure. This one, I knew, was different.

And the damn ball was the shape of a lemon!

People would probably find it difficult to believe that in a game of Munster final stature you can find yourself playing with a completely mis-shapen sliothar. But that's precisely what happened that day in Limerick.

Facing into the breeze, I deliberately placed it 'sideways' so that it would roll evenly off my hurley. 'Whatever else, this has to go over,' I told myself. Effectively, the sliothar was the shape of a rugby ball. Looking back, I should have brought it to the attention of the referee. But, in the heat of battle, you just want to get on with things.

Luckily, I connected sweetly with the ball and it sailed between the posts. Minutes later, Cormac Bonnar came on as sub and flicked home the goal that buried Cork. But it had been by no means a stress-free ride

That night, we ended up in Johnsie Ryan's pub in Oola which – being in Limerick – is a real hot-bed of anti-Tipperary feeling. Johnsie though is a Tipp man, who gives great entertainment from behind the bar after big hurling games.

Limerick people like to go in and slag Johnsie when they win a match and, when Tipp win, they tend to avoid him altogether because – in full flow – he could be hard to listen to. Johnsie you see has the distinction of being a very, very, biased Tipp man.

Nowadays though, he has a problem in that his kids are as staunch supporters of Limerick as he is of Tipperary.

Around that time, Limerick weren't real contenders for titles and Johnsie liked nothing better than to 'console' them with the comment, 'Yerra sure ye've got the tennis at Wimbledon to look forward to.'

Although in Limerick, Oola is just a mile or so from Cullen and the route taken home by most West and South Tipperary people after major games at the Gaelic Grounds.

Looking back, relief was the over-riding emotion that evening after beating Cork. It meant we were going back to Croke Park, scene of three impressive triumphs by us already this season.

The semi-final against Antrim was really a bit of a non-event. Believe me, these are the kind of games that players hate. Hugely important assignments that – deep down – you know you should win comfortably. Losing is unimaginable. You are already thinking of the All-Ireland final. To mess up here would be such an embarrassment.

In that context, I could easily understand what happened Offaly in the following year's semi-final.

You have just come from a provincial final where you have been the total focus of attention. But the atmosphere for playing Antrim is a bit like a junior game or a minor game as prelude to the main event. There is no parade, no national anthem. People are still settling into their seats. You can hear a constant hum of conversation.

And the problem is that Antrim, at that time, were good enough to make life really difficult for anybody. Traditionally, if they start going well, the supporters of three counties invariably shout their support. You sense a mood of absolute derision pointing towards you.

And the longer it remains a contest, the more nervy you become. You know that so many people in the stadium want to see the supposed 'big' team being pegged down to size. So this is the entertainment. If they're honest, most people expect Antrim to lose. But they want that slight uncertainty to be prolonged for as long as possible.

It's a real case of David trying to kick Goliath where the sun doesn't shine.

I have always considered it a snare on the way to the All-Ireland final, a kind of black hole that you have to clear. In '88, we cleared it but not without the customary hoots and guffaws of the watching comedians.

We were in the All-Ireland final, but not many had been over-impressed by the manner of our passage.

By now, I think it's fair to say that a certain amount of speculation was beginning to simmer about what exactly constituted Tipp's best fifteen. Pa O'Neill, who had been the hero of the League final, wasn't going quite as well now while Johnny Leahy had begun pushing strongly for a place.

There was a feeling throughout Tipp that Pa, although captain, might actually be under pressure to hold his place on the team.

Anyway, exactly seven days before the final, we sat down on the pitch in Thurles and listened to Donie Nealon call out the names of the fifteen who would be starting. Pa had been left out but there was absolutely no mention of who would be captain.

A couple of minutes after the announcement of the team, one of the selectors said in a matter-of-fact manner, 'Nicky, you'll be captain!'

Being perfectly honest, it really didn't matter to me. I hadn't thought much about the captaincy and I genuinely felt sorry for Pa. All of the players did. I mean he had been captain all year and now, suddenly, he was dropped for the biggest game of all.

Maybe just announcing me as captain was not the most tactful course to take. It could be argued that, with Pa gone, the job of naming Tipp's captain should have returned to O'Neill's club – Cappawhite – who were the county champions. Or, at the very least, they probably should have had an input. If that was the case, I think we could have avoided a lot of the hassle and controversy that followed.

Instead, it became a hugely contentious story with me as the undisputed bad guy.

It was said by some that I had engineered my way to the captaincy. Nothing could have been further from the truth. We all felt Pa might be under pressure to hold his place and I would have had absolutely no problem if the job was given to any other West Tipp man (God knows there were enough of us on the team).

I remember just saying to Pa, 'Jesus, I'm sorry' when the team was named. To be fair to him, he was good about it. At no point did he begin to sulk or start looking daggers in my direction.

Unfortunately, not everyone proved so generous towards me. A lot of mischief was put about, suggesting that Tipp wanted their flash boy up collecting the Cup, that they wanted to turn it into a total media circus.

Now it goes without saying that I wasn't exactly unhappy about being captain. I think – in Tipperary – it's every school kid's dream to be collecting the McCarthy Cup on the first Sunday in September. And I was no exception.

But, clearly, these were not the ideal circumstances in which to be given the captaincy, not when the repercussions almost threaten to overshadow the game.

As All-Ireland final week evolved, it got worse and worse. I got anonymous phone calls at home, I got anonymous letters. An Post had come up with special Galway and Tipperary postcards and, while I got hundreds and hundreds from well-wishers, I got a few abusive ones too.

It was being said that I had grabbed the captaincy, that I had 'shafted' Pa because of my own greed and ambition.

Looking back, the calls and letters had an awful effect on me. In the run-up to a big game, I don't want hassle and I certainly wasn't ready for the kind of grief I was getting now. From always wanting to play in an All-Ireland final, I actually started willing the week to be over.

There was speculation in some quarters as to whether Pa would bother even going to the match. Rumour had it, Cappawhite people were going to boycott it.

Hindsight I know is useless, but it was all probably so unnecessary. I know Johnny Leahy was an exceptional player who was making great strides but really we could have avoided so much hassle had Pa been left in the starting fifteen.

After all, this was to be Tipp's first All-Ireland final in 17 years. Even without this hassle, we could rest assured that the hype surrounding us was going to be absolutely immense. I tried to tell myself that the job was no more than flipping a coin, that I shouldn't let it get to me. In fact, I never even prepared a speech.

But it *was* getting to me and I knew it. I remember Fr Jack O'Neill, who is from Cappawhite, saying to me with a great laugh that it might take a couple of generations for people to get over what had happened.

That November Lattin-Cullen would play Cappawhite in a West Junior Hurling final and, sidelined with a knee injury, I came on as a second-half sub. There was an extraordinary under-current of bad feeling that evening.

Cappawhite desperately wanted to beat us for Pa O'Neill.

Naturally, it all seems an age ago now but, to put it mildly, it was a pretty unsettling affair at the time.

One thing, I suppose, that didn't help me was the incredible hype that had begun to surround Nicky English. No matter what kind of game I played in, it was all over the national newspapers if I scored. That year I played two games in the West Tipp Junior Championship and they were treated like major news stories.

One night we played a poor club team called Glengar who were putting out a hurling team for the first time in something like 40 years. I scored something like 3-10 against them and the papers went overboard about it.

In another game of that campaign, we played Annacarty's second team. Now we would have given their first team a run for it, but their seconds were desperately weak. Again I got a big score and again the newspapers carried Nicky English headlines.

The hype had become ridiculous. A spin-off of the time was that I acquired the nickname 'God' or 'Nicky God' in certain circles. While training with the county team, Joe Hayes especially was never slow to call me by it, knowing how much it embarrassed me.

But, in this context, you could see how some people might think I was getting too big for my boots.

The captaincy issue stalked me all the way into that final against Galway. Yet I can't totally blame it for my poor form on the day. I'd love to but it would be dishonest.

The truth is I was quite relaxed by the time I got to run out onto Croke Park. It was almost like a weight had been lifted from my shoulders. I was finally putting the hassle behind me, getting down to the only thing that truly interested me. Playing hurling.

Everything was so new to us, we were total innocents that day in Croke Park. We wanted to do everything right, meet the President, toss the coin, whatever the stewards instructed us to do. Typical of a team in their first All-Ireland for many years, we were concerned too much with the occasion and not enough with the match.

I know, for example, that Conor Hayes – who was due to mark me – had a few pints the night before in a pub in Parkgate Street. He couldn't lose really. All the hype was about me in particular and Tipp in general. Yet Galway were the reigning All-Ireland champions. Looking back now, it was really the perfect trap.

The final was completely unlike our Championship game with Galway the previous year. Much tougher, much tighter, it exposed us to a few harsh realities about what was required for winning All-Irelands.

Hayes did a lot of pulling and dragging on me throughout and I felt I could have got a few more frees than proved the case. Aidan Ryan was playing left corner forward and he liked to move out the field where he was free to wander. This left his marker, Sylvie Linnane – who didn't follow him – more or less free to slip across as extra cover behind Hayes and Ollie Kilkenny who was marking Pat Fox.

Kilkenny was a very good corner-back, always hard, tight and severely intimidatory. Hayes, too, was a hell of a player and Pat and myself would have had matters hard enough without Sylvie being free to move across and provide an extra barrier.

Then, of course, you had the Galway half-back line of Pete Finnerty, Tony Keady and Gerry McInerney which was, without question, the best in the business at that time.

Before we left the dressing-room, I made a short speech, the gist of which was that we had waited so long for this day. It was important we did not let it pass us by.

But, sadly, the game did just what I had warned against. It passed us by, me included.

We were incredibly naive. There was no way we were prepared to hit Galway hard that day. This, we felt, was not the kind of game in which you tried to introduce any kind of physical agenda.

It was an All-Ireland final and you played everything by the book.

We had taken a decision beforehand that, if we won the toss, we'd play against the wind. It was something decided during our morning puckaround out in Newcastle beside the team's base of Finnstown House. Not surprisingly, some people subsequently attributed it to our defeat.

But the truth is we just never played with any fluidity on the day. Personally, I was calm enough. I had tried to put all the hassle of the week out of my mind and I felt fine out on the field. But I just wasn't getting involved enough. There is a certain point in every game where you actually get comfortable with your play but I never got comfortable that day.

Galway were physically stronger than us and, for the most part, I was trying to contest puck-outs with Conor Hayes which – being honest – was an uneven contest.

Still, we reached half-time with a deficit of only four points and I genuinely believed we were going to win the game. The mood in the dressing-room was really upbeat. Our backs had hurled particularly well against the breeze but, before going back out, Donie Nealon reminded us that the wind wasn't going to win it for us. We'd have to do that ourselves.

But we never did get to them in the second-half. Declan Ryan was having a terrific game at wing-forward, scoring a total of four points from play. Conversely, his marker – Gerry McInerney – got a vital brace in return from long range.

Then we had what I considered a perfectly good goal by Johnny Leahy disallowed when referee, Gerry Kirwan, called play back for a foul on Donie O'Connell. To my mind, it was a bad decision, a wrong decision by Kirwan. He ought to have played the advantage rule.

A goal then would have put us 1-10 to 0-12 ahead just twelve minutes into the second-half. It would have been a massive psychological boost. Instead, we were still a point behind and struggling to get on terms.

With about ten minutes to go, Pat Fox hit a fantastic shot which struck Galway goalkeeper – John Commins – and was cleared to safety. It was to be that kind of day. The breaks of the ball just weren't going with us.

Still, we stayed right in contention virtually into injury-time when substitute, Noel Lane, got away from Conor O'Donovan to score the only goal of the day. That put the score at 1-15 to 0-13 in Galway's favour and we were effectively dead and buried.

Much was made of a penalty we were awarded subsequently for a foul on Cormac Bonnar. I was seen chatting to Pat Fox briefly before putting it over the bar. People couldn't understand my reasoning in going for a point with Tipperary five points down.

The truth is I didn't actually go for a point, not that it was ever going to matter. Before taking the penalty, the referee actually told me it was the last puck of the game. I don't know if you can see it on video but Sylvie Linnane started celebrating when he heard me being told that. In effect, he didn't even have to block it. The game was over.

I wanted to hit the shot hard and high and I just happened to get under the ball. It was irrelevant. The whistle went immediately after.

When you lose an All-Ireland final, you just want to get out of there as fast as you possibly can. With the way the crowd spills in, you don't really get a proper chance to shake hands with your opponents. You just want to put your head down and get to the dressing-room and bus as fast as is humanly possible.

No-one talks in that dressing-room when you get there. Or maybe, more precisely, no-one is able to talk.

There was a function for us that night at the Embankment in Tallaght and it was almost dangerous such were the numbers of Tipperary people present. Presumably, they had all booked their tickets in the belief that we would have the McCarthy Cup in our possession. We were sorry to disappoint them.

As captain, I had to give a speech. Theo English had been on to us all year that, if we were serious about winning an All-Ireland, we would have to "keep the fences up" between ourselves and women or any other distractions.

I finished my speech by thanking everyone and saying, 'It didn't work, Theo. Maybe next year we'll try it with the fences down!'

A huge crowd welcomed us back to Thurles on the Monday night and I found that incredibly emotional. As was traditional, we met the Archbishop in the Cathedral and I'm not ashamed to say I cried through a lot of the formalities.

Being honest, I think that was a culmination of everything. Not just the disappointment of losing, but the frustration at all that had gone before as well.

However, by the Wednesday, it was time to return to normality. I was due back working in the Abbey and my mother called me to get out of bed. I didn't want to. Truth is, I didn't want to face anybody. The depression was really hitting me. I couldn't bear the thought of having to talk to anybody about the game.

In fact, to this day, I've never watched the '88 All-Ireland final on television. I couldn't bear to. It is completely devoid of happy memories for me.

The repercussions of the captaincy issue lingered long into that winter. I was conscious of it for months afterwards.

Coming out of the final, I had met former Irish soccer international, Paddy Mulligan, who was a big Galway supporter. 'They asked too much of you, Nicky,' he said to me. 'Maybe,' I thought. 'Maybe not.'

The dropping of Pa O'Neill and the decision to start against the wind were widely considered the principal reasons for our defeat as the post-mortems rumbled through the county.

But, for me, we lost – above all else – because Galway were a better, more street-wise team than we were. They were more experienced than us and, when it came to the crunch, we allowed ourselves to become over-awed by the whole occasion. It was something we all vowed would never happen us again.

The next time we were in Croke Park, it wouldn't be for an occasion. It would be for a match.

Next time, we would win it.

XVII
MOVE OVER HUGO SANCHEZ, HERE COMES JOE HAYES!

DUBLIN became my new home in the summer of '89.

It was a huge, vaguely frightening decision I took in the belief that hurling medals and memories would not pay bills in later life. Playing for Tipp at such a time was an intoxicating adventure. Summer days revolved around the company of the dressing-room, the nervousness of the big day.

In many ways, my life at home was idyllic. Teaching in the Abbey, living with family in Cullen, hurling with the most talked-about team in the country. The easy thing would have been to wallow in it, to just close my mind to the outside world, to my long-term future.

But hurling had given me a nationwide profile which I knew could open doors and, when an opportunity arose to join Allied Irish Investment Managers in Dublin, the prospects were simply too tempting to dismiss.

Life as a schoolteacher was solid and rewarding but, when I thought about it, I didn't feel comfortable with the idea of just accepting the classroom as my work-place until retirement age. If I wanted to do something different with my life, now was the time to do it.

So on June 21, I pulled on a shirt and tie and reported for my first morning's work in the Ballsbridge offices of AIBIM. For the first time in my life, I was surrounded by people who knew little and cared less about the game that had dominated my life since childhood.

Looking back now, it's amusing to think of my efforts to convert them.

Maybe three weeks after my arrival, Tipp played Waterford in a Munster final televised live from Pairc Uí Chaoimh. Purely because their newest work-mate was involved, many of the AIBIM staff tuned in for the afternoon's 'entertainment'.

It was not perhaps the best game to win them over.

If anything, the contest would be recalled among the most infamous in Munster Championship history. A mean, bad-tempered, often reckless encounter in which Waterford had two players sent off, ignited huge media criticism and a lingering bitterness between the two counties that – to this day – has not been totally erased.

Returning to work in Dublin afterwards, the scars of battles visible on my body, a few work-mates looked at me as if I was some kind of deluded alien from space. It was clear they considered hurling a bewildering mess of violence and short tempers.

Luckily, I was to be granted a long summer in which to persuade them differently.

After losing the '88 All-Ireland final, 'Babs' had decided we needed a fresh impetus to our training routines. So, when we re-grouped for winter training in late January of '89, he arrived down from Dublin with a tall, athletic looking gentleman called Phil Conway.

Conway was – it emerged – a well-know athletics coach who had actually competed in the Olympics for Ireland as a hammer-thrower. Now previously, it has to be said, our training was a relatively basic, non-scientific routine of running laps of the pitch followed by skill-work and practice games.

Phil had a more intense, more sophisticated approach to preparing athletes for battle. He knew nothing about hurling, but never pretended to. And, while his name meant nothing to us that first evening in Thurles, his manner and his sincerity made an immediate impression.

'Babs' had always been a great man to organise things, especially the little details that need attending to on the day of a big game. But the truth was that we hadn't been doing enough serious physical training to be able to take on a tough side like Galway on equal terms.

I am a great believer that hard, physical training creates mettle in a team. When serious questions are asked in a game, the team that has suffered together will – invariably – rally together. And that was what we went in search of with Phil Conway.

Never before had we endured anything like the training we did out on the back field that year in Thurles. On a single night, we would rattle off fourteen 300 metre runs with Cormac Bonnar – who was a bloody animal – invariably taking it out at an incredible pace. In the muck and the sleet, we would do hundreds of sit-ups, press-ups, everything to get the body toned.

And Phil liked to give us sheets of paper to take home with us which re-emphasised the need for discipline in just about everything from diet, to social life, to sleep patterns. Suddenly, everything we did was strictly structured and regimented.

As players, we became fitter than we had ever been in our lives.

Still, some things refused to change. We played Kilkenny in a National League semi-final in Croke Park and, as John Henderson came in to challenge me, I managed to break a bone in my ankle. Early spring and I was crocked again. It had a depressingly familiar ring.

In '88, it had been my hamstring, '87 a broken ankle, '86 a punctured lung. This would have been funny if it wasn't so dispiriting.

Hobbling through the later stages of the game, I recall 'Babs' – who clearly didn't realise the seriousness of my injury – shouting at me to 'Go

Stonewall Pete – Trying to shrug off Peter Finnerty during the '89 All-Ireland Semi-Final

Ballet class – A tasteful pirouette to avoid colliding with Niall Patterson in the '89 All-Ireland Final

Now don't rush off on me – Challenging James McNaughton during the '89 All-Ireland Final

The point that never was – Kicking over the bar in the drawn '91 Munster Final

You can't be serious – The score is disallowed

You are? – The umpires dig their heels in

Eyes forward? – Distracted by something before the '91 All-Ireland Semi-Final

Best foot forward – Getting to the ball ahead of Tony Keady

The writing's on the wall – Close to breaking point

Wounded soldier – The lonely walk after a battered body seizes in the '91 All-Ireland Semi-Final

Just wasn't me Cyril! – Chatting with Cyril Farrell at half-time in the '91 All-Ireland Semi-Final

The President and me – Exchanging pleasantries with Mary Robinson before the '91 All-Ireland Final

I'm with the Big Guy! – Marching behind Cormac Bonnar before the '91 All-Ireland Final

See you next time – A consoling pat from John Henderson as my All-Ireland Final comes to an end in '91

Anyone got a spare hamstring – Think I've been here before

A friend in need! – Joe Hayes consoles me after my hamstring goes

Thumbs up – Tipp are champions again after beating Kilkenny in the '91 Final

Eye on the sky – An aerial duel during the'92 Munster Championship confrontation with Cork

Glad it's all over – Leaving the courtroom with Anne after winning damages over that magazine 'scoop'

A face in the crowd? – Momentarily distracted before this year's National League Semi-Final against Laois

Back to the future – Returning to Walsh Park for the start of the '96 Championship

Fair shoulder Dickie! – Protesting my innocence as Dickie Murphy books me during the '96 Munster Championship opener against Waterford

S'cuse me! – A tap on the shoulder during this year's Championship game against Waterford

Oh no you don't! – Trying to prevent Damien Byrne from clearing at Walsh Park this year

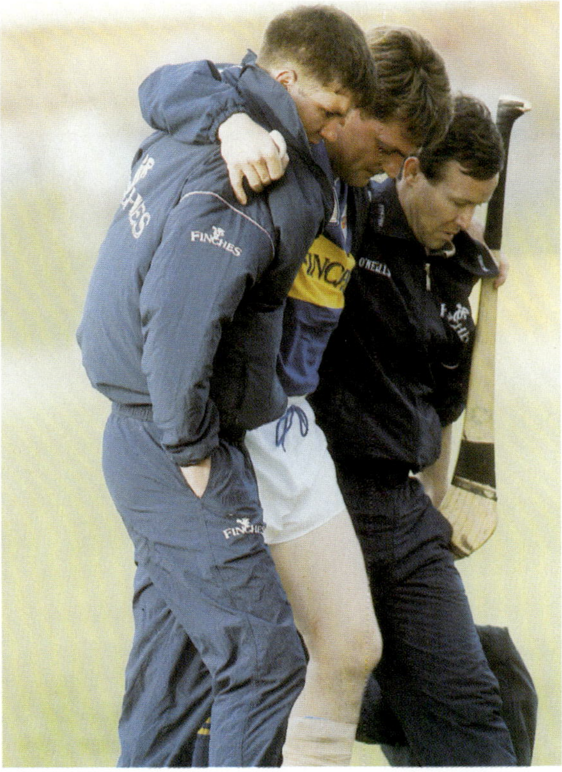

Running on empty – Helped off the pitch in Tralee '96 by Dr Gerry O'Sullivan and Brian Horgan after injury strikes again

Making a point! – Taking my score after coming on in the drawn '96 Munster Final

The gates are open – A rare glimpse of freedom in the drawn '96 Munster Final

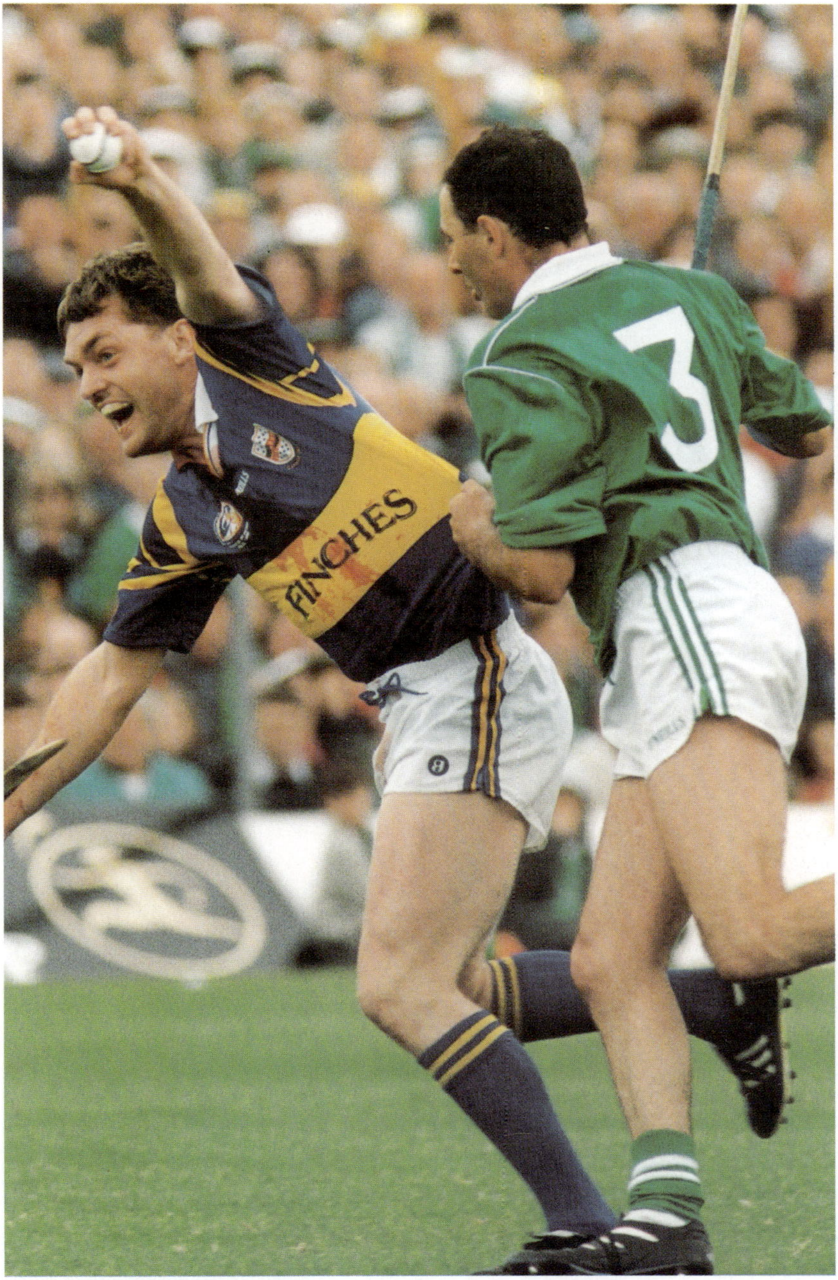

Could have been a hero! – No whistle as Mike Nash tests the strength of the fabric near the end of the drawn '96 Munster Final

Opportunity knocked! – Leaving the field after this year's drawn Munster Final

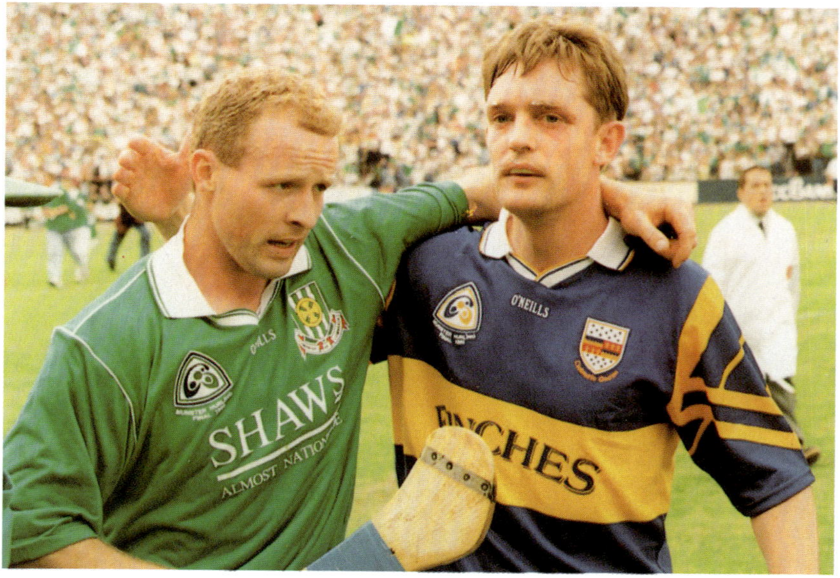

Think I'll keep this jersey! – With Stephen McDonagh after Tipp's Championship adventure ends in Cork

out to the middle of the field and win a few balls'. It would not be appropriate to print my response here.

With Michael Cleary coming on to make a big impact, Tipp won the game by a point. But, afterwards, I knew I was in real trouble with the leg. It was decided to take me on a stretcher from the dressing-room to a waiting ambulance and I will always remember the commotion outside as I appeared.

People were scrambling to get photographs of me, probably imagining that my ailment had turned out to be something more serious than a broken bone in my ankle. Not yet having moved to Dublin at the time, I was brought to a hospital which – to this day – I can't identify.

There they x-rayed the leg and, although confirming that I wouldn't make the League final against Galway, decided there was no need to put me in plaster. The absence of a plaster actually gave me false hope that I might make it for the final. But that didn't last long.

I returned to Dublin on the Tuesday where Denis O'Connor – secretary of the Supporters' Club – collected me off the train at Heuston Station and brought me to the Blackrock Clinic where the specialist immediately put me into plaster.

My mood was low going home on the train that evening. Fr Jack O'Neill met me at the station and we went to Johnsie Ryan's in Oola for a few pints. Jack had to try and humour a fairly shattered hurling man that evening.

Even the pupils couldn't help laughing when I arrived into class the following morning on crutches. When last seen, I had been just hobbling. 'What'll you be like tomorrow sir?' they asked me grinning.

Both Tipp and Galway were under-strength for the League final but it didn't diminish the game which proved an absolute classic, Galway winning 2-16 to 4-8 at the finish. No one was too despondent that evening in the losing dressing-room.

It was as if we knew there would be a bigger train coming down the track. Barring upsets, the counties would clash again in August. And Tipp felt certain they'd be ready.

Cormac Bonnar had played well in that League final but, restored to full fitness, I displaced him at full-forward for our first round Championship game with Limerick at Pairc Uí Chaoimh. Pat McGrath, at left-corner forward, was the captain.

The first-half proved a bit of an ordeal for us, the sides going in level at 1-7 each. Limerick were extremely pumped up, driven by the knowledge that Tipp – the team with all the hype behind them – had more to lose than them.

Hard words were spoken in the dressing-room at half-time, McGrath being replaced by Bonnar with me moving across to the left corner. Cormac's arrival both transformed the game and – in a sense – baptised a full-forward line that would go on to help win two of the next three All-Irelands.

Pat Fox, who – like myself – had also missed the League final was firing on all cylinders too, winning the RTE 'Man of the Match' award that night on television. It was an ironic choice given the background to Pat's inclusion.

Michael Cleary had originally been selected in Fox's place but, on the previous Thursday night in training, Pat accidentally hit Michael with the ball in a place you don't want to get hit. It meant Cleary was in no condition to play and we liked to joke with Fox afterwards that we considered him a dangerous man.

If you took his place he'd get you!

With big Bonnar flying, we demolished Limerick in the second-half, winning eventually by 4-18 to 2-11. I scored 2-4 in the game, one of the goals an attempted clearance that flew in off my leg. But the most memorable score of the day unquestionably came at the death.

It was scored by 'the legendary' Joe Hayes who proceeded to do the clumsiest somersault you've ever seen in celebration. Hugo Sanchez had the art perfected at the time and I will never forget Joe – his big arse barely able to get off the ground – offering a Clonoulty version.

To put it mildly, it wasn't pretty.

Mind you, the marks for artistic impression weren't terribly high either on July 2 when we returned to Pairc Uí Chaoimh for a provincial final we had all presumed – in our innocence – would be against Cork. The fact that live TV coverage had been arranged identified the certainty with which people generally anticipated that '89 would bring a third consecutive Tipp-Cork Munster final.

Of course, Waterford had other ideas. Some considered it a freak result when they drew their semi-final against the Cork men but, when they blasted home five goals to win the replay, not many were inclined to be dismissive anymore.

A pity, then, that they lost their heads on the big day.

I make no apologies for saying that I believe Waterford let themselves down in the '89 Munster final. I said it then and I repeat it now. Too much of the pulling they did that day was wild and dangerous. They just didn't go out to play the ball.

Maybe they had chips on their collective shoulders from the way the press considered them rank outsiders. Maybe they believed they weren't getting the kind of respect that was their due. I don't pretend to know what their motivation was that day in Cork. All I do know is that they were their own worst enemies.

After being taken off in the Limerick game, Pat McGrath now lost his place and the captaincy went to Bobby Ryan. Thankfully, it proved a largely peaceful, conflict-free arrangement which kept Bobby away from the kind of grief I had endured the previous summer.

As games go though, it proved a terrible eye-sore. Waterford's approach was ill-disciplined and menacing, so much so that referee – Willie Horgan – had his hands full keeping things from boiling over. To be fair to Willie, his main concern was to protect players. And this he managed reasonably well.

Having scored with almost my first touch from play, I then ran for and missed a ball resulting in Timmy Sheehan and myself colliding head-on. It was a full clash of faces really, but completely accidental. I was badly stunned and I think Timmy had a broken nose.

'Jesus,' I thought. 'This is all I need at the start of a Munster final.'

As the game evolved, we were always in control on the scoreboard. Waterford's indiscipline was costing them frees all over the field and I had one of those days where I felt like I couldn't miss. My tally at the end of the game would be 0-8 from frees, 0-5 from play which I was more than happy with.

But it was not a game to treasure in the memory-bank.

As the contest drifted away from them, Waterford's frustration boiled over and the two players who were sent off – Noel Crowley and Damien Byrne – could have little argument with Willie Horgan's judgement. It ended with Tipp winning 0-26 to 2-8 and the game, sadly, splattered all over the following morning's front pages.

One amusing incident highlighted the way Phil Conway's arrival had pretty radically altered Tipp's approach to fitness. During the second-half, it was decided that John Cormack should start warming up in preparation for replacing Colm Bonnar.

Without saying anything to the selectors, Conway took him into the tunnel where he started a specific, structured warm-up routine. Next thing, there was a stoppage in the play and Donie Nealon turned around to discover that Cormack was nowhere to be seen.

'Where the hell is he?' Donie bellowed before John and Phil emerged a little sheepishly from the tunnel. It was taking time for Tipp to acclimatise to Conway's professionalism.

I've often looked at the video of that game since to see if my immediate impressions were in any way harsh on Waterford. But the reality is, in my opinion, that some of the swinging in the game was downright unacceptable. There were Waterford players who seemed to have no interest in the ball that day.

And the tragedy was that we had a live television audience to witness the fact.

XVIII
THE KEADY AFFAIR AND WHY SYLVIE NEVER FORGAVE ME!

NO game I've ever been part of ended in as much emotional chaos and bad feeling as the 1989 All-Ireland semi-final against Galway.

It was a contest that will forever be associated with the infamous 'Keady Affair', the controversial banning of Galway's centre-half back for allegedly playing a club game in New York without receiving proper clearance. Keady's 12-month suspension ignited a conspiracy theory in Galway that was to seriously pollute their relations with Tipperary.

You see Tony's 'sin' was to play for a Laois club against a Tipp club and, when the latter raised their objection, it was automatically assumed that they were doing so with the tacit approval of the Tipperary County Board.

Nothing could have been further from the truth.

Through the weeks leading into our semi-final confrontation, Tony Keady's name never left the pages of the newspapers. Galway were bidding for their third successive All-Ireland crown and it was mischievously implied in some quarters that this was Tipp's way of stopping them.

The whole affair dominated the Westerners' build-up to the semi-final with their team-manager, Cyril Farrell, hinting one morning in the *Irish Press* that they might actually withdraw from the semi-final in protest.

'Babs', as I recall, issued a statement meanwhile distancing Tipperary from the matter and, when Galway's appeal came up before Central Council, our county secretary – Tommy Barrett – actually spoke out strongly in favour of reinstating Keady.

Unfortunately, Galway still lost the appeal and a distinct shadow hung over Tipp's third big Championship collision with Farrell's men in as many years.

Funnily, going into the game, we were oblivious to that shadow. There was such a focus, such a single-minded hunger to our campaign that year, the papers could have announced the outbreak of World War Three and I'm not sure it would have bothered us.

To us, this was make-or-break time. It was a game we simply had to win. No ifs, buts or maybes. Lose to Galway for a third summer running and we would just have to accept that we were inferiors on the hurling field.

With Phil Conway's training, we were in the best shape of our lives going into that semi-final. People like Declan Carr, Johnny Leahy and Cormac Bonnar had established themselves impressively in the team while Bobby Ryan was surprising everyone with his resourcefulness at centre-back.

At the very least, we were going to make it hard for Galway.

The year before we had been almost timid in our behaviour, delighted to be in a final and determined to behave impeccably. Afraid to push or jostle. Afraid to play hard hurling.

This was different. As far as we were concerned, the game could be played in Croke Park, Thurles, Ballinasloe, Lattin wherever. It didn't matter a damn to us. We were going to take them on physically if need be. We were going to win this game no matter what it took.

For us, the Keady affair was no more than a trivial side-show. We felt certain that no matter who Galway put out against us, we'd have the measure of them.

A lot had been made in the post-mortems to the '88 All-Ireland final of how Galway seemed to have little difficulty in imposing themselves physically on Tipperary. It was said that maybe we lacked the 'bite' of past Tipp teams, that we were easily intimidated.

'Babs' had been quoted in a controversial *Sunday Independent* article criticising Galway's physical approach to the game. All in all, the message seemed to be that we didn't have the requisite steel.

That, I think, more than the Keady business focused our minds going into the '89 semi-final whereas Galway – stupidly in my opinion – allowed themselves become totally distracted by the injustice inflicted on one man.

Considering their track record against us, I would have thought Cyril Farrell would have been better off reminding his team of how they had the upper-hand on us. If I was in charge of Galway at the time, I would have been telling them, 'Look, we've beaten this crowd two years in a row. And we've beaten them because we're better than them.'

Anyway, I believe Galway arrived into Croke Park that day totally paranoid about the circumstances depriving them of their centre-back. Tipp, on the other hand, travelled like a team that could not fail.

And the difference showed.

Mind you, I think all of our heads were spinning a little running out the tunnel that day, knowing from the sheer intensity of noise, that Antrim were after pulling off one of the great upsets in hurling history. Sitting in the dressing-room beforehand, we could tell something incredible was happening outside.

Normally all you hear is the sporadic cheering in response to scores, but this noise was far more intense, far more sustained. It seemed like the

Hogan Stand was shaking such was the commotion.

When confirmation reached us that Antrim had in fact beaten Offaly, Donie Nealon brought us together in the middle of the floor and said what – in reality – all of us were thinking. 'Look,' he said. 'This is the All-Ireland final.

'Win today and you've won an All-Ireland medal!'

It may seem insensitive from an Antrim perspective to record those words but the reality of the time was that Galway and Tipperary were probably a distance ahead of the other hurling counties and certainly well clear of Antrim. We knew in our heart of hearts that everything we had worked for was now on offer against Galway.

The Antrim and Offaly players were gone in by the time we left our dressing-room. It was only afterwards that we heard of Offaly's gesture in giving the Antrim lads a guard-of-honour off the pitch. It was a very decent thing to do but I'm not sure I would have been able to manage it, given the devastation you feel at losing a big game.

Maybe that's more a reflection on me though than the Offaly players.

As for the game, Tipp's first-half display was probably the best I can remember in all my time wearing the blue and gold. Right through the field, we completely out-hurled Galway. Psyched up to the limit, we were just on fire from the first whistle.

Declan Ryan knocked Michael Coleman to the ground in one momentous early collision while Cormac Bonnar was giving Conor Hayes a torrid time. Physically, we were no longer second-best. But one man, above the rest of us, was ready to die if need be that day.

The year before, Pat Fox had been ruthlessly pulled and dragged around the place by Ollie Kilkenny. To rub salt into his wounds, Kilkenny had – at one point – patted him on the head when Pat put an effort wide. It was a gesture that incensed Fox.

I knew that Fox was going to do his utmost to ensure that Ollie Kilkenny would remember him in 1989.

Still, despite our early dominance, Galway kept in touch through two goals – one at either end of the first-half – from Eanna Ryan. The first was a bit of a nightmare for Ken Hogan, a weak shot sneaking in under his legs. The second was a shot from an acute angle that flew high into the net even though it looked like Ryan was going for a point.

We could hardly believe it going in at half-time having played so well but to be leading by only two points. It was demoralising. Dominating all over the field, we just couldn't put Galway away. If anything, they now had to be the happier of the two teams.

You could almost feel the apprehension in our dressing-room at half-time. This was our All-Ireland final and Galway were still breathing down our necks.

The second-half was just a few minutes old when Pat Fox delivered on his promise and struck a brilliant goal. Now Pat and I had an understanding whereby, when either one of us was under pressure on the ball, we would just play it across field to the opposite corner. And that's what happened this time.

I played it over towards Pat's corner and he did well to catch it in front of Kilkenny, turning him in in the process. When Pat Fox gets the ball a yard ahead of you while running towards goal, it's over. He is almost impossible to hook or block because he hits the ball so high up. Off his left-side, he can hit it brilliantly in a tight space.

That day, he never broke stride while burying the ball past John Commins for a goal that finally gave us some leeway. I can still remember the net shaking and the sense of relief that flooded through us all.

But almost immediately the wind seemed to strengthen in our faces, bringing with it rain and a whole new set of doubts. We were going to have to slog this one out to the death.

Mid-way through the half an incident occurred which, if I'm honest, I've always felt bad about since. A Tipp seventy was coming in and, as the ball was going wide, Sylvie Linnane hit me on the side of the head. I'm not sure what he hit me with – the hurley or his elbow – but Sylvie *did* hit me.

Now I wasn't mortally wounded or anything, I was never going to die. But Sylvie was the type of defender who liked to dish out a bit of punishment and I saw this as an opportunity to subdue him a little. By going down, I reckoned I'd get him booked and thereby warned about his future conduct.

While I was lying on the ground, one of the Galway selectors – Bernie O'Connor – ran in, presumably pretending to the officials that he was a Tipperary mentor – and told me to get the hell up again. The real Tipp mentors, meanwhile, were telling me to stay down.

Sylvie, too, came over and tried to pull me up off the ground but Cormac Bonnar jostled him away.

Next thing, I heard the crowd roar and realised Sylvie was being sent off. I was shocked and, being honest, a little disappointed with myself. He didn't deserve to be sent off.

I had always considered Sylvie and myself to be reasonably good friends and this was not the type of thing you wanted happening to a friend. About a year later, I met him at a pub opening in London and he was still pissed off with me. 'I was very mad with you,' he told me. I replied that I hadn't meant to get him sent off but I don't think he'll ever accept that.

The bottom line is that he just shouldn't have been sent off.

Sylvie's dismissal seemed to steel Galway for a bigger effort. Down to fourteen men, they came at us with everything they could muster. You could see it in their eyes that they considered this incident just another stage in an on-going conspiracy against them.

Within sight of the winning post, Tipp grew jittery. Our hurling no longer had the fluency of before. We were living on our nerves, praying for the final whistle.

The match was almost over when Michael McGrath charged recklessly into Conor O'Donovan with both knees raised. Now 'Hopper' was never a mean kind of player but I felt that his actions were those of a man whose concentration was now less on the game than the 'injustice' being heaped on Galway.

The whole Keady business was now closing in on Cyril Farrell's team. It was clear that they felt referee, John Denton, was part of the grand conspiracy.

As McGrath walked across the pitch having got his marching orders, Johnny Leahy said something tactless in his direction and 'Hopper' hit him. The whole thing was a mess and Denton's final whistle was greeted by as much jeering and booing as cheering.

The atmosphere in the stadium was terrible. A real bitterness descended and, in many ways, a mean tradition between Galway and Tipperary was born. It was regrettable but I'd be lying if I said that, at the time, it bothered the Tipp players.

If the circumstances were unfortunate, the bottom line was that we had achieved what we set out to do. There's no doubt in my mind that we were a better team than Galway in '89. If anything, the controversy just distracted people from that fact.

We had completely out-played them in the first-half only to be pegged back by two lucky goals and the second-half dismissals clearly worked as much to our detriment as theirs. That evening, returning to the Burlington Hotel, the mood was one of achievement and anticipation. We knew we were going to be All-Ireland champions.

We knew that at, at last, we were going to get the medal we had longed for all our lives.

At the time, I was staying in Terenure and – that night – Pat Fox and myself stayed in the same room. Both of us were on an incredible high. Pat, especially, because he had had his revenge in no uncertain terms on Ollie Kilkenny.

We woke at about eight o'clock the following morning and just lay there chatting about the game. In fact, we started the day by opening a bottle of champagne, the only drink in the house.

If only 'Babs' could have seen us!

XIX

THE NUMBER SIXTEEN BUS FROM TERENURE FOR A DATE WITH DESTINY

MAYBE the only aspect of All-Ireland final weekend 1989 that truly surprised me was the gravity of Antrim's disappointment in losing.

I hope that doesn't sound condescending because it's certainly not intended that way. Of all opposing teams I've been with after major games, few proved wittier or more down-to-earth than Jim Nelson's men. We actually had a great sing-song and joke-telling session down in the dungeon bar of Kilmainham Castle on the Monday after the final.

Talking to them about the match, I couldn't help but be struck by their frustration. To a man, they were saying how much they genuinely believed they were coming down to Dublin to take home the McCarthy Cup. Tipperary winning had definitely not been part of their script.

You might think it a strange admission, but I was astonished they ever seriously believed they'd beat us. I remember thinking 'Jesus, I thought I *knew* we had this won before it even started. I always felt so certain that we'd win.'

You see, a week before the final, I sat down late on the Saturday night in Cullen and watched a video of Antrim's semi-final defeat of Offaly. When I got up from the television, I turned to my father and said 'There's just no way this team can beat us.'

The kind of hurling we were playing at the time, so quick, so fast, so physically powerful just had to be too much for them. We had a good system going, we were in a rhythm and I knew from the video that our first touch was much better than theirs.

Looking at it logically, maybe Ciaran Barr might have caught a few high balls but – otherwise – I just couldn't see where they were going to cause us trouble.

Being honest, I think that was the mind-set we all took into that final against Antrim. Sure, we were wary. After all, not one of us had a senior All-Ireland medal to show for our years wearing the blue and gold. But the wariness came especially from a knowledge that our people would never ever forgive us if we lost this.

Looking back, the weekend was nowhere near as stressful as it had proved the year before. I remember being in work on the Friday night until about seven in the evening. Being in Dublin, I almost felt detached from what was coming. Work-mates had their own lives to lead and it was clear the All-Ireland final might as well have been happening in Outer Mongolia as far as most of them were concerned.

At home in Tipperary, a controversy had erupted over the decision to stage a home-coming concert in Semple Stadium where – effectively – our supporters were going to be charged an entrance fee to see the Cup. In hindsight, we were probably being more than a bit disrespectful to our opponents.

If ever Antrim needed motivating, they surely got it from the news that Tipp had their celebrations already planned long before either team even hit Dublin.

Still, I can't say any of the players gave two damns about the controversy. Here was another one of those stories that filled so many pages of newsprint but which made little impact on those behind the dressing-room door. As far as we were concerned, we were going to win the Cup and worry about festivities only when we had that Cup safely in our hands.

That said, it was certainly another reason why we simply couldn't afford to lose the game.

Another element of controversy surrounded wing-back, Paul Delaney, in what was essentially a follow-up to the 'Tony Keady affair'. It was being alleged that Paul had played a couple of games illegally in London and that, if he played in the final, Tipp might be vulnerable to an objection.

Rumours started to fly in the build-up and, after consultation with officials, it was decided that 'Mossy' would have to sit out the final. It was a sensitive time with so much flak having flown over the Keady business and referee, John Denton's, semi-final performance being clinically dissected in some of the Sunday newspapers. Tipp felt under pressure to be seen to do everything above board and, unfortunately, 'Mossy' was the one to suffer.

I could be melodramatic about the reaction within the squad to the news that Delaney was being left out. But the truth is that, going into an All-Ireland final, players are so self-absorbed they don't really have much time to worry about team-mates.

No question, everyone felt genuinely sorry for him. Paul deserved to win an All-Ireland in '89. I always think, if you go back to the replayed Munster final of '87, he was one of our main men in Killarney. He played a lot of that game at centre-back where he did a fine marking job on Teddy McCarthy who would have been in his prime then.

Delaney had come from nowhere to do that. Now, with the biggest day of his life beckoning, he was being told he would have to sit things out. It was a hard blow for him to take.

My memory of 'Mossy' the day we won the All-Ireland in '89 is of him walking around in his blazer, looking a little detached from everything. It must have been one of the most trying days of his life.

On the Saturday night, I travelled into the Burlington Hotel to meet the rest of the team. Sitting upstairs on the number sixteen bus in from Terenure, juggling a sliothar in one hand, I felt I hadn't a care in the world. My hurleys and boots were already gone in and I was completely calm.

Inside the door of the hotel, Declan Carr was having his photograph taken with Neil Kinnock and signing autographs. As I went to book in, Jimmy Magee grabbed me and did an interview for RTE. I remember saying to Jimmy that this was a game I would not let pass me by.

We all felt that way. The trappings and trimmings of All-Ireland final day would mean nothing to us this time. We were there to win. End of story.

Over dinner that night, we all tried to reiterate the need for clear minds. We reminded ourselves of the damage Barr, Olcan McFetridge and 'Sambo' McNaughton had done to Offaly. 'Let them get a run on you and you're in trouble,' we said.

Cordoned off from the general public on the seventh floor of the hotel, some of the lads pucked a sliothar up and down the corridor just to pass the time. As ever, we watched the 'Up for the Match' programme on RTE and, before going to sleep, Pat Fox and myself drank a pint each in the room. We felt none of the apprehension or unease of '88. A little nervous yes, but not apprehensive.

The day we awoke to was absolutely perfect for hurling. Mild and calm with no wind to speak of, it was heaven-sent for any self-respecting team.

We had our customary puck-around that morning in St. Michael's behind the Merrion Centre and deliberately left it late before departing the hotel for Croke Park. Streets were virtually deserted as we made our journey across the city, the sirens of the Garda out-riders bringing bemused expressions from the few who were out walking.

All was pretty calm in the dressing-room beforehand, everyone going through the little rituals that comfort them at such moments. All through, Phil Conway kept calling out the time remaining before we vacated the dressing-room.

Phil was like a computer print-out...'Twenty minutes to going out'... 'Fifteen minutes to going out'...'Ten minutes'...

As the sense of urgency increased, the selectors said their piece – Donie Nealon's voice, as ever, sending shivers down our spines. Then Bobby jumped up, called us to the middle of the floor and prepared to give his battlecry.

Just as Bobby prepared to speak, Phil's voice could be heard in the background saying, 'six minutes to going out'

Bobby was suddenly flummoxed. 'Six minutes?' he said. 'Jesus, what I have to say won't take six seconds!' And we all sat down again.

Being honest, the game never proved much more than a comfortable stroll to the title. Antrim had massive support on Hill 16 and their players were definitely motivated for a big effort. But we got in front early and never subsequently relinquished our stranglehold on the game.

Gary O'Kane was the man dispatched to mark me and – here – I think Antrim were being a bit naive. At the time, I would estimate Gary was no more than a 19-year-old and maybe not experienced enough for a corner-back role in such a high pressure game.

Still, my own start, was a little nervous. Only the second ball I got, I tried to pass down along the line to Cormac Bonnar but tripped and over-hit it, the ball trickling harmlessly wide in front of the Nally Stand. It looked absolutely terrible and I remember thinking, 'Christ, here I go again in an

All-Ireland final.'

Then the first free we got was right in front of the Cusack Stand and the whole of Hill 16 seemed to start whistling and jeering as I bent over the ball. Psychologically, this was a big moment for me. If I missed, I knew the jeering would get worse every time I prepared to take a free. 'This,' I thought, 'could ruin my whole day'.

But I struck the free as sweetly as I could and, thankfully, it sailed straight over the bar. The Antrim fans never whistled after that. At least, if they did, I didn't hear them.

Everything seemed to go with us as the game moved towards half-time, Declan Ryan finding the Antrim net from 50 yards for a goal that could hardly be deemed intentional. It meant we went in at the break 1-13 to 0-5 ahead and, in most peoples' eyes, already safely home.

Typically, Donie Nealon did most of the talking in the dressing-room. He told us to forget about the lead we had. He reminded us of '68, of how Tipp had blown a big lead against Wexford. 'There is no lead!' Donie bellowed.

To be fair, Nealon was right. Our track record suggested we weren't a good second-half team. If we got careless now, it was not beyond the bounds of possibility that we might blow it.

As it happened, we held our concentration – Pat Fox's early second-half goal effectively putting the seal on the victory we craved. Antrim never dropped their heads and, in a tighter game, the second-half goals of Aidan McCarry, Brian Donnelly and Donal Armstrong would without question have left us facing crisis. Instead, there was an edge of celebration to everything we did.

Declan Carr was majestic in the middle of the field, soaring to make great catches, powering his way through the action, hitting ball off either side. Although I ended up collecting the award myself, Declan would have been my choice that day as man-of-the-match.

An under-rated player, Declan was a real joker in the panel, always taking the piss out of someone. Because of this, there were a lot of people who didn't particularly like him, who actually liked to see him playing badly in a Tipp jersey.

The trouble with Carr was that you never knew for sure when he was being serious. If you went for a drink with him, he was quite capable of saying he was going to the toilet only to disappear for the rest of the evening. It was that kind of careless, irresponsible approach that exasperated some people.

But Carr had real presence on a hurling field and that was unquestionably his finest hour in a Tipperary jersey. I remember him scoring one outrageous point from under the Cusack Stand in the first-half that no-one else on the team would have had the nerve to try. Being honest, hitting it from where he did was ridiculous.

Believe me, had it not gone over, we would have been cursing him in the full-forward line. But over it went. And that kind of summed up Declan's day. Maybe Tipp's day too.

I doubt if Bobby Ryan got the ball in his hand even once at centre-back but it didn't matter. Despite their final score (3-9), Antrim were never seriously in a challenging position.

The game ended in dream-like fashion for me with that spectacular goal at the Canal End on the stroke of time. It came from a beautiful ball in from Aidan Ryan which, as it went past me, I noticed was fizzing with back-spin. Instinctively, I thought to myself, 'This is going to sit up perfectly as it hits the ground'.

And it did. The ball just hopped up beautifully in front of me and I hit it first time past big Niall Patterson to complete the scoring. Tipp had scored 4-24 and I was attributed with 2-12 of that total, equalling the individual scoring record for an All-Ireland final.

Much as I'd like to hold onto that piece of history, I think now's the time to come clean and admit that I had very little input into the other goal and it probably should have been put down to Cormac Bonnar.

It came mid-way through the second-half when I made a run goalwards before passing to Cormac who batted the ball against a post. As it came back out to him, big Bonnar effectively put the ball in the net even though it hit my hurley on the way in.

The truth is, all I was concerned about as he hit it was getting out of his way. The fact that it made contact with my hurley was purely accidental.

Admittedly, it wasn't a matter of much discussion in the Tipp camp when that final whistle went and our supporters came flooding in across the pitch from every corner of Croke Park. Unlike the year before, I wanted to just stand there and soak up the celebration. To shake every hand, accept every hug.

One of the few clearcut memories I have is of Noel Ryan, who has been collecting and mending the hurleys for Tipp as long as I have been involved with the county team, running in and taking my hurley from me.

Another memory is of a few of my neighbours from home coming up to embrace me. Fellas like Christy Ryan, Sean Crowe and Neil Hassett – captain of the first team I had ever won a medal with 17 years earlier – got to me which is amazing when you consider the thousands who came onto Croke Park when the final whistle went in that All-Ireland. It has never ceased to amaze me how it's invariably your club-mates who are first up to you when the final whistle goes.

A friend of mine always made the point that club supporters are more loyal to their players than county supporters. And I don't think there's any doubt about it.

Bobby made a fine speech (he had to be there for something!) and we got ourselves showered and dressed before getting the bus back to the Burlington and on then to a special reception at Leopardstown Racecourse. Out in Leopardstown, we were introduced individually to a huge crowd from the parade ring which I think most of us found a little embarrassing.

A few friends of mine going back to my UCC days in Cork – John Grainger was one of them – managed to get out there and it was great to see them. We had a hell of a night that went on long into the early hours.

After the customary Monday lunch in Kilmainham, we set off on the team coach for Thurles, stopping along the way for a meal in the Montague Hotel outside Portlaoise. Now, to put it mildly, this meal seemed a little unnecessary.

After all, most of us had had a fry for breakfast, we had been at the traditional 'day after' lunch at about one thirty and now – no more than three hours later – we were sitting to the table again. Joe Hayes, in his own inimitable style, put it most succinctly when he wondered, 'What are all the f...ing dinners for?'

Back on the bus then, we continued the long, historic homecoming. A massive crowd greeted us as we crossed the county boundaries at Fenner Hill and I will always remember the face of a guy called Mick Ryan, the Mayor of Urlingford no less, standing at the front of the bus with a bottle of champagne in his hand.

We all knew Mick as 'The Bricker' and, with a bonfire lit, he wanted the entire Tipp team to get off the bus. Now Denis O'Connor, who was running the itinerary virtually to the split second, knew that if we got off the bus there was very little chance we'd all manage to get back on. Chances were we'd just get mixed up in the huge crowd and disappear.

So 'The Bricker' was told no-one would be getting off and I will never forget the anger on his face. He just couldn't take this, the fact that the team wasn't getting off the bus in Fenner Hill. But that was the strict instruction. Apart from a few quick calls of nature, no-one would be getting off before Semple Stadium.

As we got close to Thurles, another controversial decision was taken. Because of the huge crowds, it was decided that we would take a back-road into town, with the lights on the bus turned off. Traditionally, Tipp teams would have driven right up into Liberty Square but here we were almost sneaking our way around in darkness.

The question everyone was asking afterwards was, 'Who turned off the lights?'

This definitely created bad feeling and was to be a topic of discussion in the local papers for many months to come. But, again, it's important to tell the truth from a player's perspective. The reality is that we hardly even noticed how we got to the stadium. We just wanted to get in there and see the crowd.

As things worked out, anyone I spoke to afterwards managed to get into Semple Stadium that night without paying. Like most things in Ireland, if people really want to get in for nothing, they'll get in for nothing. And, anyway, I think most people had acknowledged that it was a little ridiculous expecting people to pay money to see the McCarthy Cup.

I will never forget my first glimpse of the crowd gathered. It was absolutely enormous, somewhere I believe between 30,000 and 40,000. And, after all the worries about bad feeling, the atmosphere was just fantastic.

Before being introduced to the crowd, we had a few beers in the dressing-room we had been using all year for training. That felt strange. Sitting around in our blazers instead of jerseys, bottles of Budweiser in our hands instead of water.

The craic was brilliant as Joe Dolan and the Wolfe Tones provided the entertainment, Dolan resplendent in a fairly tight-fitting Tipperary jersey.

In fact, my abiding memory of the evening is of sitting in Glasheen's pub around two in the morning with Joe belting out all the old familiar numbers to an absolutely spellbound audience. We were packed in like sardines and the crowd seemed to know the words of every single song.

That was the almost surreal way the homecoming ended for me.

Sitting in Glasheen's with Joe Dolan and friends. Not feeling a care in the world.

XX
'YOU WON'T BELIEVE THE TEAM...'

LITTLE signals betray a community that is beginning to unravel.

Before we lost our Munster and All-Ireland crowns in the summer of 1990, it's fair to say that the Tipperary players had become aware of friction in the dressing-room. For whatever reason, it was clear that 'Babs', Theo and Donie were no longer the harmonious group of previous campaigns.

You could just sense a certain distance creeping into their relationship. This was to be their fourth Munster Championship campaign in charge and a distinct weariness seemed to have taken hold.

As players, too, I think we had all become a little careless.

Winning the All-Ireland after so many years in the wilderness sent us off on something of a celebratory merry-go-round which – if we're brutally honest – didn't really end until the following March.

My own life was changing at an incredible pace now. On November 4, 1989 Anne and I got married in Waterford with Ian Conroy as my 'best man' and Fr Michael O'Brien as chief celebrant. Hurling was being pushed a little downward in my list of personal priorities.

Between parading the McCarthy Cup and planning holidays, Tipp became something of joke in the National League. If anything, we started playing the part of big-shots a little too comfortably.

Every town and village wanted their moment with the Cup and my own place, Cullen, was no exception. Although my club Lattin-Cullen is effectively based in Lattin, I am most definitely from Cullen and the locals wanted that fact recognised.

So on the Friday night before Tipp played Cork in the League, most of the team came down to our village in miserable wind and rain to be introduced to the crowd by Jimmy Magee. We had a great night and I really appreciated so many of the lads travelling.

That Sunday, Tipp were hammered by Cork after which my club held a dinner-dance in honour of the team in Emly. I had to speak at the dinner and made the point that both Pat Fox and myself – who hadn't played in the game – were 'probably Tipp's two best players on the day'.

It was all a bit of a laugh to us and, looking back, our attitude was terrible. We had become far too big for our boots.

That January we went on holidays to Florida and, here again, the innocence of earlier years had clearly left us. Two years previously, when the team holidayed in the Canaries, 'Babs' had us out training every day.

We might have looked ridiculous running up and down the beach but at least it showed that we were focused as much on the future as the past. In Florida, we just enjoyed ourselves and came home overweight and under-motivated.

As Phil Conway went to work on us, our League form threatened relegation. We ended up going to Nowlan Park for our final game against Kilkenny in genuine danger of going back down to Division Two.

The match ended in a draw after Joe Hayes inexplicably kicked a ball out over the sideline and, from the resultant free, Kilkenny got an equalising goal in injury-time.

We were all pretty subdued in the dressing-room afterwards while 'Babs' held a little radio up to his ear. Normally, he would be doing this to get the results from a race meeting somewhere. But, this time, he was listening for news from New Ross where Wexford were playing Galway.

If Wexford won, Galway – not Tipp – would be relegated.

Anyway, the game was level right at the death when Jimmy Houlihan put over a huge free to send Galway down. It sparked incredible scenes in our dressing-room. Everyone started shouting and hugging one another.

Joe even got up and made a bit of a speech about how the Irish rugby selectors had been on to him because of his knack for finding touch! We were thrilled with ourselves even though it had taken a Wexford man to keep us in Division One.

And it was hard that evening to believe that we had been so uninterested in our early League games. Truly, time is a strange and wondrous thing.

The following Friday, we took off for Toronto where we were to play the Allstars in the famous Skydome. Being honest, it was probably the last thing Tipp needed at that time. Another week on the beer.

Toronto was, admittedly, a brilliant experience. The games there were being sponsored by A&P Dominion, a major supermarket chain run by a Tipperary man called John Dunne.

A crowd of 20,000 turned up to see us beat the Allstars comfortably in a match televised live at home. We won 5-15 to 3-11 and, while the stadium was absolutely breath-taking, I have to say the surface was far from ideal for hurling. Essentially, it was concrete with a mat on top and you would certainly get badly burnt or cut if you fell on it.

Still, that has to go down as probably the most enjoyable of all the Allstars trips I was on. Because the game was going out live at home, there was more of an edge to it than had been the norm.

That then was St Patrick's weekend in Canada. We returned home to the boom of Phil Conway's voice and the dictates of his leaflets. Tipp had been drawn away to Limerick in the first round of the Championship and, to put it mildly, that made us apprehensive. You see, laps of honour can soften a team and we knew there were few counties in the country that would take greater pleasure from dethroning Tipperary than Limerick would.

They had always been a difficult team to beat but now men like Mike Houlihan, Ciaran Carey and Gary Kirby were beginning to come through. And it was obvious they would be hugely motivated.

But Limerick, at the time, also had an incredible capacity to shoot themselves in the foot and it happened again here when Mike Barron was sent off after only 15 minutes for pulling on Cormac Bonnar from behind. After that, we were always pretty comfortable with substitute, Dinny Ryan, coming on to get the goal that ended Limerick's resistance.

Tipp won 2-20 to 1-17 but, if we were honest with ourselves, there had been no real rhythm or tempo to our performance. As often happens at such times, I suppose we only saw what we wanted to see.

With my old friend, Fr O'Brien, now in charge of our Munster final opponents – Cork – the hype machine took over. There was an enormous build-up to the game and more and more you could sense that Tipp were being sucked into some kind of trap.

Cork would be coming to Thurles as underdogs and it was a role they positively savoured. Over the years, they have always virtually willed opponents into writing them off and the summer of '90 was no different.

We trained in Semple Stadium on the Tuesday before the game and all of us could tell there was friction amongst the selectors. While we worked out under Phil Conway's instructions, 'Babs', Theo and Donie sat above in the VIP section of the new stand trying to agree on a starting fifteen.

I knew I'd be playing left-corner forward and that Johnny Leahy would be at left-half because 'Babs' had told him he'd be on Seanie McCarthy and that he should be trying 'to catch the ball over him.'

But, as we did our warm-down and stretching exercises, there was still no sign of the three of them moving. So we left them there and went into the dressing-room, wondering what on earth it was that could be delaying them.

Tipp did have a share of injury problems. Bobby Ryan and Declan Carr had both been suffering from blood infections while Cormac Bonnar was clearly not 100% fit. But, surely, the task before them wasn't as complex as they were making it seem now.

Eventually, when we had all showered, 'Babs' came in and walked over to the corner where Pat Fox and myself were sitting. 'You won't believe the team that is picked for Sunday,' he said to us. I remember thinking immediately that it was a strange thing for a manager to say.

Mind you, he was right. We couldn't believe it.

Leahy was playing at full-forward although he had been named in the corner. Conor Stakelum was in at left-half forward. There was no place for either Colm or Cormac Bonnar. Bobby was named at left-corner back with John Madden – who had virtually come from nowhere – named in the other corner.

The centre-back position had been given to John Kennedy who would be captain.

Most of us were speechless when we heard the team. I remember I travelled back to Dublin that night with Phil Conway. Now Phil was a brilliant trainer but he never pretended to know much about hurling. So our conversation on the road home was a little one-sided.

I was telling him how apprehensive I felt. 'I don't think that team is good enough to win the Munster final,' I told him. 'We have a better team than that but it won't be playing.'

That week, Tipperary people generally seemed confused by the make-up of the team. Like most of them, I simply couldn't understand the peculiar logic employed by 'Babs' and Co.

I knew in my heart that Cork would be delighted Cormac Bonnar hadn't been selected. He had come on to break their resistance in the '88 Munster final and just had a tendency of doing well against them.

Still, the team was picked and we had to go with it. Then 'Babs' came out with the immortal line that has since gone down in Munster final folklore.

Interviewed on TV by Ger Canning 24 hours before the game, he used the expression 'Donkeys don't win Derbies.' There's little doubt he used it in a completely innocent manner but, as soon as I heard it, the alarm bells started ringing.

Knowing Fr O'Brien, I sensed instinctively that this was precisely the kind of thing he would seize upon to motivate his players. There was nothing he ever liked better than for his players to be going into a game with a collective chip on their shoulders.

In fact, Cork – generally – have always been brilliant at turning a harmless remark into some kind of motivating force.

I remember in '86, the Mayor of Galway making some inane comment about the McCarthy Cup coming across the Shannon and Cork using it as if it was some terrible insult. In his victory speech after the All-Ireland final, Tom Cashman even held the Cup up and roared 'This is for the Lord Mayor of Galway.'

Now, four years on, Tipp had fallen into exactly the same trap. 'Babs' would spend the next few years almost monotonously telling Cork hurling teams how good they were, trying desperately to repair the damage.

But the damage was done. And Tipp were to pay the price.

We started the game very poorly and only Conor Stakelum really kept us in touch. The rest of us were terrible. Johnny, as expected, was struggling at full-forward so, incredibly, the selectors decided to put Fox in there.

Now this was the last place in the world I would have been moving Pat to. We all knew how worried Denis Walsh was about him in the corner but, by putting him at full-forward, you were effectively taking Fox out of the game.

Mind you, worse was to follow.

We had steadied ourselves with two goals coming up to half-time, Michael Cleary getting the first and me the second. That put us five points in front and it seemed like we might just be ready to pull away.

But then, just before the interval, John Madden put the ball out needlessly for a line-cut and, from Kieran McGuckin's delivery, big Mark Foley rose almost unchallenged in the Tipp square to bat the ball home.

The goal completely undermined our mood. We went into the dressing-room feeling utterly deflated. Having been in a position of authority, we now had Cork snapping at our heels and – deep down – most of us sensed the balance of the team was all wrong.

Fox and myself sat discussing things in the dressing-room. Things hadn't really gelled between us in the first-half but we were both confident we'd get it right eventually. The Cork full-back line was nervous and we knew it.

Then they called out the team that would be starting the second-half and Pat's name was missing. I couldn't believe it. None of us could. The selectors had decided to replace him with Dinny Ryan.

I don't mean to be in any way offensive towards Dinny here. He was a good player but nowhere near Pat Fox's league. The decision bordered on incredible.

To the day I die, I will remember running back out onto the pitch for the second-half and the announcement being made across the tannoy. 'Dinny Ryan replaces Pat Fox on the Tipperary team.' There was such an explosion of colour and noise from the Cork supporters you would have thought they had just scored another goal.

Red and white flags seemed to be predominant everywhere. Psychologically, Tipp had just taken a huge step backwards.

Even had Cormac Bonnar been brought in, the blow of losing Fox might have been softened. Cork hated facing big Bonnar but, being fair, I'm not sure he was going well enough at the time to make an impact.

The point though is that Dinny Ryan, for all his talents, did not frighten Cork in any way. Pat Fox did. The switch amounted to a desperate own goal.

Gradually, Cork got on top of us in the second-half, chasing everything like a pack of demented wolves. Foley was running riot at centre-forward and would finish the day with a personal tally of 2-7. He hit balls that day that he never would again. He couldn't miss.

Having played with him on a successful Fitzgibbon Cup team, I knew Mark Foley had bundles of talent. But I never expected him to do what he did that day in Thurles. The truth is no-one did.

Colm Bonnar managed to stop the Tipp rot a little when he replaced the ailing Declan Carr, and we actually recovered from six points down to trail by the narrowest margin possible with just eight minutes remaining.

I spent most of that second-half playing at full-forward and it was one of the best performances I gave in a Tipperary jersey. Feeling really strong and confident, I always sensed I would win any balls that came my way.

But the roof caved in when Foley got his second goal and, just before the end, John Fitzgibbon rubbed salt into our wounds by drilling home Cork's fourth. Tipperary's reign was over.

Little was said in the dressing-room afterwards. What was the point? Recrimination is useless when the horse has already bolted.

That said, it was one of the hardest defeats I think I have ever had to digest in a Tipperary jersey. We were in our prime as a team between '89 and '91 – both physically and in terms of skill. Being honest with ourselves, we knew we made Cork look good that day in Thurles.

A combination of self-delusion, softness from a winter of celebration, bad team selection and careless words cost us dearly. Fr O'Brien was never quoted as saying that he used the 'donkeys' quote to his team's advantage but you didn't have to be a rocket scientist to know that he would have.

It was all Cork supporters spoke of afterwards and the *Cork Examiner* carried the heading that Monday morning of 'Not bad for donkeys.' And if supporters were obsessed with it, what do you think the team and mentors were using?

But that had been just a slip of the tongue for which 'Babs' and the rest of us paid dearly. What was far more difficult to accept was the illogical team selection.

I will never agree that our best team took the field for the 1990 Munster final. Nor will I ever agree that the decision to replace Pat Fox at half-time made the remotest semblance of sense. Here was a game that Tipp blew, pure and simple.

And that was the evening I went for my few much-publicised drinks with Fr O'Brien. Not because I was hurting any less than Tipperary followers everywhere. Not because my ambitions had all been satisfied the year before.

I went for a few drinks with him simply because I considered him then – as I do now – a friend.

We talked about everything that evening except hurling. The way I wanted it to be. Because I sensed – as we all did – that the honeymoon was over for Tipperary now.

XXI
'IF I HAD DUCKS, THEY'D DROWN'

THE mind plays mischievous games.

We all like to rationalise great hurling battles, to tidy up the most momentous happenings with cold, logical brush-strokes. There must always be a reason for someone winning, always an excuse for those who lose.

But, sometimes, we fool ourselves in thinking that games can be just parcelled by words and pictures.

How can anyone parcel '91 from a Tipperary perspective? The truth is no-one can. Emotions jack-knifed that summer in so many different directions, I'm not sure any of those of us involved ever truly stopped to absorb the happenings fully.

You see all through that Championship, Tipp had their foot to the floor. We had to. There was no soft game for us that year, no chance to amble and admire the scenery.

The pressure was evidently on 'Babs' after the 'donkeys affair' of the previous summer. I think it's fair to say that this was probably the first year since his arrival as manager that there was any evidence of his own people beginning to doubt him.

If ever a year in hurling taught me never to be presumptuous, this was it.

Tipp went into '91 with so many demons swirling about our ears. After losing to Cork the previous summer, an imitation memorial card started arriving through letter boxes. It read 'In loving memory of the Tipperary hurling team – Born, Croke Park 1989. Died, Thurles 1990. Sadly missed by Tipperary people everywhere. Will always be remembered by the champions, Cork.'

The popular jibe was that we were the 'great one-in-a-row' Tipperary team. It seemed the hurling world was having a great laugh at our expense.

The truth is, of course, that Tipp have never been short of enemies. Because we have borders with so many other hurling counties, local rivalry is a common ingredient to our games. And spite is easily summoned.

When Tipp play neighbouring counties like Kilkenny, Limerick, Galway, Offaly, Clare, Laois and Waterford, the games are invariably laced with a certain venom. Ask people from virtually any of these counties and they will tell you that Tipp are 'arrogant' or 'cocky' in a hurling environment.

I know that, as a county, we have probably fewer friends in hurling than any other.

That thought comes to mind now because of the way '91 started for us. We lost arguably the most pathetic National League semi-final ever played on a scoreline of 0-7 to 1-7 against Offaly in the Gaelic Grounds. The game was played in horrible conditions and Tipp looked an absolute and total shambles.

I watched it from the sideline because of a calf strain, as did Pat Fox and Cormac Bonnar. After the game, we convened back in the Limerick Ryan Hotel for a meal during which I was approached by John O'Donoghue who had replaced Theo English as a selector.

O'Donoghue was in a fairly aggressive mood. 'So what's the story with you, are you ever going to play again?' he asked with more than a hint of sarcasm.

Given the nature of Tipp's performance, I could understand his frustration. But it was as if he was implying that I was faking my injury. And that is something I have never ever done.

Mentally, Tipp looked to be in real trouble that evening. There was a strange lethargy within the camp that seemed to be inhibiting us from even discussing our problems frankly.

It felt like we were going nowhere.

Carr, as captain, was finding himself in an increasingly invidious position. His form was no better than average and there seemed a real danger that he might follow the examples of previous captains – Pa O'Neill and Pat McGrath – by losing his place on the team

But the following week, Declan asserted himself in a way that took everyone by surprise. After training one night, he attacked everybody. He attacked the management – which was unheard of – and he attacked fellow players to their faces.

I missed the session but, by all accounts, Declan found time to criticise me too. No-one escaped what he wanted to say that night. Carr knew that we were in trouble, that too many people were just wrapped up in their own worlds.

He was a great talker and the effect that night had on everyone was quite amazing. Suddenly, Tipperary had a captain. And a strong one.

In taking on the management team especially, Declan had shown a willingness to jeopardise his own position for the benefit of the team. It was a pivotal moment in Tipp's year.

Another speech that touched important nerves came from county chairman, Mick Maguire, the night before we opened our Championship campaign against Limerick in Thurles. Mick comes from the same parish, the same club as myself and would have a sharp understanding of the rivalry that exists between Tipp and Limerick.

'Look' he said that evening 'if Tipperary were playing South Africa, Limerick would be shouting for South Africa.' It was a line that always lingered in my mind afterwards. Because it often struck me that guys from mid-Tipp and North Tipp could never quite comprehend the depth of rivalry between those of us living in the west of the county and our Limerick neighbours.

I still recall that meeting in the Park Avenue as one of the best I've ever attended. It struck the perfect chord for what lay ahead.

As it happened, we went on to beat Limerick pretty easily. Yet again, they had a man sent off against us – this time Anthony Carmody for a pull on Michael Cleary. But we were never really in danger even before Carmody's dismissal with Johnny Leahy playing his best game yet for Tipperary.

Twelve minutes from the end, I ran through to score a goal that was no more than window-dressing in a fourteen point victory. Little did I know then that it would be my last Championship goal for Tipperary.

One significant happening in that game was the departure of John Kennedy with a damaged cruciate ligament in his knee. John never played for Tipp again.

He was replaced, eventually, by Michael Ryan that day. I say 'eventually' because I believe there was a slightly comical exchange on the sideline before Michael got into the action. Donie Nealon had told him to start warming up but 'Babs' almost choked when he saw who was running up and down the touchline.

'Jesus, we can't bring in Mick Ryan,' roared 'Babs'. 'He's not ready for this.'

They argued but Donie was insistent. 'He's going in, let him in,' he said. So Michael Ryan went in, played majestically and has been wearing the Tipp colours ever since.

I often thought about his performance that day and wondered at his calm. He would have been no more than 19 or 20 at the time. If 'Babs' had said to me at that age to get back in the dug-out – I'd have gone back in. But Mick didn't give a damn about 'Babs' or anyone.

He just wanted to get in there and hurl. And, credit to him, he did that brilliantly.

With Limerick beaten, our motivating force became Cork's incredible big-game record on their own territory. They had never lost a Championship match in Pairc Uí Chaoimh and were unbeaten in Championship at any Cork venue for 70 years.

Now we were hungry for them. Vengeful from the year before, conscious of how they had stopped us from becoming the first Tipp team to win four Munster titles in a row.

But, beyond that, I think we were also painfully conscious that people didn't really rate the All-Ireland we had won in '89. Sure, we could argue that we beat everyone put in front of us but Limerick, Waterford and Antrim were scarcely giants at the time while the defeat of Galway had hardly been without its scars.

So we went to Cork a driven team, a team committed to winning back its self-respect.

Seventeen minutes into the game our plans and aspirations seemed to lie mangled in Pairc Uí Chaoimh. Leading 0-3 to 0-2 after seven, we proceeded to concede three goals in the next ten minutes and actually looked in serious danger of being humiliated.

Our full-back line, especially, was in terrible trouble with Kevin Hennessy having a distinct edge over Conor O'Donovan.

This day was to be a watershed in my career. It was to be the first day I genuinely started to feel vulnerable on a hurling field. The first day, things that had for so long come naturally to me started to seem difficult.

I got an early chance to score off my left side but pushed the ball wide. Five minutes later, an identical opportunity arose and I delivered an identical result. It was to have a huge effect on my confidence. In fact, it knocked the stuffing out of me.

Just after Cork had got their goals, Johnny Leahy gave me a great pass in a goal-scoring position and, inexplicably, I dropped the ball out of my hand. Johnny followed up though and buried it in the net.

Probably the only constructive thing I managed in the whole half was to hook Ger Cunningham, take the ball off him and score a point. Overall, I was desperately unsettled. Nothing seemed to be coming easy.

We went in at half-time lucky to be only four points down. It was decided that Noel Sheehy would move across to replace the injured O'Donovan at full-back with Michael Ryan coming into the corner.

Gradually, Tipp clawed their way back into the game to get to within two points but Cork stirred themselves again and, suddenly, John Fitzgibbon struck for a goal that seemed certain to bury us.

It was a brilliant goal, one of the best I've ever seen – whipped low and venomously along the ground past Ken Hogan.

'Fitzy' was a good friend of mine and someone I always had great time for. I can still remember him come running out after scoring and jumping into the air exactly as Christy Ring would jump. Ring, you see, was 'Fitzy's' idol.

If anything, he was lost in a time-warp because of his adoration of Ring.

He cocooned himself in the hurling world of the fifties and sixties. 'Fitzy' loved that tradition and wouldn't ever tolerate a bad word being spoken about Christy Ring.

That day in Cork, as he ran out the field, I knew he was imagining himself as Ring having buried Tipperary.

But Tipp weren't buried. Pat Fox, brilliantly, got behind the Cork defence to whip home a critical goal, reducing the margin to four points with ten minutes remaining.

Michael Cleary, Leahy and Fox were all flying now and – almost manically – we chased Cork down until the sides were level. It was then I had another opportunity to rescue my day and blew it.

A great chance broke to me as I raced towards Ger Cunningham's goal and I remember thinking 'This is it, I can't miss this one.'

It would have the perfect time to hit the net. As Cunningham froze, I tried to place it beyond him, to score with subtlety rather than power. Until then, I had done everything right, taking it on the run, sprinting clear of the covering players...

But I couldn't finish.

The ball hit Cunningham on his shoulder and I just wanted the ground to open up beneath me.

I couldn't believe what was happening. The day had gone so badly from start to finish and here I was missing a gilt-edged chance to win the day for Tipperary. It was as if I had been mesmerised by the mere sight of the goals.

Looking back, the early wides had unsettled me and I never managed to recover. Nine times out of ten, that ball would have been buried in the back of the net. But this was the tenth time. I felt like screaming as the ball was cleared.

It seemed to just encapsulate my day then when Kevin Hennessy then got a ball beneath the stand and scored an incredible point from the touchline to put Cork ahead in injury-time. 'Oh f...ing hell,' I thought. 'That's the end of it.'

But, of course, this was to be no ordinary summer.

Before I knew it, I was racing in on the Cork goal minus my hurley and kicking the ball over the bar for an equaliser. I knew immediately it was over but the umpire, after some hesitation, signalled wide.

The look on Pat Fox's face captured exactly how we all felt. It was a crazy decision. I've often spoken to Ger Cunningham since and there was never any doubt in his mind that it was a score. Unfortunately, the TV camera angle was inconclusive so RTE could not prove emphatically that the ball went over the bar.

But, if you look at the respective reactions of the players, you will see immediately what they all thought. Tipp players had their arms in the air, Cork players dropped their heads.

At the time, I was almost incoherent with rage. I couldn't believe the decision. Couldn't believe that after such a wretched day personally, Tipp were now being deprived a second chance by an umpire who was stuck under a post when he should have been behind the goals.

Six months of hard work were now going down the tubes because of one man's mistake. At least that was how it seemed.

I have met the umpire in question several times since and he still maintains that the ball was wide. But anyone who could see it from a proper angle will tell you that he was wrong.

Thank God, Noel Sheehy managed to win the resulting puck-out and Fox's nerve held to sweep over a brilliant equalising point with the last stroke of the game. But it had been far too close for comfort.

We could have been out of the Championship because of an umpire's error.

I couldn't lift myself to be upbeat in the dressing-room afterwards. We were all happy to have survived but I knew that my own contribution had been inadequate. A journalist asked me for my assessment.

'If I had ducks, they'd drown,' I told him.

The replay was set for two weeks later and we didn't resume training until the Friday night. I was desperate to get out on that training pitch, to wash away the memories of one of my most frustrating performances ever in a Tipp jersey.

Work was now confining me to the car a lot and I arrived at Semple Stadium that evening about 40 minutes early and itching to get a hurley in my hand.

Once training started, I was in a really bullish frame of mind. There was so much pent up energy inside of me. I wanted to be hit by people and to hit back. I've always believed that you should train as you intend to play. Training hard does something for both body and mind. It makes you feel cleansed somehow. Makes you feel strong.

So that night, I just wanted to take on fellas, to score goals, to start putting balls over the bar, to exorcise the demons of Pairc Uí Chaoimh. I wanted fellas to come and thump me, to challenge me.

So the practice match started, I got the ball and took off on a goal-bound run. Noel Sheehy came to meet me. My natural jink takes me off the left foot onto the right. So I feinted to fly right past him and next thing... BANG... I was on my back in agony. The hamstring.

'What have you done?' I asked myself. I knew I was in real trouble.

Now this was the first time I really got to know Liam Hennessy. Liam had taken over from Phil Conway as trainer and he was to become one of the most important men in my hurling life and that of the other Tipp players over the next few years.

While Phil had done a great job technically, his lack of hurling knowledge restricted the role he could play within the panel. Liam was different. Coming from Cappawhite, he was passionate about the game.

To this day, I can only marvel at his genius as a trainer and psychologist. If Liam wants to, he can make a nuclear holocaust seem like a Christmas party. I couldn't count the number of times he has lifted me from the edges of despair when I felt like throwing in the towel because of a new injury.

And this was just such an occasion.

I was close to tears as I limped into the dressing-room, knowing that the pull was bad. The pain meant nothing to me. It was just the devastation, the awful realisation that I had no chance of playing in the replay.

John O'Donoghue and physio, Willie Bennett, were inside but little was said between us. Truth is, little could be said. So I just showered and headed away to spend the night in Cullen.

Hennessy called over the following morning and immediately went to work on me. He persuaded me to keep putting ice on the leg and started convincing me that, of course, I'd be ready for the replay. I believed him because I had to.

So I took a week's holidays from work and we did everything in our power to get the leg right.

On the Friday night before the game, Liam was attending a wedding at the Royal Marine Hotel in Dun Laoghaire. He rang me from the hotel and told me to come on down so that he could have a look at how the leg was progressing.

That was a measure of his commitment. There I was running around the lawns of the Royal Marine Hotel under Hennessy's supervision while the wedding guests inside probably never even realised that he was missing.

Looking back, I never had the remotest chance of playing but I think Liam realised how important it was just to keep me believing. All along, I was trying to persuade myself that I would have something to contribute in the replay. It was better than moping at home.

On the morning of the game, we had Mass in Templemore before going to Thurles and having the customary puckaround in St Patrick's College. Not surprisingly, it was decided that Donie O'Connell would start instead of me.

I was totally depressed. For me, the whole year was effectively gone now. I will always remember driving down to the ground on the bus and supporters looking in the window at me, gesturing to find out whether I was in or out.

I just nodded my head each time and they'd throw their eyes to the Heavens. This was to be the day of all days for Tipperary hurling and I wouldn't be a part of it. Even now, that rates as the biggest regret of my life.

Maybe the place to start with the '91 replay is mid-way through the second-half when a Kevin Hennessy goal put Cork nine points clear. The score was 3-13 to 1-10. Ger O'Neill and myself had been sitting in the dug-out, watching the slaughter unfold.

At that point, I turned to Ger and told him that the game was over. I reasoned that Cork were going to get at least five more points before the finish. That meant Tipp would have to get fourteen just to draw the game.

'No chance,' we both agreed. 'We've absolutely no chance.'

It had been around this time that 'Babs' told me to start warming up. There was a big cheer when I got up out of the dug-out. I'm honestly not sure if they actually intended putting me on at that point but I'm certainly thankful that they didn't. The truth is my leg wouldn't have lasted two minutes out there although I would have been stupid enough to try it. For me to go on would have been ridiculous.

Warm up? I didn't have a bloody leg to warm up.

My memories now are largely of chaos in the dug-out. People have this notion that everything is calm and calculated on the sideline. The truth is a certain bedlam rules. And I don't think Tipp's dug-out was any different to what others would have been in this regard.

What do you do when you're nine points down? Apart from prayer, your options are pretty limited.

So how did the game turn? Well, Joe Hayes had certainly started winning ball around midfield but, more to the point, he was delivering it well to the forwards. Colm Bonnar was hounding Tony O'Sullivan who had come out to midfield and Johnny Leahy had moved to wing-back where he was now lording it.

But, with fifteen minutes remaining, Tipp were still six points down when Fox delivered one of the greatest goals I have ever seen scored.

Chasing a long ball, he looked no better than third favourite to get there first when, somehow, he managed to flick it left-handed past a startled Ger Cunningham. I don't believe there is another man alive who could have done that.

It was Fox at his brilliant best. The goal was about speed, strength but – maybe above all – bravery. And Pat was never short any of those virtues.

That score was the catalyst. Suddenly, the tide turned and Tipp went after Cork like greyhounds coursing hares. No-one could have been prepared for the scenes that followed.

With ten minutes remaining, a ball dropped from the sky and Declan Carr flicked home a stunning equalising goal. The drama was now in full flood. Again the crowd invaded the pitch, just as they had done after Fox's goal. Emotions were spinning manically.

Cork rallied and the battle swung upfield and down, our eyes following every movement, as if we were sitting in on some crazy tennis game.

Michael Cleary and Cormac Bonnar pushed Tipp two points clear when, with the game in injury-time, Tony O'Sullivan dropped a Cork free short and Tomas Mulcahy flicked the ball against an upright. I will never forget that moment.

It was as if time stood still, the sliothar bouncing off the upright and away to Colm Bonnar who cleared. Colm had been standing just outside the post whereas two Cork players were on the inside. Basically, had the ball bounced inward, it would have been a goal. That was how close we were to going out!

The rest proved something of a fairy tale. If I live to be a hundred, one of the highlights of my life will be seeing Aidan Ryan charging through attempted clearances from Seanie O'Gorman and Richard Browne before, incredibly, burying the ball in the Cork net.

I say 'incredibly' because Aidan had never in his life scored a goal for Tipperary. Not before or since. He just didn't think goals and yet here he was scoring one of the all-time greats.

It was, I suppose, a moment to epitomise the day.

That put Tipp five points clear and, although Fitzgibbon goaled a late free for Cork, two Michael Cleary points ensured the game was safe.

Maybe the greatest match ever played had ended in triumph for Tipperary.

Cork complained afterwards, arguing that Ger Cunningham had to endure abuse from the throngs that spilled through the Killinan-end wire after Fox's goal. It was said that stones had been thrown at the goalkeeper.

I don't pretend to know what people did or said when they came out through that wire but I doubt if it was a match-winning factor.

This was, without question, the greatest Tipperary victory I ever witnessed. The team had, effectively, come back from the grave.

Walking down into the square afterwards, it was as if an electric current was just shooting through the town. The atmosphere was quite incredible. Joe Hayes and myself went into a crowded pub downtown and were followed in shortly afterwards by a friend of Joe's from Clonoulty called Jimmy Morrissey.

Jimmy had a big banner with him which read 'Bring on Joe Hayes!'

That was all Joe needed. He launched into one of his trademark commentaries on the game just ended, taking full credit – it goes without saying – for turning the tide in Tipp's favour. Being fair to Joe, he had more than played his part.

'Babs' was there too and I can always remember him getting into a heated argument with some Cork supporter who started jibing him about the 'donkeys' remark of twelve months previously.

Every Tipp man was on a high, me included. With two more weeks to get my leg right, I now had a real chance of playing against Galway in the All-Ireland semi-final. It was time to return to Liam Hennessy's psychology.

Time to get my mind working on my body.

XXII

SOCKS DOWN, TRYING TO APE THE INCREDIBLE HULK

IT wasn't me.

Even now, I can hardly believe my eyes when I watch the video of that All-Ireland semi-final against Galway in '91. The guy wearing the number fifteen jersey for Tipperary is a stranger. A stranger who's lost control.

Many months after that game, Richie Stakelum said to me 'That wasn't Nicky English out there.' Richie knew precisely what he had seen.

Here was a day when frustration – maybe desperation even – got the better of me. Two more weeks of physio on the injured hamstring had brought me closer to full fitness. But I still wasn't right and I knew it.

Because Féile was on in Thurles, Tipp were now training in Templemore. I attended every session but only to undergo more physio treatment from Triona Maher on top of what I was already getting on a daily basis in Dublin. It was soul-destroying having to watch the others train.

All this time, I was travelling up and down with 'Babs', Declan Carr and Conal Bonnar. Joe Hayes and the lads liked to slag us about that, to hint that this was a cosy arrangement, that the team was obviously being picked in the car. Needless to say, this wasn't true.

But I was selected for the Galway game basically because I managed to train at our final session. So maybe you could understand the lads having a few suspicions.

Even though the leg didn't feel great, there was just no way I was going to willingly step aside for this game. I was still desperate to exorcise the memories of Pairc Uí Chaoimh.

Looking back, I wasn't remotely relaxed about the match.

My normal game has always been a patient one. But, this time, I was virtually bursting to get the ball. I had my socks rolled down and I was like the incredible hulk charging frantically around the field.

It was as if I wanted to crash into someone, anyone. I wanted to prove that I was still solid, that I could play at this level and not feel in any way vulnerable.

All the pent up frustration of the last few months now came bubbling to the surface.

The reality is that I knew in the back of my mind I was not ready for that Galway game. Maybe that's why I went into it with such a manic attitude. I was like a tiger set loose from his cage and Heaven help anyone who got in my way.

The only truly constructive thing I can recall doing in the game was a little 'dummy' in the first-half which sent Carr racing clear towards goal. Basically, as the ball came towards me, I knew that Brendan Dervan was right behind me so I stepped over it, completely fooling him.

Funny, but it's one of the most pleasing things I've ever done on a hurling field and it came from a game in which I had a total nightmare. It was the kind of thing you might imagine Kenny Dalglish doing on a soccer pitch but, being honest, I think it reflected the only moment in that game when my head was working properly.

It left the ball at Carr's feet in an unmarked position about forty yards from goal. He lifted it, sprinted away and then, sadly, blazed the ball wide.

It was just as well that Tipp, at the time, were really humming. Because

I was going to be of absolutely no assistance that day.

One of the first balls I went for, I collided heavily with a Galway player – the impact separating an AC joint in my shoulder. Soon after, I went charging into another challenge and got caught by a defender's backswing. The impact opened a cut that would require eight stitches above my left eye.

Basically, I was rushing and racing into everything. Just trying to release this thing inside of me. Trying to wash away the memory of Pairc Uí Chaoimh.

At no point was I willing to stop and take a deep breath. I was moving around like a mad man, looking for someone to barge into.

After maybe 25 minutes, with my shoulder smashed and my jersey soaked with blood, the almost inevitable happened. Somebody got a ball out on the wing and, instinctively, I cut inside to create an option. Soon as I accelerated... BANG... the hamstring went. My day was over.

The Galway crowd jeered me as I limped off the field, a broken-down hurler with nothing left to offer.

Their jeers, I suspected, were a legacy of '89. But there must have been a share of frustration too because, even with me labouring, Tipp were winning comfortably. In fact, goals by Cormac Bonnar and Michael Cleary had us an incredible nine points up at that juncture. And Galway seemed incapable of raising an argument.

Back in the dressing-room at half-time, I knew I was on a different wavelength to the others. Their mood was so upbeat, so self-assured.

I sat in a corner of the room, my eye, shoulder and leg throbbing. Tipp were flying and I could no longer stay with them. They were now able to win games easily without me. That message was ringing loud and clear now. I had become superfluous to the cause.

Sitting there, it just felt like my whole world had collapsed around me. I was exasperated. As bad as my body felt going into the game, it now felt like it was barely held together with pieces of twine.

I couldn't stop myself from quietly crying.

It was a stupid thing to do really. There was still a game to be won and the lads were trying to focus on the 35 minutes ahead. They had to go out and be men again and here I was blubbering quietly like a baby. That just made me even more angry with myself.

I got stitched up, then showered and watched what was left of the second-half in my track-suit. Tipp won the game 3-13 to 1-9. They looked unstoppable.

One unforgettable moment for me from the second-half was a penalty save by the Tipp defence. It was not so much the execution as the response that really identified the team's mood.

Paul Delaney was never a man for showing much emotion but, at that moment, he was shouting at Colm Bonnar. And Colm was shouting back. 'Yes, yes, yes,' he was saying.

To me, that just identified the incredible spirit now in the team. A spirit put there by Liam Hennessy. Because it was Hennessy who got the backs talking to one another like that. It was Hennessy who had brought people out of their shells.

Right through '91, I felt the spirit of Hennessy was manifest in everything that Tipperary did. He just ignited a great energy, a great power in people.

I had seen that power in Mick Ryan's shoulder charge on Tomas Mulcahy during the Munster final replay. And I saw it many times subsequently as Tipp marched on to the All-Ireland crown.

'Babs' was a brilliant organiser with a good hurling brain. But Hennessy was the link between management and players. He was the communicator who kept us all going.

I would give him enormous credit for the role he played in '91. Not just for the psychology he used on me, the way he cushioned me from despair. But for the bond he created within the squad, for the openness and the sense of unity among players.

The evening of that semi-final, we had a meal out in the Lough and Quay pub in Clondalkin. I remember Matt Kavanagh, who drove the bus, trying to cheer me up by telling me I'd be alright for the final.

'If I play in this All-Ireland Matt,' I told him. 'It'll be a miracle.'

My body was in an absolute mess that evening. I was in ribbons. I had just torn my hamstring for the second time in three weeks. Ligaments in my shoulder were also torn.

And now I had a black eye too, with a neat bit of embroidery above it. I really looked the part of the wounded soldier.

XXIII
FOX – THE ONE MAN FULL-FORWARD LINE

FEW managers ever gambled going into an All-Ireland final like 'Babs' did in '91.

Injuries savagely disrupted Tipperary's preparations. Like myself, Cormac Bonnar had torn a calf muscle while Bobby Ryan was carrying a very bad ankle injury. None of us could train.

Right until the team was named, I really wasn't sure if the selectors would pick me. No amount of physiotherapy was ever going to get me 100% fit in time to face Kilkenny. The bottom line was that, if I played, I was almost certain to be a marginal figure in the game.

I've often thought about it since, wondered why they risked so much by putting me in when someone like Conor Stakelum was an obvious and fit alternative.

I'll forever be indebted to them for sticking with me.

The fact that Tipp won ensured that there would be no repercussions over team selection. But I went through a crisis of conscience beforehand. I kept questioning myself, wondering whether or not I should say something to the selectors.

By nature, players have a capacity to delude themselves when injury calls. I'm no different. If I feel there is any way I can conceivably contribute to the team, I want to be there.

I don't think it's so much dishonesty as pig-headedness. Players want to play, end of story. I've yet to meet the man who was happy to sit in a dug-out when he could have been out in the middle of the action.

Being truthful, with Cormac also injured and – if anything – more doubtful than me, I knew I couldn't really pull out anyway. But it played on my mind a lot.

I kept asking myself 'Am I going to be as good for Tipp at number 15 in this game as anyone else would be? Would Conor Stakelum be a better option?'

It's a terrible way to approach an All-Ireland final. Probably the worst frame of mind imaginable. You should be 100% healthy, both physically and mentally, going into the biggest game of the year. I was neither.

We had returned to Thurles for our last night of training and a colleague of mine at work, John Moriarty, drove me down to Semple Stadium. On the journey home I remember saying to John that there was just no way I could see myself finishing the game.

On that Saturday night we were staying in the Burlington Hotel and I went up to Cormac's room to see what his mood was like. Cormac said he felt his leg was coming good.

While we were talking, Pat Fox came in. Fox looked at me and said that the team wanted a 'man-of-the-match' performance from me in the final.

I said, 'Jesus Pat, I just know I'm not going to last 70 minutes.'

Fox, typically, laughed it off. He was well accustomed to my nervousness before a big game. 'You'll be grand,' he chuckled.

Later, at the team-meeting, Fox stood up and made an incredible statement. Looking back, I think he realised that he would be playing with two 'crocks' in the full-forward line the next day. He knew in his heart and soul that he would have to do the work of three men.

'Just give me the ball,' he told the players. 'Just give me the ball and I'll take the Kilkenny backs apart.'

In my time with Tipp, no-one had ever made such a brazen declaration. It was an amazing thing to do given the scale and pressure of the occasion.

But you had to hand it to Fox. He felt that he had the measure of his direct opponent, Liam Simpson. And, sure enough, he went out the next day and proceeded to break Kilkenny hearts.

Scoring 0-5 from play, Pat Fox was man-of-the-match – more or less as he had promised.

Fox apart though, it was hardly a vintage Tipp performance.

'Big Bonnar' and myself struggled with our injuries while Bobby was in real trouble with his ankle at centre-back where Christy Heffernan threatened to over-run him in the first 20 minutes. Eventually, Conal Bonnar took over there and actually did a superb job but at least Bobby had the satisfaction of finishing the game.

Not surprisingly, I didn't.

My problem was not so much winning ball as doing something constructive with it. I felt as if my hamstring was just being held together by threads and the worry was constantly there that it would go again.

Despite looking the better team, Kilkenny had to settle for mere parity (0-9 each) going in for the half-time interval.

Early in the second-half, I actually got around Bill Hennessy only to drive the ball wide from much the same position I had twice missed in Pairc Uí Chaoimh. My confidence was almost as threadbare as my leg.

But, before I departed, I suppose I did have the satisfaction of playing a role in the only goal of the game. I took possession from a line-ball and turned to break away from Hennessy. But, by now, I was limping badly and there was no power in my right leg.

For a split second, he held me but then I turned straight into him and kind of caught him under my arm. Hennessy let go but I didn't have the legs to go around him so, effectively, I just stayed leaning in on him.

The whistle went for a free to Tipperary. Even though there had been a slight foul initially, it was – without doubt – a harsh decision.

We all know what happened next, Michael Cleary mis-hitting the free and it catching the entire Kilkenny defence napping by dipping into the net, reputedly off Liam Walsh's hurley. 'Skippy' quite plainly just went to tip it over the bar. But the Gods above had made their choice.

Shortly afterwards, Conor Stakelum – who had replaced 'Big Bonnar' – was tussling for a ball in the corner and I made a diagonal run towards Hill 16. It was at that moment that the hamstring went. Being honest, I was surprised it had lasted so long.

As I dropped to the ground, Eddie O'Connor came over and started shouting at me to 'get off the f...ing pitch'. At the time, Kilkenny were beginning to get a little momentum going and he thought I was deliberately trying to stall things.

But there was nothing phoney about the pain I now felt. The hamstring was in tatters. My Championship was over.

It's funny how lonely it can feel limping off a field even when you're surrounded by 70,000 people. I had to walk around behind the Hill-end goal where Kilkenny supporters gave me a nice little fanfare of abuse.

The solitary walk back to the dug-out seemed to take forever. When you go off in such games, you become utterly superfluous to the equation. Mentors are in the business of winning and an injured player becomes an invisible player.

I suppose that's the hard, insensitive side of sport. You might be at your lowest ebb but you can't expect people to be worrying about your feelings when there is an All-Ireland title still up for grabs.

So I knelt in front of the dug-out and, like everyone else in blue and gold, just willed the minutes away.

It was nerve-wracking watching helplessly from the sideline. I remember especially Liam Fennelly flashing a couple of shots just the wrong side of the post and – at the very death – Ken Hogan saving from Eamonn Morrissey after Adrian Ronan lobbed in a high ball.

But, strangely, there was always a certain calm about Tipperary on the field. It was as if the team *knew* that they had the measure of Kilkenny. As if the tradition of past meetings between the counties just gave Tipp an edge in confidence.

When I was younger, I was totally dismissive when people talked of how 'tradition' could influence games. But the older I got, the more substance I could see in the argument.

Tipp were always comfortable playing Kilkenny. We would certainly have preferred to play them than, say, Wexford at any given time. If we had a choice between them and Galway for All-Ireland final opponents, believe me would always have chosen Kilkenny.

When you think back to 1986, there wasn't one member of the Cork panel that believed Galway could beat them in the All-Ireland final. Tradition gave them that inner confidence and I've no doubt that it stood to them on the day.

Although Tipp won narrowly enough in '91 (1-16 to 0-15) and at least three of us were really in no fit state to play in an All-Ireland final, I don't believe we were ever truly fearful of Kilkenny. It was as if we just *knew* we were going to win.

As if tradition was our safety net.

I never did get to score in that, my last All-Ireland final. Thinking about it afterwards, it seemed a little incongruous that of the three finals I played in, I contributed virtually nothing in my first ('88), was attributed with an all-time scoring record in my second ('89) and then played like a statue in my third ('91).

No matter what way I looked at it, the year had been an absolute disaster personally. And it left me with a strange conflict of emotions.

Tipp, after all, had just won the perfect All-Ireland. Effectively, they had answered all those who sniped about '89 being a 'cheap' or 'soft' title. In beating Limerick, Cork, Galway and Kilkenny, they had silenced all the sceptics.

Looking back, it had been a year that opened with so many doubts and uncertainties. It was argued initially that we had no full-back line worthy of the name. Now Paul Delaney, Noel Sheehy and Michael Ryan could lay legitimate claim to being the best triumvirate in the country.

Fox, obviously, was the hero of the final. But people like Conal Bonnar, Johnny Leahy, Declan Ryan and captain, Declan Carr, had been magnificent too when the game was there to be won. Being honest, everyone had had their moments at some point on the journey.

Me? I suppose I had scored a goal against Limerick but there was precious little else of my year to cut out for the scrap-books.

The incredible thing is that I never did pull a hamstring again after the summer of '91. Maybe that was down to the fact that, as I lost my speed, I just wasn't putting the same pressure on my legs. But it's amazing how something that completely blighted my hurling five years ago never did return.

The celebrations and homecoming were far more natural, spontaneous events than they had been two years previously. Everyone was more relaxed, more comfortable with what had been achieved. It was as if we now knew how to celebrate an All-Ireland win.

I can remember on the night of the game, Bobby, Donie O'Connell and myself just left the official function once Fox got his man-of-the-match award and found a relatively quiet little corner in the Burlington bar.

There was far less frenzy than there had been in '89. The supporters were more inclined to just leave us to ourselves, to give us our own space.

Going home on the Monday evening was a beautiful experience. There are few more intense rivalries in hurling than Tipp-Kilkenny so the journey through Urlingford and Johnstown had a special resonance. Michael Cleary and myself sat right at the front of the bus and you couldn't but be taken by the sheer joy on Tipperary faces as we crossed the county border. It all seemed so natural this time. So comfortable.

This time, there was no clandestine route home, no lights being dimmed to conceal our identities. This time, we went straight in the front door, bringing the McCarthy Cup on its traditional route right into Liberty Square.

Once we got there and everyone was introduced to the crowd, there was little left to say or do. The group fragmented, most of us eventually ending up in the Park Avenue for a few drinks.

One of the nicest things for me was the thought that I wouldn't have to go to physio the following morning. For almost three months now, my days had been shaped around the treatment table. I was weary of the routine. Glad to be free finally of the constant, gnawing uncertainty.

On the following Saturday, Anne and myself would be taking off for a two week holiday in Portugal. The back of my right leg was black as coal from the base of the hamstring right down to the calf and it would certainly draw a few funny stares when I pulled on a swimming togs.

But the holiday was a perfect opportunity to relax and re-charge batteries.

I was now approaching 30, an age when some players were inclined to start thinking about retirement. It often struck me that some players of that vintage seemed to retire after virtually every All-Ireland final they played in. But, for me, nothing could have been further from my mind.

This was a time I couldn't possibly have given up. In my heart and soul, I knew I had to come back. I had to prove that I wasn't a washed-up hurler.

The year had been a shambles for me and I wanted to erase whatever question marks now lingered. Fit and strong again, I was sure I could contribute to another All-Ireland win for Tipperary.

But, of course, that All-Ireland was not to come for me. In many ways, my legs would never fully recover from the traumas of '91.

XXIV
CORK 'BALANCE' THE BOOKS

MEMORIES can be long and dangerous in hurling.

Bad blows liberate bad blood and old wounds can fester for months and years in silence. Even a loose comment, a throwaway barb can survive for years in the back rooms of a vengeful mind.

When you trample on a team, it is advisable not to forget the look on their faces as you leave.

Because always, always there is another day.

One of the more controversial cameos to the epic '91 Munster final replay had been Declan Ryan's blow on Jim Cashman at a time when Cork looked to be well in control. I don't know if Declan meant it, but it was a bad blow and one for which he could legitimately have been sent off.

As the two of them went up for a high ball, Declan seemed to pull very low and subsequent replays of the incident certainly didn't do him any favours.

Cashman's hand was injured by the contact made and Cork people argued vehemently afterwards that it was a significant turning point in the game. Whether or not that was an exaggeration, there could be no denying that the incident seriously diminished Cashman's presence.

Tipp, certainly, would have been aware of the feelings generated that day in Thurles. Not alone was it humiliating for Cork to surrender a nine points lead, they also had the added sense of being sinned against by flying

Tipperary ash.

Eleven months later, we travelled south to begin the defence of our Munster and All-Ireland crowns against Cork in Pairc Uí Chaoimh. As opening assignments go, this was about as forbidding as they come.

We stayed out in the Blarney Park Hotel the night before the game and, somehow, I could sense the team was a little flat. Now I was definitely susceptible to pessimism at the best of times but there was just no way the ferocious hunger of '91 was still there with us.

At the team-meeting, I tried to articulate my fears. I remember saying that Cork were going to go for us like never before and, for Tipp to survive, we would simply have to play harder than they were prepared to.

Somehow, I just got the feeling that we weren't fully focused, that guys just weren't as hungry as they needed to be.

Cork had been seething for a year and now we seemed to think we could stroll into their backyard and just quietly remove them from the Championship. It was never going to work like that.

True to form, they came out that day incredibly pumped up for battle. At the very start of the game, there was a little melee and I actually recall Tony O'Sullivan swinging at one of our players. That should have told us all we needed to know.

If Tony – one of the most sporting players you could meet – was in the mood to fight, it was a sure sign that Cork were up for the game.

Tipp got to the end of a desperately tight, tense first-half leading by a point. But, just before we went in for the break, an incident occurred that was to have a huge bearing on the outcome.

Cormac Bonnar went charging towards the Cork goal but was met full in the chest by Denis Mulcahy. Just as he was hit, Bonnar kicked the ball and Ger Cunningham flicked it out for a '65'.

Incredibly, the ball was just waved wide, Cork being penalised neither for the dangerous charge on Bonnar or the fact that Cunningham had put the ball out over his own end-line. Insult had been heaped on injury.

'Big Bonnar' didn't seem to know where he was after the collision and could not reappear for the second-half. In fact, it was to be the last anyone would see of the Fox-Bonnar-English full-forward line.

Injuries had always been the bane of that triumvirate. I doubt if we played ten games together in the four years we were accepted as Tipp's first choice.

But this was a cruel way to end.

Bonnar's departure was a massive blow to Tipperary. That said, it was never likely to generate much sympathy in a Cork crowd still mindful of what had happened Jim Cashman a year before in Thurles.

The writing was on the wall for Tipperary as we returned for the second-half. Physically, it was being put up to us. And I don't think we really had the stomach to respond.

Hunger is such an immense factor in hurling games at this level. Top inter-county teams are usually relatively even in terms of talent. The winners and losers are invariably separated – above all – by force of will.

Tipp, at the time, were probably a little better than the others but there were days when the team just didn't seem to have the proper appetite for battle.

That day in '92 I suspect was the first sign of a softening in the Tipperary team. As John Fitzgibbon and Tomas Mulcahy scored second-half goals for Cork, there was very little response from Tipp. When it was put up to us physically, we looked vulnerable. We looked a team ready to crack.

And I'm not sure that would have happened in '91.

It was desperately disappointing to be part of what was happening. Because I think, effectively, we had given up long before the final whistle.

And that was inexcusable.

Brian Corcoran emerged the star of the show that day for the marking job he did on Pat Fox. Corcoran certainly played well but Pat was clearly below his best. In most instances, Fox was getting to the ball ahead of Corcoran but his first touch kept letting him down and the Corkman spent the day sweeping up breaking ball.

I had a great chance to turn things around for Tipp and possibly exorcise my own personal demons ten minutes from the end. But I couldn't take it.

As I raced in towards Ger Cunningham, I was obsessed with the thought of making absolutely sure that we got a goal. Rather than shoot myself, I passed inside to Fox and the pass was a bad one.

On reflection, I should definitely have shot myself and maybe my decision was down to a basic lack of confidence. I had worked so hard to get myself physically right for this moment and now my whole year was condensed into that one decision.

I know a lot of people said afterwards that the 'English of old' would have buried the sliothar in the back of Cunningham's net. And maybe he would have.

I ended the game scoreless and, if Tipp had been done few favours by the referee, we also knew that our most fundamental problems lay deep within ourselves. Declan Ryan got a late goal to give the scoreline a respectable look but, long before the end, we were a beaten team.

All the negative signals we had taken a few weeks previously from our losing League final display against Limerick in the Gaelic Grounds had been rudely reaffirmed here. There was something lacking in the fibre of the team.

We had led Limerick 0-11 to 0-3 at half-time in that game only to virtually acquiesce for the remainder. It was an astonishing collapse, but one largely overshadowed by the raucous celebrations of Limerick's supporters.

So accustomed to losing games against Tipperary, Limerick's response to Ray Sampson's late winning point was to celebrate wildly. It was the first time they had beaten us in a game of any significance for many years.

The next morning's newspapers focused more on Limerick's courage than Tipp's strange queasiness. In hindsight, the latter might have been more relevant.

Buoyed by their victory, Limerick went to Pairc Uí Chaoimh full of confidence for the Munster final but were ripped asunder by a rampant Cork. It was an odd but surprisingly pleasant experience going to that game as a spectator.

Tipp had been involved in the previous five Munster finals and I suspect, deep down, there might have been a certain relief among players to actually get a breather from the pressures.

It was actually lovely to be able to have a few beers and watch the game dispassionately.

The flip side, of course, was seeing Limerick get totally destroyed and knowing that, in a proper frame of mind, Tipp would have had a great chance of going all the way to the All-Ireland final.

Galling too to think that, after my own hardships of '91, my legs were now in perfect working order.

I was fighting fit but there was nothing left to play for.

Or so I thought. It just so happened that the year would end on an incredible high for me.

One of the most precious medals I possess was won on a filthy day that November.

It is a county junior championship hurling medal collected after Lattin-Cullen staged a dramatic late surge to beat North Tipp opponents, Ballinahinch, in a memorable final.

For years, this had been an ambition within the club but we endured a couple of disastrous seasons immediately prior to '92 and some of us probably despaired that we would ever see the day. But it came to pass on that wretched evening in Cappawhite and I will never forget the feeling.

People have often wondered why I never bothered to join a bigger club, given the profile I received from hurling with Tipperary. While at UCC, I had a share of offers from Cork clubs and, since moving to Dublin, some of the city clubs have approached me too.

Why didn't I join?

Well to be honest, if I ever had doubts about staying with Lattin-Cullen, that day in '92 erased them. To win that Championship gave me as big a thrill as anything I've ever won in a Tipperary jersey.

The game seemed to have gone away from us until we managed to score an unanswered 1-2 in the last five minutes to scramble home by two points.

It was the first county hurling championship that the parish had ever claimed and the celebrations went on for many weeks afterwards.

All my life I have played with the club. It used to be that the other players would joke to me that I was 'stuck' with them. Now I tell them that they're stuck with me!

There is a sense of place in playing for your home club that I don't think I could ever have attained elsewhere. Look at it this way, that junior medal won with Lattin-Cullen meant so much more to me than any Cork or Dublin senior championship could ever have done.

Even a few years ago, when we joined forces with Annacarty, I'm not sure it would have meant as much for us if we went on and won the Tipp senior Championship.

Being fair, the club has never been demanding of me so my loyalty hasn't called for any tremendous sacrifices.

Generally, we could put out a decent football team but hurling was always a more difficult battle. Through the late seventies and early eighties especially, Lattin-Cullen were good enough probably to have won a county senior football title.

We actually got to the county semi-finals in 1980 but Galtee Rovers beat us.

Hurling, effectively, was the poor relation although there were sporadic successes. The ground broken in '92 might actually have given way three years sooner but for the presence of a young Johnny Leahy in the Mullinahone teams that contested the West junior hurling final and intermediate football final against us in '89.

Johnny was a real hero in Mullinahone as he was bringing them back virtually from nowhere at the time. They beat us in the hurling. We won the football.

Just like the county scene, clubs are effectively divided into quite separate categories. There are the major clubs that carry a virtual obligation to be winning trophies all the time. Then, there are the others for whom – most of the time – competing is the thrill and winning an occasional bonus.

Last year, Lattin-Cullen got to another Tipp county senior football semi-final but, again, we just couldn't quite take those last few steps for the bigger prize.

The people I've played with at club level are friends for life and the memory of that day in '92 will stay with me to my grave. Our goalkeeper back then was Eddie Morrissey who was 47 at the time.

Eddie first played with Lattin-Cullen in 1963 and, when we finally got around to winning that junior title, he had two brothers and two sons on the team with him.

It was the kind of team-sheet you wouldn't come across in the 'Big Smoke'.

XXV
MISS IRELAND AND ME

BOBBY Ryan was never a man to tip-toe with something on his mind.

'What kind of a f...ing eejit are you?' he yelled as he came into the bedroom. It was about quarter to eleven on a Saturday night in February of '93 and we were staying in the Carrickdale Hotel near the border a few miles south of Newry.

Tipperary were playing a League game against Down in Ballycran the following day and, although just a substitute, I had been feeling tired and decided to go to bed early. Bobby had gone for a few drinks and I became a bit agitated with him now for disturbing me.

'What are you on about Bobby?' I snapped.

'Are you going out with some woman in Dublin?' he asked.

'What?'

'I was just talking to Skippy (Michael Cleary) down there and he says there is something in a magazine about you going out with Olivia Treacy.'

'What in the name of Jesus are you on about?' I said, lifting myself from the pillow.

'Skippy says it's in a magazine, down in black and white. What's the story? Is it true?'

I looked across at Bobby and gasped, 'You can't be f...ing serious'.

Straight away, I picked up the phone and rang Anne. She was at home in Waterford that night because her sister, Susan, was over from England for the weekend. 'Look' I said 'Bobby says there's something in a magazine about me.'

I couldn't believe I was having to make this phone-call, but – if someone had written this – it was better Anne heard it from me first. She was as incredulous as I was and said she would check it out the following morning at the local newsagent's.

That morning, we went to eleven o'clock Mass and I thought about going to 'Skippy' and saying something. But I decided it was best to leave things until I heard back from Anne.

Down in Waterford, she couldn't bring herself to check the magazine in question so she sent Susan in instead. Susan signalled out through the shop window that it was true.

The magazine claimed that 'Former Miss Ireland, Olivia Treacy, is rumoured to be seeing Tipperary hurler, Nicky English.'

Anne rang me with the news and I couldn't believe my ears. I knew who Olivia Treacy was but had never met her in my life. Now we were supposed to be having an affair!

So, while my wife was down in Waterford trying to come to terms with this 'revelation', I was a few hundred miles away preparing for a game of hurling. It felt too bizarre for words.

Sitting on the bench that day, my mind was a thousand miles away from hurling. I just could not believe what was happening. The magazine in question had already been on the shelves for ten days and God only knew how many people had now read it.

I sat thinking that the story could have such serious implications in every aspect of my life. Firstly, it could wreck my marriage. Anne was, clearly, upset and confused and I could hardly blame her.

But there was also the question of my work. I remember wondering what on earth my employers would think. As an investment advisor, I had to be seen as someone with a certain integrity. The last thing I needed was to be depicted as a married man-about-town.

With about ten minutes to go, 'Babs' sent me on in a game that had its share of needle. Down were still angry over a newspaper article by Declan Carr the previous August in which he claimed that teams of their status had no business playing in an All-Ireland semi-final.

The game was ferociously contested right to the end when miraculously – given my mental state – I managed to score the winning point.

It seemed to take forever to get home that evening and Anne was already in bed by the time I got in. I wanted to talk to her, to stress how ludicrous the story was, to make sure she understood that it just wasn't true.

I mean even thinking about it all now is a little unreal. How could a magazine just write this? How could they just print a blatant lie without a thought for the damage it might do?

I had never met Olivia Treacy in my life. In fact, as the story developed, it would become clear that she was just as bewildered and annoyed as I was by the article.

Unfortunately, people tend to see the written word as gospel. Or, at least, they are inclined to argue that there is rarely 'smoke without fire.' The very fact that Bobby Ryan had to ask me if it was true showed the kind of damage this was doing. Bobby knew me as well as any man and yet even he was beginning to wonder.

First thing next morning, I went in to see my boss in AIB. I wanted to bring up the subject with him before he brought it up with me. To put my cards on the table. This was the kind of rumour that would obviously impact on my job if it gathered any momentum.

As it happened, the magazine had already been seen by people within the bank. Business-wise, it was obviously a black mark.

That same day, I met my solicitor and he immediately sent a letter to the magazine. They subsequently issued an apology, accepting totally that the story had been untrue.

But I felt that 'sorry' wasn't really worth the paper it came written on.

It struck me that sometimes an apology appears not necessarily because a story printed has proved untrue but because, legally, it is just a little dangerous. I wanted people to *know* the story was nonsense. I needed them to know that.

At first, admittedly, I had no conception of just how far the rumour had flown. But, slowly, the full scale of it began to dawn.

One day my mother went to visit a friend in hospital and started chatting with another visitor. When she said that she was from Cullen, this man responded 'Isn't that where Nicky English comes from?'

Maura said it was. She knew she should have told him who she was but I suppose this was her way of testing the waters. She wanted to see if he would make any reference to the magazine story. And that was her mistake.

'Is there any truth in the rumour that he's supposed to be carrying on with a model above in Dublin?' the visitor enquired. My mother had already seen the magazine but nothing could have prepared her for hearing it put so bluntly.

It was obvious now that the impression people were taking from the story was that, effectively, I had lost the run of myself in Dublin.

In training with Tipperary now, the people who knew me best – like 'Babs', Joe Hayes, Bobby and Pat Fox – tried to lighten my mood by slagging. But, slowly, they began to realise just how serious the thing had become. Soon enough they just dropped the subject.

The whole thing, naturally, was having a bad effect on Anne and my own mood started to deteriorate. Looking back, it was the toughest time I ever endured.

By and large, my life has been a bed of roses. I have faced no great personal grief apart from an uncle I was reasonably close to dying. Effectively, hurling has shaped my moods.

But here, for a time, the game just ceased to matter. I remember playing the National League semi-final that year against Cork in Semple Stadium and getting cat-calls from the crowd during the parade. It was just impossible to concentrate on anything.

Maybe a month later, as the Championship opener against Kerry loomed, I remember Anne took herself away for a week's holidays. Mentally and physically, I was feeling absolutely jaded. I remember saying to a friend of ours, Mary McCormack, how tired I felt. That, for the first time in my life, I didn't want to go training that evening. That I didn't want to hurl.

Basically, I just wanted to lock myself away, to forget about all that was happening.

Mary told me to keep going, to take myself down to Thurles and not give in.

That night I pulled a thigh muscle that would keep me out of the Kerry game. It would also, effectively, ensure that I was only a substitute for the subsequent Munster final against Clare. But there was so much going on in my head, I didn't really give a damn.

I just got to the stage where I recoiled from everything, where I wanted to hide. More and more, I was getting these cat-calls from the terraces, having snide comments made to me on the playing field.

Typical of this was a game later that summer with Lattin-Cullen in the Junior Sevens. We were playing a Clare team and, out of the blue, one of their players started to have a go at me about my alleged 'affair'.

This guy didn't really know me but the rumours had, by now, gathered such momentum, the magazine's lie was now openly in the public domain. It seemed the whole country had seen the article, nobody the retraction.

We had long since decided that the only option available to me was to go to court. I simply had to get a public platform for the truth. This rumour had taken hold like a bush fire and it was throwing my whole life into turmoil.

Just how deeply affected I was struck me on the day of the Munster final. That afternoon at the Gaelic Grounds, I wore the number17 jersey in the Tipperary dug-out and remember actually feeling relieved to be in there. My instinct was just to hide, to stay away from the pitch where someone might say something derogatory.

Never before or since have I been happy to be left off Tipp's starting fifteen. But that day it just felt safer to be sitting with the other substitutes and team officials.

But how can you portray those feelings to a jury of strangers?

The thought of taking the stand in the High Court and talking about my personal life just filled me with a certain terror. The only other time I had been in court was as a witness to a motor accident.

Now I would have to take the stand to deal with barristers. To talk about the most private aspects of my personal life. My mother and father would have to be there with me too. I remember wondering what was going through their minds.

Could they ever have imagined that my hurling career would lead me to this juncture?

All my life, I have been very guarded about my privacy. I have never been in the habit of discussing relationships with anyone – parents included. That's just my nature.

Now, simply to undo someone else's error, I found myself facing the prospect of having to take the stand and face questions about my relationship with my wife. The prospect made me almost sick with fear.

It was never going to be too difficult to mount a case for damages. My life, Anne's life, the lives of our parents had all been hugely affected by one piece of ludicrously careless journalism. I needed to take this as far as I could, to show that this kind of 'reporting' was simply not acceptable.

But I found the prospect of having to discuss it all in court more than a little daunting.

The case eventually came up before the High Court in February of '95. I will never forget that morning, the absolute terror I felt at the ordeal that seemed to lie ahead. But, thankfully, I never did have to take the stand.

It just never came to that. Aware of the weight of evidence against them, the magazine agreed a settlement with which I was happy. Money, quite honestly, had never been my motivation. I wanted just to walk out of that court-room publicly acknowledged as an innocent man. I wanted the rumour buried for once and for all.

If I live to be a hundred now, I don't ever want to endure that kind of trauma again. Of all the hurling venues I've played in, none has ever unnerved me like the High Court managed that morning.

And, to this day, I have never actually met Olivia Treacy.

She is obviously a beautiful-looking woman and, some months after the court case, I saw her on St Stephen's Green. I was walking along with a friend of mine from work, John Moriarty, when suddenly we saw her coming towards us.

John and I almost froze as she approached. It was one of those surreal moments where everything seems suspended in slow motion. We stood there staring, wondering if she might recognise me as the man who was once, supposedly, having an affair with her.

But Olivia didn't know me from Adam and kept on walking.

I was just another wide-eyed stranger.

XXVI
ELEPHANT MAN

IT was the dirtiest blow I ever took on a hurling field.

Through the last fifteen years, I've faced some of the hardest, supposedly most fearsome men in hurling. For sure, I've come across my share of intimidation.

Hurling is a physical game. You don't expect defenders to be sheepishly compliant when you're hell-bent on getting through to the goal behind them.

Ultimately, though, there is a line of behaviour you trust will not be crossed. In the wrong man's hands, you see, a hurley is a pretty lethal weapon. So trust is fundamental to playing the game.

During one match, indelibly printed on my mind, I believe that this line was crossed. It was during the National League semi-final against Cork played in Thurles three years ago. I've tried many times to rationalise what happened and to locate some fragment of explanation for the incident.

But the fact is that when the hurley was whipped flush into my face, the player responsible was pulling towards his own goal!

The incident happened about 15 minutes from the end of a tight game when I caught a ball in the left-half forward position.

Taking the ball in my left hand, I held out my right to shield myself from the marker. Suddenly, he just pulled across me, the bas of his hurley slamming into my face. It was an unbelievable blow and I went straight down.

Even now, when I think about it, I get angry. At the time, shock numbed all my senses and, after a little treatment, I actually played on to finish the game. You see, initially, the damage done didn't look too worrying.

The cut inflicted was small, requiring just one stitch. But I had suffered internal injuries, the extent of which would only come to light that evening.

Unfortunately, the incident wasn't highlighted on television. In early spring, matches aren't dissected and analysed to anything like the extent we have become accustomed to once the Championship gathers steam in summer. So effectively, the culprit – who was sent off – seemed to be getting off lightly as far as I was concerned.

The only consolation for me was that his manager, Fr Michael O'Brien, did not let the incident pass without comment and I will always have great respect for the way he subsequently came out in criticism of the blow that mangled my face that day.

O'Brien was asked about the incident after the game and remarked in the national press, "I always tell my team to play the ball. I'll not take that sort of nonsense from any man." It was a brave move. A manager does not endear himself to the public by criticising 'one of his own'. People would have seen that as a kind of betrayal, to side with a player from an opposing team against a player from his own dressing-room.

I know the stance he took caused problems for him later on.

But in view of the severity of the blow and the circumstances, it was to his eternal credit that he did not stay silent.

The extent of the damage inflicted dawned on me after the game – which Tipp lost – as both of my eyes began to swell and blacken.

I went to work the following morning and was quite a picture turning up with two black eyes, both of them now virtually closed.

Gradually the pain became just too intense and, as the morning wore on, I had to excuse myself from work and go home. My head felt like it was going to split and I was beginning to look a little like 'The Elephant Man'.

That week, I went to a soccer international at Lansdowne Road, the damage to my face safely concealed behind dark glasses like a boxer the morning after a 12-round epic. Niall Quinn had given me a ticket for the players' post-match function and I went into the reception feeling more than a little self-conscious.

Eventually, curiosity got the better of some of the players and they asked me to remove the glasses. I will never forget the look on their faces when they saw my eyes.

Someone pointed me out to Jack Charlton and he came over to ask what had happened. I think he thought I must have been a mugging victim or someone recuperating from a bad car accident.

'I was playing a hurling match,' I told him.

Charlton was absolutely incredulous. 'You're all daft, you lot,' he gasped. 'How anyone will play that game without being paid for it is beyond me.'

I suppose it must have looked a little ridiculous to the superstars present. Some of them would have been earning as much as £6,000 a week without ever having to worry about taking the kind of blow I had taken.

It was, without question, the worst thing that ever happened me on a hurling field. I must admit I still find it difficult to forgive the player for what happened to me that day. And I have the photographs to remind me of the damage.

I don't know how the player in question felt at the time. But it was a disappointment to me that at no point did he either apologise or enquire afterwards about my well-being.

I would consider myself friendly with a lot of rival players I've encountered over the years. Men like Ger Cunningham, Tony O'Sullivan and Tomas Mulcahy were involved in some of the most momentous Cork-Tipp battles of the last decade and a half.

But all are gentlemen who knew the extremes you could and could not take the rivalry to.

As a rule, differences on the field were never taken beyond the perimeter fence. No quarter is asked or given in Championship games especially, but you don't acquire a hatred for someone just because they hit you hard.

I mean few people were more physical over the years than Galway's Sylvie Linnane. Sylvie always played hard and it was certainly not beyond him to draw the occasional wild swipe. He liked to act gruff and confrontational.

As most people know, I had my own little run-in with him during the 1989 All-Ireland semi-final.

But, at the end of the day, Sylvie went out to hurl. He didn't see his job in any kind of cynical way. In other words, he wasn't a player focused exclusively on upsetting the man he was marking.

I was always struck by how vocal that Galway team could be. Even now, I can hear their voices bellowing across Croke Park. People like Linnane, Hayes, Finnerty, Keady and the Kilkennys urging and cajoling one another to greater effort.

It always seemed to me that Tipp, by comparison, were pretty quiet.

Tony Kilkenny was one of the worst players I ever faced in terms of getting beneath your skin. I would put it that he was good at being destructive.

Not in any kind of vicious way, you understand. It's just that he was happy to annoy an opponent for 70 minutes even if it meant sacrificing his own game. Tony would be content to grapple with you all day in the knowledge that it was keeping you out of the game.

Ollie, too, saw his role essentially as one of knocking people out of their rhythm.

One player I never seemed able to get on with was Cork defender, Dermot McCurtain. We clashed first during my senior Munster Championship debut in 1982 and it was pretty much downhill from there.

It started when somebody struck Donie O'Connell and he fell to the ground bleeding. Determined to prove my manhood, I immediately went in search of the culprit.

Donie seemed to think that McCurtain was to blame so I ran across and hit him the proverbial 'box in the gob'. As you might expect, it wasn't much appreciated.

We clashed again during the drawn Munster final of '87 when, effectively, we just started trading blows in the middle of the field. The referee moved in and, mysteriously, went to book Denis Mulcahy and myself.

Mulcahy's facial expression made it patently clear that he was an innocent man so the referee, realising he had the wrong person, let us both off with a warning.

Looking back, Mulcahy was probably the toughest opponent I ever faced. He was quick off the mark and, physically, very strong. I always found him pretty fair and was surprised by the way in which he removed Cormac Bonnar from our '92 Championship clash at Pairc Uí Chaoimh.

It always struck me that, had that incident happened a year earlier, the entire Tipperary team would have been in on top of Mulcahy before he could draw breath.

But the severe hunger had left us then, the kind of hunger that all successful Championship teams must carry. The hunger of Clare in '95 and Wexford in '96.

It is not a thing you can create through someone just roaring at you in the dressing-room. No, it has to go deeper. Sometimes, the best thing that can happen a team going into the Championship is to have some gripe or needle in the back of their minds against the opposition.

It amuses me when I hear people say that that Tipperary team didn't win as many All-Irelands as they should have. In my book, we should be thankful for what we got. Just think of the great players who never even came close to lifting the Liam McCarthy Cup.

Until September, I would have categorised George O'Connor of Wexford among them. George's commitment to the cause was nothing short of astounding as his county seemed to flounder from one hard luck story to another.

Watching him climb the steps of the Hogan Stand this year was one of the truly memorable pictures of the Championship.

I also always had huge respect for an old comrade of his, John Conran. One of my stronger points as a player was my ability to catch high balls but, when I think of Conran, I think of cold, miserable days in Enniscorthy and Conran plucking puck-outs from over my head.

The guy was a phenomenal wing-back who deserved the kind of prize that George had to wait so long for.

Another guy who sticks in my mind for his fielding is Galway's Gerry McInerney. I had always considered him the weakest of the famous Galway half-back line, having marked him at one point in the '87 All-Ireland semi-final.

But, when we faced Galway in '93, McInerney lined out at centre-back and broke our hearts (mine particularly for a while) with his majesty beneath the high ball.

I've had my share of little altercations through the years but, generally, I'd like to think that I'm not walking from the game with too many enemies.

By and large, players don't trade insults on the field. If anything, it's a lot more civilised out there than most people seem to imagine.

Funnily, some of the most fearsome opponents I've encountered have also turned out to be most decent of men.

When I was playing against him, I always considered Brendan Lynskey a real rough diamond.

But I've gotten to know him in the last few years and he happens to be a thorough gentleman. In many ways, the complete opposite of what I imagined him to be on the field.

Now I wouldn't dream of driving past his door without stopping for a chat.

There are many other countymen too whose friendship I hope to keep long into my retirement.

Maybe part of the mellowing process that comes with age is a realisation that the 'enemy' don't always have horns coming out of their foreheads.

XXVII
'YOU WERE THE ONE WHO LAUGHED AT US'

MURPHY'S Law seemed my constant companion through much of '93.

The blow in Thurles allied to rumours about my private life and a subsequent calf muscle injury all gelled into something of an on-going nightmare.

I missed the opening Championship game with Kerry and was just a substitute for the Munster final clash with Clare. Now there was a day when nothing could have gone wrong for any Tipp man.

Or could it?

Tipp demolished Len Gaynor's team in that final by 3-27 to 2-12 having led by fourteen points after just 24 minutes. It was a freakish kind of game in which everything the team attempted just seemed to come good.

Long before the end, they were just going bananas in the forwards, scoring virtually at will. Clare's heads were down and the game, in many ways, deteriorated into a training run for Tipperary.

Anthony Crosse had taken over from Cormac Bonnar as our full-forward and, on this evidence, looked like he was going to fit seamlessly into the big man's shoes. But then the game was so lacking in a seriously competitive edge, it was difficult to make any definitive judgements.

I was sent on midway through the second-half and helped myself to four points from play as the massacre was played out. It was a meaningless performance that shouldn't have had any long-term repercussions. But sadly, from my viewpoint, nothing about this summer was proving simple.

The first score I got was set up for me by Declan Ryan. He got the ball right in front of the Clare goal and seemed to hold it for an age before tapping it across to me for one of the easiest points imaginable.

Declan would have had no problem scoring himself and I was well aware of that. If anything, I felt he was treating me like a bit of an old cripple by holding onto the ball so long to set me up in a scoring position.

So, having scored, I looked across at him and grinned. I felt as if he was helping me like you'd help an invalid. If anything, I felt that he was having a bit of a laugh at me.

Little did I know that that moment would burn a hole in certain Clare minds. Given time, it would emerge that many Clare people thought I was laughing at them, that I was poking fun at the predicament they now found themselves in.

If I'm honest, I can see now how it must have looked to them. Tipp were winning in a canter and here was this 'smart alec' coming in off the bench to have his bit of fun at their expense. But nothing could have been further from my intentions.

I just found it more than a little amusing that one of my team-mates would go to such lengths to 'take the piss' out of me.

Sadly, Clare players and supporters took it that we were trying to make fools of them and maybe – if the roles were reversed – I would have reacted in exactly the same way. But the truth of the matter was that, if anything, the joke was on me, not Clare.

It was an incident that would crop up in less than pleasant circumstances over the next couple of years. Twelve months later, when Clare took their revenge, I was verbally abused by one of their supporters who was drinking in the Limerick Inn.

'You were the one bollocks who was laughing at us last year,' he roared at me.

It turned out that Anthony Daly and his team-mates had used the incident as a huge motivating factor for revenge in '94. Even before that game, I had become aware of how deep-rooted the feelings were.

There had never been any hint of hatred between Tipp and Clare but now it existed in full flood.

Actually, it even cropped up again when we played Clare in our first League game of '95. It was played in Ennis and Daly let Pat Fox and myself know fairly bluntly what he thought of us.

Anyway, having demolished Clare in '93, Tipp went to Croke Park as virtually unbackable favourites for their semi-final game with Galway. The week before that game, 'Babs' was quoted as saying that the whole country wanted to see a Tipperary-Kilkenny final.

It subsequently emerged, that the Galway team played a tape of 'Babs' interview repetitively during their bus-ride to Croke Park. Then they proceeded to rip into us like never before.

Not for the first time, too much had been read into an emphatic Tipperary performance. Having swaggered out of Munster, we were probably just what Galway ordered.

There was controversy even before we got to Dublin with team-captain, Michael O'Meara, being dropped from centre-back to allow Bobby Ryan resume in a position from which he had won two All-Ireland medals. The Toomevara man thus became Tipp's third captain to be dropped in mid-Championship in five years.

All in all, there was an air of presumption about Tipperary that day in Croke Park. Even our supporters only travelled in small numbers, most seemingly saving themselves for the 'big one' with Kilkenny.

As it happened, we played pathetically on the day. Galway weren't exactly exhilarating either but an early mistake by Ken Hogan – a feeble shot bouncing awkwardly off his hurley across the line – gave them the kind of impetus they needed.

I have often looked at the video of this game and would genuinely regard it as the poorest of the major Galway-Tipp collisions in recent years.

Tipperary were dealt a massive blow ten minutes from half-time when Declan Ryan had to go off with a bad knee injury. Declan's departure took a lot of Tipp's physical presence from the forward line.

But the problems were compounded on the sideline when it was decided to make a double substitution, Colm Bonnar also being called ashore. The decision hinted at panic and the body-language confirmed it.

Galway led comfortably at half-time and the atmosphere in the dressing-room was one of pandemonium. It was as if we trailed by twenty points the way everyone was shouting. Even the team doctor, John Keating, lobbed a few unexpected grenades in the players' direction.

I will always remember especially the comment of one Tipperary selector. He shouted that there were some of us who, if we lost, would never see Croke Park again. 'You might as well throw your boots into the Liffey,' he said.

I had no problem with what he was saying. In fact, time showed him to be absolutely right. A lot of us never did get back to Croke Park afterwards.

It was the timing that he got wrong. He should have delayed saying his piece until we were ready to leave that dressing-room. It would have been the perfect parting shot as we went thundering down the tunnel for 35 minutes of make-or-break.

Instead, it was said the moment we arrived in and everyone was left sitting there, fidgeting with apprehension. If anything, the timing of his outburst left us more jittery.

The second-half went no better than the first, our sense of general panic remaining pretty much intact. We started accumulating wides at a crazy rate and, despite getting close, we never managed to haul Galway in.

I was as culpable as anyone, pulling an effort from the 21-yard line badly wide and – generally – feeding on the panic. Then we had Ramie Ryan and Paul Delaney crashing into one another on the Cusack Stand side, Ramie being stretchered away after a lengthy stoppage.

I've often looked at the video since and it was a terribly poor game. To this day, I'm convinced that Galway expected to lose it but were just pleasantly surprised by the chaos in Tipp's play.

The day after, we met for a few pints and – not for the first time – discovered that out of the Championship, you were left to your own devices. For a day, you could forget your sorrows and just enjoy each other's company. In Tommy Wright's pub on the quays, we met for a presentation to Cormac Bonnar who had retired.

Joe Hayes became self-appointed master of ceremonies and typically, started giving a commentary about Colm being 'taken off again'. Every now and then, Joe would look out the window and groan, 'Oh God, there's another pair of boots going down the Liffey.'

Joe was calling the event 'The Bonnars' farewell to Croke Park'.

He was one of the great characters of the dressing-room during my time with Tipperary and also a man that 'Babs' had great time for.

In '93 he had been suffering from an ankle injury and was going particularly badly when 'Babs' dropped him. So Joe rang 'Babs' wife, Nancy, and protested that surely he couldn't be dropped after his service to Tipp since '87.

On this particular day, we were playing a challenge match against Laois in Thurles and, while those of us based in Dublin were driving down with 'Babs', he told us of a phone conversation he had had earlier with Joe.

'Babs' had said to him, 'You'll have to play against Laois tonight for me Joe. I'll play you in the middle of the field. I'll give you your chance.'

Joe was protesting that he was injured, that he couldn't play. 'It's like signing my own death warrant,' he argued.

Afterwards, he would reveal that he bought some kind of fancy isotonic drink for 'twenty two quid' to try and get himself right for the game. 'Didn't know whether to throw it into the bath or drink it,' he admitted.

Anyway, Joe arrived into the dressing-room that evening without as much as a hurley. Mick Ryan, who was still one of the younger guys on the panel, had a beautiful new hurley which Joe took off him, protesting that this was 'an emergency'.

Then he went over to Colm Bonnar who was to play alongside him in midfield. Now it never made the slightest difference to Colm who he was asked to mark because he really wouldn't recognise one opponent from the other.

But that day, Laois would have big Niall Rigney in the centre of the field and Joe just didn't fancy his chances against him. So he said to Colm, 'Look, I'm gone. Will you take Rigney?'

Colm agreed that he would. The truth was that he wouldn't have known Rigney from the other midfielder and, actually, managed to identify him before the throw-in only because of the name written on his hurley.

So Joe goes out and hurls all around him, sticking over something like four points in the process. Rigney, meanwhile, cleans out Colm who is then dropped for Tipp's next game.

Joe is picked.

So you can see the irony of his little cabaret act the day after Galway knocked us from the Championship.

People might find these kind of images difficult to relate to a team that has just been beaten in an All-Ireland semi-final. But you train so hard for the Championship that, when it ends prematurely, all you really want to do is switch off.

You have been so disciplined, so structured in your life for the previous six months that you need some kind of release valve.

We all knew that this Tipperary team was fast approaching a crucial crossroads in its existence. Individually, some of us knew too that time might just be catching up on us.

Cormac Bonnar had retired – reputedly under management's persuasion – earlier in the year and I was certainly becoming aware of my own feelings of vulnerability on a hurling field. More and more it was being said that Tipp lacked a certain 'steel' at the business-end of games. It was implied that our attitude was a little suspect. That we didn't like it when a physical challenge was put up to us.

It was a thought that would sit with me through the coming winter.

Personally, I had started to feel a little soft. I was beginning to wonder whether or not I still had the physical toughness for hurling at the highest level. As a new season dawned, I became aware of a definite sense of apathy within the Tipp panel. And, if anything, I shared it.

Liam Hennessy got those of us who were Dublin-based training up in St Columba's College on Tuesday nights. People like Brendan Carroll had joined the panel and his appetite for training on those miserable winter nights just seemed to remind me of my own decline.

At the end of January, with 'Babs' away in Dubai, we played a challenge match against county champions, Toomevara, and lost heavily. It was a pathetic match and it was impossible to feel in any way positive about the season ahead.

A week later, we were expected down for training in Thurles the same day as the Railway Cup final. This was the first time in years I hadn't been selected to play for my province. My attitude shocked me.

Rather than harbour disappointment, I felt only relief that I wouldn't be driving all the way to Ennis where the game was being played. In fact, I didn't even go to Thurles the same day, as Hennessy had the flu. There was just no way I was interested in travelling on my own.

As the League resumed, we lost our supposed 'revenge' match against Galway in Nenagh after which 'Babs' turned on us furiously in the dressing-room.

On the drive back to Dublin that evening, I talked long and hard with Anne about whether or not I should just pack it in. I had scored a goal in the game – my first goal in a competitive inter-county assignment for exactly two years – but there was little to feel enthused by.

Still, as winter mellows into spring, a hurler's appetite invariably returns. Even the bleakest of scenarios somehow brightens when you notice the slight lengthening of the evenings and the softening of the frost.

So many times, I have been totally devoid of appetite for the game in January and February only to sense the hunger return in March. It's human nature. When sleet is stinging your face, you can think of many places you'd prefer to be.

That spring, I travelled across to London with Mayo footballer – Willie Joe Padden – to help launch a new GAA lotto scheme there. It was a trip that really brought home to me just how utterly hurling had shaped my life since childhood.

While in London, I renewed acquaintance with my old friend and team-mate, Martin McGrath. I had played minor, under-21 and senior inter-county hurling alongside Martin and I've often thought that the three points he scored against Cork in Killarney in 1987 were three of the most important points ever scored for Tipperary.

Martin is exactly the same age as me, but he had been living in London for five years now. And he was married with three little children, all of them girls.

It felt strange to be sitting there listening to him talk about family life, about driving the kids to school or ballet classes, about going to parent-teacher meetings. It seemed so out of character for the guy I used to go training with.

My problem, of course, was that I kept clinging to the past.

Martin was after announcing his retirement, his club having just won the London Championship. I couldn't help thinking how contented he looked and sounded.

At home, the shape of the Tipperary team was now beginning to change. People like Ken Hogan, Bobby Ryan, Donie O'Connell and Conor O'Donovan were gone from the scene and I was very much considered one of the elder statesmen.

Weary of the leg injuries that had started to blight my career, I decided that maybe the best medicine was just to try strengthening them by playing in every game available. And that's exactly what I did.

Challenge games, pitch-openings, every kind of football match with Lattin-Cullen, I submitted myself happily to them all. I had decided to blank injuries from my mind and I actually began to play really well again.

Tipp, too, started to move with a fresh momentum and – suddenly – the pessimism of winter gave way to new hopes and ambitions.

After a week of fractious debate over the venue, we played Kilkenny in a League quarter-final at Croke Park and beat them well (2-18 to 1-12). Pat Fox and myself scored the Tipp goals.

Cork were our semi-final opponents and again I found the net but it had the look of a fairly token effort as we went in at half-time trailing 1-2 to 0-10. But Tipp were transformed in the second-half with Anthony Crosse absolutely exceptional and we went on to take what most presumed was a significant psychological scalp for the summer with a 2-13 to 1-13 victory.

A week later we would meet Galway in the final but, by now, I had probably started to ask a little too much of my legs. On the day after the game, I played golf before driving to Dublin that night and then driving back down on the Tuesday evening for training.

On the Wednesday, I went to play a bank match for AIB at the St Vincent's ground in Dublin. I had pushed a step too far.

Just jogging out onto the pitch before the start, I felt a familiar stab of pain from my calf. I had pulled a muscle without even touching the ball.

People often asked me afterwards what, on earth, I was doing playing in a bank match just four days before the League final. But you have to understand that the bank team is, effectively, my club in Dublin. I'm very involved with them and it's difficult to say 'no' when you're asked to play.

Anyway, for the previous three months or so, I had played virtually every game I could for club and county without even once sustaining an injury of any kind. I felt certain that the more I played, the stronger I was becoming.

It became pretty obvious immediately that I was now out of the League final even though Liam Hennessy, typically, never gave up hope. The game was being played in Limerick and, on the Sunday morning, he had me out running up and down a school field to see how the leg responded.

Even though it was tightening right from the start of the fitness test I tried to convince myself that it wasn't too bad and succeeded only in making it far worse. I was out alright and, with our Championship game against Clare only three weeks away, had now done enough damage in the test to ensure I would be under real pressure even to make that.

A virtuoso performance from Johnny Leahy enabled Tipp beat Galway comfortably to claim our first League title since 1988. It also meant that Tipp would be roaring favourites for the Munster Championship.

I started to panic a little as my leg proved slow to heal. Twice during the build-up to the Clare match I actually tweaked the injury in training but didn't want to say anything for fear of Liam Hennessy's reaction.

Meanwhile, Leahy – in the form of his life – was out of the game after badly injuring his ankle while playing a Championship match for Tipperary's footballers. I was at home in Dublin the day that happened, listening to commentary of the game on radio.

And, somehow, I knew that Johnny was going to get injured. Don't ask me how. Just sitting there, listening I had this almost ghoulish sense that something was going to go wrong.

With Johnny gone and Paul Delaney also injured, I was desperate to be passed fit. On the night before the game, Hennessy gave me another fitness test. Almost immediately, the leg broke down.

The repercussions would prove long and spiteful over Johnny and I failing to make the team that faced Clare. Johnny was out because of a football game, me because of a match with the bank that they managed to win by ten goals even without me.

Tipperary supporters just couldn't seem to understand how our commitment had been channelled anything less than exclusively towards the county's hurlers. Even some supposed friends were inclined to 'have a go.'

It would be a talking-point in the county for the remainder of the summer.

'Babs', to be fair, never took it out on us. He understood how Johnny's high level of fitness that summer was as much a legacy of training with the county football team as with the hurlers. Seamus McCarthy was, thus, as entitled to his commitment as anyone else was.

'Babs' knew too the kind of pressure I was under to play those games with the bank. In the light of what was to happen, I appreciated the fact that he didn't start taking cheap shots at me for missing the Clare game.

After all, it was to be his last game in charge of the team.

I remember on the night before the game, Aidan Ryan turned to me and said, 'Jesus, they really hate you down in Clare.' Aidan was friendly with one of the lads on the Clare panel and he had left him in little doubt in relation to their feelings about the '93 Munster final.

It subsequently emerged that Clare were using their anger towards that incident as a huge motivating factor for the game. It had been bad enough to be annihilated by Tipperary in the '93 Munster final. But to be laughed at into the bargain – which was how they had read things – was something they could never tolerate.

From my viewpoint, it was bad enough to be missing the game through injury but to then hear that I was such a fundamental part of Clare's motivation really rubbed salt into the wound.

In the dressing-room before the game, I said a few words to the players. I told them that they probably had no idea of the depth of feeling that was driving Clare into this game.

Now here we were having swanned into Limerick as League champions, the whole country expecting us to win comfortably. And in the room next to us, Clare sat seething.

In many ways, we were sitting ducks.

Pat Fox and myself had agreed as much on the bus-ride to the ground. Clare were on offer at ridiculous odds of 3/1 to beat us. 'You know something?' Pat said. 'If I was a betting man, I'd put a few bob on Clare today.'

I can recall a sense of total frustration, watching the game from the bench. Tipp had plenty of possession but their hurling was never fluent and they just couldn't put an incredibly driven Clare team away.

Always it seemed we were vulnerable to a sucker punch and it came four minutes from the end when Tommy Guilfoyle – who had already scored a goal – got in front of goalkeeper, Jody Grace, to flick a high ball to the net.

Seconds earlier, Fox – who had been sent on to try and save the game – blazed a goal-effort inches over the Clare bar. Somehow, you sensed, the Gods had decreed this would be a day of Clare vengeance.

I didn't even go into the dressing-room when it ended. Johnny Leahy and myself just took ourselves away as quickly as we could from the throng of jubilant Clare and hostile Tipp supporters. I honestly believed my inter-county career was over.

'Babs' would almost certainly go now and a new management team might prefer to start with a clean slate, to discard the old order. I felt I couldn't argue if they did.

As it happened, 'Babs' announced his resignation immediately after the game and I genuinely felt sorry for him. He had brought us from nowhere and now his eight year tenure was ending with a Championship defeat in May.

Yes, May 28 and we were out of the Munster Championship. It was the first time in my career with Tipp that we had been removed from the race so early

Some time later, Limerick would destroy Clare in the Munster final.

XXVIII
'PAT, WE'RE GONE, WE ARE FINISHED'

NOT one of us could have predicted the management team that would replace 'Babs'.

Fr Tom Fogarty's name was always in the hat because of his successes with Tipperary's minors but no-one imagined that Ken Hogan and John Kennedy would be his lieutenants. Both are actually younger than me and would have worn the county jersey for a shorter period of time.

Their appointment took me completely by surprise.

Privately, I had already decided that I wanted to hurl on into '95. Whatever doubts I harboured about my own appetite for the game, I just knew that I couldn't walk away from it all under the clouds of '94.

It would have been lovely to send 'Babs' off with an All-Ireland win but this was definitely the right time for him to go. That said, his departure left an incredible void in the Tipp dressing-room. Fr Tom was a completely different kind of character. A thoroughly gentle man who rarely lost his temper and who tried, as much as possible, to evade the spotlight.

'Babs' had been larger-than-life throughout his tenure. He loved the media focus and, on many occasions, manipulated it to his advantage. On other, well documented days, his tongue could get him into trouble and leave Tipp under more pressure than was necessary.

I spoke to Fr Tom shortly after his appointment and he said that I'd be welcome to rejoin the panel after Christmas. It was exactly what I wanted to hear. On the one hand, I wanted time to recharge my batteries. But, on the other, I needed to know that the new management team believed Nicky English still had a future in the Tipperary jersey.

It felt strange rejoining the panel and seeing Ken and John operating in their new capacity. Both had always been well liked during their playing days but now, by necessity, a certain distance would have to emerge between them and their former team-mates.

Our first League game of '95 was against Clare in Ennis, the day Anthony Daly let Pat Fox and myself know exactly what he thought of us. A new rule had been introduced whereby you could only catch the ball once now on a solo run and that definitely made it difficult for Tipperary.

We had trained extremely hard on the previous Tuesday and Thursday nights and I remember feeling absolutely shattered during the second-half. I had managed to score a couple of first-half points off Brian Lohan but, as the game wore on, our tiredness really showed and Clare ran out emphatic winners.

The next game was against Cork in Pairc Uí Rinn and it was not a contest I would remember with any great fondness.

The court case I had taken over allegations about my private life was held on the previous Thursday. All the pent up stress and apprehension just flooded out of me that day. Anne and myself met up with with some close friends and celebrated well into the early hours.

I wasn't working the following day so, again, we ended up having a few drinks and, basically, exorcising all the frustrations and tensions of the previous 18 months. It was as if an incredible weight had been lifted from us.

All in all, I think I was mentally and physically jaded by the time Sunday came. I tried really hard in the game but it was as if my legs just wouldn't listen to the signals from my head.

It was one of the few occasions in fifteen years that I can remember pulling on a Tipperary jersey when I might well have been better off just sitting at home.

The reality is that you just can't function properly on a hurling field if you're feeling exhausted. And that day in Cork, hard though I tried, I knew I was wasting everyone's time.

We lost heavily and I subsequently pulled a calf muscle in our next game against Laois. Tipp would barely avoid relegation from Division One and our absence from the League play-offs meant a protracted build up to our opening Championship encounter against Waterford at Pairc Uí Chaoimh.

Waiting for that game to come was more than a little unsettling. There were now a lot of new faces in the panel and, apart from Liam Hennessy, the whole back-room staff had changed.

It was impossible to know exactly what was going through the selectors' minds simply because you didn't know what signals to look for. With 'Babs' there had always been one telltale sign.

If 'Babs' stopped talking to you at training sessions, you knew – instinctively – that you weren't going to make the team. It happened to me for the '93 Munster final when I was coming back from injury.

'Babs' just stopped communicating with me and, long before the team was announced, I knew I wouldn't be in it.

This time, I was more than a little relieved to hear my name being called out and, of course, we went on to give Waterford a terrible hiding. Pat Fox came on as a second-half substitute to score 2-4 and we were all thrilled with the quality of our performance.

Later that evening, a few of us went to Larry Tompkins' pub across from the railway station in Cork where we watched the 'Sunday Game'. There had been a flare-up during the second-half of the game but, as no-one was sent off, it never really struck us as being of any great significance.

But the incident came across really badly on television and I will always remember Michael Ryan looking at it and groaning.

Former Antrim player, Ciaran Barr, highlighted the incident on the 'Monday Game' 24 hours later and the debate that ensued prompted the Munster Council to use video evidence in suspending both Ryan and Paul Delaney.

Not for the first time, there seemed little sympathy doing the rounds for Tipp even though this was a virtually unprecedented course of action by the provincial council. Neither Ryan or Delaney had been censured in the referee's report but both were now out of our semi-final against Limerick.

What followed was, in many ways, reflective of Tipp's history.

When we play extremely well, there is a tendency in the county to become a little cocky and presumptuous. Tipp were always vulnerable after their best performances.

When I think back on that Waterford game, we really rubbed it in to them. Goals were flying in almost for fun and we started playing flashy, arrogant hurling. If you were on the wrong end of it, you could see why people hated us.

I actually chipped a bone in my ankle during the game and had to have a pain-killing injection before we faced Limerick. Unlike previous years, I was now extremely relaxed about my hurling. Fatalistic if you like.

I had decided that there had been too much tension in my game virtually since '91. This time, I felt looser, more self-confident. My attitude amounted to *'Que sera sera.'*

But little things can punch big holes in a man's mind.

The week of that Limerick game, my car was broken into and the radio stolen. It happened right outside the house and our dog, 'Blaze', started barking furiously on hearing the intruders. It seems that they were probably worried that he might come out after them, so they flipped the boot-lid and took out one of my hurleys just in case.

There were five in the boot but, unfortunately, they took the wrong one.

I didn't realise exactly what had happened until the following morning when I came down to find the boot partially open. And, sure enough, my worst fears were realised as I looked inside. My favourite hurley was gone.

It's hard to explain just how the right hurley can, basically, become an extension of you when you're playing. No two hurleys are identical and, as such, they all have a quite distinct feel when you are using them.

You can go for years using one that you don't particularly like. I should know. I have done.

But in '95 I felt I had found the perfect hurley. It was just the right size, just the right weight. Using it against Waterford, my touch was really good. In my career, I might have come across maybe five hurleys that I considered perfect. This was one of them and now someone was probably using it for fire-wood.

The first chance I got against Limerick, I mis-hit it, the ball dropping harmlessly into Joe Quaid's hand. It was an easy chance and I'm still convinced I'd have scored if I wasn't 'acclimatising' to a new hurley.

These are the little things that make a difference in big games. Limerick would win the match by a single point so it was hard not to dwell afterwards on thoughts of what might have been.

The game was incredibly tight all through and, although I scored two points and played reasonably well, I was extremely conscious now of how Tipp needed other, more pivotal figures to shine if we were to win the game. Guys like Johnny Leahy.

Johnny played centre-field and I don't think he would disagree with me saying that it was probably one of his worst matches ever in a Tipperary jersey. Subsequent events have shown that Johnny was carrying a lot of demons that would eventually come to the surface.

I felt that day that Johnny didn't really want the ball and he was eventually moved in to corner-forward.

Deep down, I think it's only now that Johnny has come to realise how he has wasted a few years of his career. He is one of the best hurlers I have seen but that day Johnny just wasn't fit enough.

This was a tragedy for Tipperary because, on his day, he is such an inspirational player. I would put Johnny up there with the Brian Whelehans and the DJ Careys. He is a fantastic man to win the ball and lift everyone around him.

During the game, I was moved out to wing-forward which, basically, was Johnny's proper position. It was a bad decision. I felt I was just barely able to hold my own in the corner and was no longer capable of contributing significantly from the wing.

I also thought that Liam McGrath could have been used at centre-forward to curb the inspirational play of Ciaran Carey. Limerick, generally, and Carey, specifically, were not as fit in '95 as they had been in '94 and Tipp failed to take advantage of that.

A huge sadness overcame me when I heard the final whistle. For me, this was the end. I had made my mind up to retire.

Walking from the dressing-room, one of the first people I met was my father. 'You have given us some great years,' he said to me emotionally. 'And I have enjoyed every minute of it.'

It was a little sobering to hear him say those words. Obviously, he thought that I was gone too.

I had told Fr Tom in the dressing-room that I was retiring. He asked me not to make any announcement. 'You played well,' he said. 'And you still have more to offer.'

But the decision seemed a clearcut one to me. All the driving between Dublin and Thurles for training, all the injuries and the set-backs had taken their toll. Living in Dublin, it becomes very difficult to get yourself psyched up for another six months of hard work.

You stop for a while and you go a little soft. Thinking about where I stood now, I said to myself, 'Look, I am going to be no better next year. And, who knows, maybe a little worse.'

That night I went with some of the lads to a disco in Cashel. As the drink flowed, my mood became more melancholy. As long as I live, I will remember looking around the disco at the people and their detachment from the disappointment I was feeling.

Most of them, I imagined, hadn't even bothered going to the game. Tipp had had a small enough following in Cork that day and it seemed to me that the fever of '87-'91 had now left our supporters.

I stood there, looking around this disco and thinking to myself that nobody really gave a damn. Thinking about how I was killing myself to make the journey up and down from Dublin after all these years and that, really, nobody seemed to care too much anymore.

When the disco ended, I left with Pat Fox and we walked together down the street. 'Pat, we're finished, we're f...ed, we're gone,' I said to him.

Fox shouted 'We're not f...ed,' and the two of us started arguing on a street in Cashel at about half three in the morning. Across the road, there was a crowd gathered outside a chip shop and they must have wondered what the hell we were going on about.

I felt incredibly depressed. For fifteen years of my life, I had hurled for Tipperary and it seemed a terrible thing to have to close that door now. I had spent fifteen years living for that corner of the dressing-room I could call my own.

Now, I was certain, that part of my life was over. It had ended that day in Pairc Uí Chaoimh and here I was now arguing with one of my best friends outside a chip shop in Cashel in the early hours of a Monday morning. Worse than that, I could see from the faces of people around us that they were just incapable of understanding the intensity of our disappointment at being out of the Championship race.

It just seemed that no-one gave a damn anymore.

XXIX
MY SECOND HOME

IT'S not the prettiest room you've ever seen.

In fact, it's ugly. A big, grey, high-ceilinged vault wrapped in the coldest concrete. But it's always been clean. Clean and comforting.

From the first day I walked in, I chose a place in the left corner. It's where I've sat for the past 16 years. Sat and laughed and listened.

Everyone has their territory in this room. When I first walked in, this was where Noel O'Dwyer togged out. Twelve years later, when he returned as a selector, Noel was still drawn to this same wall.

You see, in time, every one of us became a slave to habit.

Everyone except Pat Fox that is. Pat is the gypsy of this congregation, always shifting, moving quietly from one harbour to the next without apparent preference.

The rest of us? Life just wouldn't feel right if our routine was tampered with.

I've shared this corner with many team-mates, many friends. Richie Stakelum sat here. So too Donie O'Connell, Bobby and Aidan Ryan, Joe Hayes and even 'Babs'.

Now only Aidan and myself remain, jostling for space with Liam Cahill and Paul Shelly. Decades are being bridged in this little corner.

This year I wanted, above all, to hurl again in Thurles.

To sit in this cold room with the hum of a great crowd overhead.

I know I'll miss this place. I'll miss the rawness of a big-match day, the little nervous images of men biding their time before going to battle.

Always the same faces queuing for a rub from Willie Bennett's coaxing hands. People like Paul Delaney, Noel Sheehy, Conal Bonnar and myself growing fretful for fear Willie will run out of time before he gets to us.

There's Sheehy and Colm Bonnar always talking, Fox always quiet. There's Declan Ryan's booming laugh and his air of easy calm. Declan always looked so in control, so comfortable to be sitting there.

Maybe it was an act but I don't suppose he'll ever tell me.

There's Johnny Leahy always playing with the ball, flicking it, tapping it off the stone floor. Johnny talks to people now, likes to get them going.

He's grown so much from the shy kid I remember when he first came through in 1988.

There's Liam Hennessy with his briefcase and his kit-bag, taking control from the moment he walks through the door. Fit and confident, structuring everything around the findings of his stop-watch.

There's the queue for the toilet, the high-fives and back slaps that are meant to mellow nerves.

There's Aidan, so quiet and pasty-looking people think he must be timid. Hasn't been the same since he had his 'heart attack' a few years back! If only they knew what we know about Aidan's toughness.

There's Colm, always stretching the last little strains out of his perfectly sculpted body. Our Mr Universe, that's Colm.

There's little Georgie Frend, never afraid to say his piece. A small, slight man who wins respect with every syllable.

Certain faces linger too, long after they've departed. Donie O'Connell always jibing Bobby and Bobby exploding with the laughter.

Cormac Bonnar working meticulously on his bandages, one forming a bandanna across his thinning forehead, a hundred others meshing to knit protection for his leg.

Remember the '91 All-Ireland final? He was like a mummy running out on the field.

There's 'Babs' with his monster kit-bag, always jabbing and blackguarding someone.

There are the goalkeepers with their solid disciplines. Pat McLoughney, John Sheedy, Ken Hogan, Jody Grace and now Brendan Cummins all hopping a sliothar off the toilet wall.

There's Fox, watching and waiting. Constantly forgetting to bring his own towel and looking around to see who has been silly enough to leave their's within his reach before they shower. There's big Jim Keogh from the Silvermines, a real gentleman who always had the right words. Ian Conroy, Jack Bergin and Seamus Power too.

I've shared this place with so many friends, I hate the thought of leaving.

Bonds have formed here that I genuinely believe will never be broken. We have gone through so much together. When I think of Leahy this year and his problems, I think too of Joe Hayes and other team-mates, how genuine they proved as friends.

If I'm ever in trouble, I know there are men from this room who would look out for me. They have done so on the field so why should it be any different now? I'd like to think they know too how I'd be there for them.

That's the great legacy of these four walls. The friendship. The sense of loyalty.

This year ended far too quickly for us. It ended in another, less comforting room where the walls were closer and the air a little thin. It ended in Cork with Ken Hogan shouting out the question every one of us had to answer.

'Have we got the bottle lads? Do we want it badly enough? Do we?'